CASENOTE® Legal Briefs

CIVIL PROCEDURE

Keyed to Courses Using

**Yeazell and Schwartz's
Civil Procedure
Tenth Edition**

Authored by: Publisher's Editorial Staff

. Wolters Kluwer

Copyright © 2019 CCH Incorporated. All Rights Reserved.

Published by Wolters Kluwer in New York.

Wolters Kluwer Legal & Regulatory U.S. serves customers worldwide with CCH, Aspen Publishers, and Kluwer Law International products. (www.WKLegaledu.com)

To contact Customer Service, e-mail customer.service@wolterskluwer.com, call 1-800-234-1660, fax 1-800-901-9075, or mail correspondence to:

Wolters Kluwer
Attn: Order Department
P.O. Box 990
Frederick, MD 21705

Printed in the United States of America.

1 2 3 4 5 6 7 8 9 0

ISBN 978-15438-0729-5

About Wolters Kluwer Legal & Regulatory U.S.

Wolters Kluwer Legal & Regulatory U.S. delivers expert content and solutions in the areas of law, corporate compliance, health compliance, reimbursement, and legal education. Its practical solutions help customers successfully navigate the demands of a changing environment to drive their daily activities, enhance decision quality, and inspire confident outcomes.

Serving customers worldwide, its legal and regulatory portfolio includes products under the Aspen Publishers, CCH Incorporated, Kluwer Law International, ftwilliam.com, and MediRegs names. They are regarded as exceptional and trusted resources for general legal and practice-specific knowledge, compliance and risk management, dynamic workflow solutions, and expert commentary.

Format for the Casenote® Legal Brief

Nature of Case: This section identifies the form of action (e.g., breach of contract, negligence, battery), the type of proceeding (e.g., demurrer, appeal from trial court's jury instructions) or the relief sought (e.g., damages, injunction, criminal sanctions).

Palsgraf v. Long Island R.R. Co.

Injured bystander (P) v. Railroad company (D)

N.Y. Ct. App., 248 N.Y. 339, 162 N.E. 99 (1928).

Party ID: Quick identification of the relationship between the parties.

Fact Summary: This is included to refresh your memory and can be used as a quick reminder of the facts.

NATURE OF CASE: Appeal from judgment affirming verdict for plaintiff seeking damages for personal injury.

FACT SUMMARY: Helen Palsgraf (P) was injured on R.R.'s (D) train platform when R.R.'s (D) guard helped a passenger aboard a moving train, causing his package to fall on the tracks. The package contained fireworks which exploded, creating a shock that tipped a scale onto Palsgraf (P).

Rule of Law: Summarizes the general principle of law that the case illustrates. It may be used for instant recall of the court's holding and for classroom discussion or home review.

🏛 RULE OF LAW
The risk reasonably to be perceived defines the duty to be obeyed.

FACTS: Helen Palsgraf (P) purchased a ticket to Rockaway Beach from R.R. (D) and was waiting on the train platform. As she waited, two men ran to catch a train that was pulling out from the platform. The first man jumped aboard, but the second man, who appeared as if he might fall, was helped aboard by the guard on the train who had kept the door open so they could jump aboard. A guard on the platform also helped by pushing him onto the train. The man was carrying a package wrapped in newspaper. In the process, the man dropped his package, which fell on the tracks. The package contained fireworks and exploded. The shock of the explosion was apparently of great enough strength to tip over some scales at the other end of the platform, which fell on Palsgraf (P) and injured her. A jury awarded her damages, and R.R. (D) appealed.

Facts: This section contains all relevant facts of the case, including the contentions of the parties and the lower court holdings. It is written in a logical order to give you a clear understanding of the case. The plaintiff and defendant are identified by their proper names throughout and are always labeled with a (P) or (D).

ISSUE: Does the risk reasonably to be perceived define the duty to be obeyed?

HOLDING AND DECISION: (Cardozo, C.J.) Yes. The risk reasonably to be perceived defines the duty to be obeyed. If there is no foreseeable hazard to the injured party as the result of a seemingly innocent act, the act does not become a tort because it happened to be a wrong as to another. If the wrong was not willful, the plaintiff must show that the act as to her had such great and apparent possibilities of danger as to entitle her to protection. Negligence in the abstract is not enough upon which to base liability. Negligence is a relative concept, evolving out of the common law doctrine of trespass on the case. To establish liability, the defendant must owe a legal duty of reasonable care to the injured party. A cause of action in tort will lie where harm,

Issue: The issue is a concise question that brings out the essence of the opinion as it relates to the section of the casebook in which the case appears. Both substantive and procedural issues are included if relevant to the decision.

though unintended, could have been averted or avoided by observance of such a duty. The scope of the duty is limited by the range of danger that a reasonable person could foresee. In this case, there was nothing to suggest from the appearance of the parcel or otherwise that the parcel contained fireworks. The guard could not reasonably have had any warning of a threat to Palsgraf (P), and R.R. (D) therefore cannot be held liable. Judgment is reversed in favor of R.R. (D).

DISSENT: (Andrews, J.) The concept that there is no negligence unless R.R. (D) owes a legal duty to take care as to Palsgraf (P) herself is too narrow. Everyone owes to the world at large the duty of refraining from those acts that may unreasonably threaten the safety of others. If the guard's action was negligent as to those nearby, it was also negligent as to those outside what might be termed the "danger zone." For Palsgraf (P) to recover, R.R.'s (D) negligence must have been the proximate cause of her injury, a question of fact for the jury.

Concurrence/Dissent: All concurrences and dissents are briefed whenever they are included by the casebook author.

▶ ANALYSIS
The majority defined the limit of the defendant's liability in terms of the danger that a reasonable person in defendant's situation would have perceived. The dissent argued that the limitation should not be placed on liability, but rather on damages. Judge Andrews suggested that only injuries that would not have happened but for R.R.'s (D) negligence should be compensable. Both the majority and dissent recognized the policy-driven need to limit liability for negligent acts, seeking, in the words of Judge Andrews, to define a framework "that will be practical and in keeping with the general understanding of mankind." The Restatement (Second) of Torts has accepted Judge Cardozo's view.

Analysis: This last paragraph gives you a broad understanding of where the case "fits in" with other cases in the section of the book and with the entire course. It is a hornbook-style discussion indicating whether the case is a majority or minority opinion and comparing the principal case with other cases in the casebook. It may also provide analysis from restatements, uniform codes, and law review articles.

Quicknotes
FORESEEABILITY A reasonable expectation that change is the probable result of certain acts or omissions.

NEGLIGENCE Conduct falling below the standard of care that a reasonable person would demonstrate under similar conditions.

PROXIMATE CAUSE The natural sequence of events without which an injury would not have been sustained.

Holding and Decision: This section offers a clear and in-depth discussion of the rule of the case and the court's rationale. It is written in easy-to-understand language and answers the issue presented by applying the law to the facts of the case. When relevant, it includes a thorough discussion of the exceptions to the case as listed by the court, any major cites to the other cases on point, and the names of the judges who wrote the decisions.

Quicknotes: Conveniently defines legal terms found in the case.

Wolters Kluwer Legal & Regulatory U.S. is proud to offer *Casenote® Legal Briefs*—continuing thirty years of publishing America's best-selling legal briefs.

Casenote® Legal Briefs are designed to help you save time when briefing assigned cases. Organized under convenient headings, they show you how to abstract the basic facts and holdings from the text of the actual opinions handed down by the courts. Used as part of a rigorous study regimen, they can help you spend more time analyzing and critiquing points of law than on copying bits and pieces of judicial opinions into your notebook or outline.

Casenote® Legal Briefs should never be used as a substitute for assigned casebook readings. They work best when read as a follow-up to reviewing the underlying opinions themselves. Students who try to avoid reading and digesting the judicial opinions in their casebooks or online sources will end up shortchanging themselves in the long run. The ability to absorb, critique, and restate the dynamic and complex elements of case law decisions is crucial to your success in law school and beyond. It cannot be developed vicariously.

Casenote® Legal Briefs represents but one of the many offerings in Legal Education's Study Aid Timeline, which includes:

- *Casenote® Legal Briefs*
- *Emanuel® Law Outlines*
- Emanuel® *Law in a Flash* Flash Cards
- Emanuel® *CrunchTime®* Series

Each of these series is designed to provide you with easy-to-understand explanations of complex points of law. Each volume offers guidance on the principles of legal analysis and, consulted regularly, will hone your ability to spot relevant issues. We have titles that will help you prepare for class, prepare for your exams, and enhance your general comprehension of the law along the way.

To find out more about our law school tools for success, visit us at *www.WKLegaledu.com* or email us at *legaledu@wolterskluwer.com*. We'll be happy to assist you.

A. Decide on a Format and Stick to It

Structure is essential to a good brief. It enables you to arrange systematically the related parts that are scattered throughout most cases, thus making manageable and understandable what might otherwise seem to be an endless and unfathomable sea of information. There are, of course, an unlimited number of formats that can be utilized. However, it is best to find one that suits your needs and stick to it. Consistency breeds both efficiency and the security that when called upon you will know where to look in your brief for the information you are asked to give.

Any format, as long as it presents the essential elements of a case in an organized fashion, can be used. Experience, however, has led *Casenote® Legal Briefs* to develop and utilize the following format because of its logical flow and universal applicability.

NATURE OF CASE: This is a brief statement of the legal character and procedural status of the case (e.g., "Appeal of a burglary conviction").

There are many different alternatives open to a litigant dissatisfied with a court ruling. The key to determining which one has been used is to discover *who is asking this court for what*.

This first entry in the brief should be kept as *short as possible*. Use the court's terminology if you understand it. But since jurisdictions vary as to the titles of pleadings, the best entry is the one that addresses who wants what in this proceeding, not the one that sounds most like the court's language.

RULE OF LAW: A statement of the general principle of law that the case illustrates (e.g., "An acceptance that varies any term of the offer is considered a rejection and counteroffer").

Determining the rule of law of a case is a procedure similar to determining the issue of the case. Avoid being fooled by red herrings; there may be a few rules of law mentioned in the case excerpt, but usually only one is *the* rule with which the casebook editor is concerned. The techniques used to locate the issue, described below, may also be utilized to find the rule of law. Generally, your best guide is simply the chapter heading. It is a clue to the point the casebook editor seeks to make and should be kept in mind when reading every case in the respective section.

FACTS: A synopsis of only the essential facts of the case, i.e., those bearing upon or leading up to the issue.

The facts entry should be a short statement of the events and transactions that led one party to initiate legal proceedings against another in the first place. While some cases conveniently state the salient facts at the beginning of the decision, in other instances they will have to be culled from hiding places throughout the text, even from concurring and dissenting opinions. Some of the "facts" will often be in dispute and should be so noted. Conflicting evidence may be briefly pointed up. "Hard" facts must be included. Both must be *relevant* in order to be listed in the facts entry. It is impossible to tell what is relevant until the entire case is read, as the ultimate determination of the rights and liabilities of the parties may turn on something buried deep in the opinion.

Generally, the facts entry should not be longer than three to five *short* sentences.

It is often helpful to identify the role played by a party in a given context. For example, in a construction contract case the identification of a party as the "contractor" or "builder" alleviates the need to tell that that party was the one who was supposed to have built the house.

It is always helpful, and a good general practice, to identify the "plaintiff" and the "defendant." This may seem elementary and uncomplicated, but, especially in view of the creative editing practiced by some casebook editors, it is sometimes a difficult or even impossible task. Bear in mind that the *party presently* seeking something from this court may not be the plaintiff, and that sometimes only the cross-claim of a defendant is treated in the excerpt. Confusing or misaligning the parties can ruin your analysis and understanding of the case.

ISSUE: A statement of the general legal question answered by or illustrated in the case. For clarity, the issue is best put in the form of a question capable of a "yes" or "no" answer. In reality, the issue is simply the Rule of Law put in the form of a question (e.g., "May an offer be accepted by performance?").

The major problem presented in discerning what is *the* issue in the case is that an opinion usually purports to raise and answer several questions. However, except for rare cases, only one such question is really the issue in the case. Collateral issues not necessary to the resolution of the matter in controversy are handled by the court by language known as *"obiter dictum"* or merely *"dictum."* While dicta may be included later in the brief, they have no place under the issue heading.

To find the issue, ask *who wants what* and then go on to ask *why did that party succeed or fail in getting it*. Once this is determined, the "why" should be turned into a question.

The complexity of the issues in the cases will vary, but in all cases a single-sentence question should sum up the issue. *In a few cases*, there will be two, or even more rarely, three issues of equal importance to the resolution of the case. Each should be expressed in a single-sentence question.

Since many issues are resolved by a court in coming to a final disposition of a case, the casebook editor will reproduce the portion of the opinion containing the issue or issues most relevant to the area of law under scrutiny. A noted law professor gave this advice: "Close the book; look at the title on the cover." Chances are, if it is Property, you need not concern yourself with whether, for example, the federal government's treatment of the plaintiff's land really raises a federal question sufficient to support jurisdiction on this ground in federal court.

The same rule applies to chapter headings designating sub-areas within the subjects. They tip you off as to what the text is designed to teach. The cases are arranged in a casebook to show a progression or development of the law, so that the preceding cases may also help.

It is also most important to remember to *read the notes and questions* at the end of a case to determine what the editors wanted you to have gleaned from it.

HOLDING AND DECISION: This section should succinctly explain the rationale of the court in arriving at its decision. In capsulizing the "reasoning" of the court, it should always include an application of the general rule or rules of law to the specific facts of the case. Hidden justifications come to light in this entry: the reasons for the state of the law, the public policies, the biases and prejudices, those considerations that influence the justices' thinking and, ultimately, the outcome of the case. At the end, there should be a short indication of the disposition or procedural resolution of the case (e.g., "Decision of the trial court for Mr. Smith (P) reversed").

The foregoing format is designed to help you "digest" the reams of case material with which you will be faced in your law school career. Once mastered by practice, it will place at your fingertips the information the authors of your casebooks have sought to impart to you in case-by-case illustration and analysis.

B. Be as Economical as Possible in Briefing Cases

Once armed with a format that encourages succinctness, it is as important to be economical with regard to the time spent on the actual reading of the case as it is to be economical in the writing of the brief itself. This does not mean "skimming" a case. Rather, it means reading the case with an "eye" trained to recognize into which "section" of your brief a particular passage or line fits and having a system for quickly and precisely marking the case so that the passages fitting any one particular part of

the brief can be easily identified and brought together in a concise and accurate manner when the brief is actually written.

It is of no use to simply repeat everything in the opinion of the court; record only enough information to trigger your recollection of what the court said. Nevertheless, an accurate statement of the "law of the case," i.e., the legal principle applied to the facts, is absolutely essential to class preparation and to learning the law under the case method.

To that end, it is important to develop a "shorthand" that you can use to make marginal notations. These notations will tell you at a glance in which section of the brief you will be placing that particular passage or portion of the opinion.

Some students prefer to underline all the salient portions of the opinion (with a pencil or colored underliner marker), making marginal notations as they go along. Others prefer the color-coded method of underlining, utilizing different colors of markers to underline the salient portions of the case, each separate color being used to represent a different section of the brief. For example, blue underlining could be used for passages relating to the rule of law, yellow for those relating to the issue, and green for those relating to the holding and decision, etc. While it has its advocates, the color-coded method can be confusing and time-consuming (all that time spent on changing colored markers). Furthermore, it can interfere with the continuity and concentration many students deem essential to the reading of a case for maximum comprehension. In the end, however, it is a matter of personal preference and style. Just remember, whatever method you use, underlining must be used sparingly or its value is lost.

If you take the marginal notation route, an efficient and easy method is to go along underlining the key portions of the case and placing in the margin alongside them the following "markers" to indicate where a particular passage or line "belongs" in the brief you will write:

N (NATURE OF CASE)
RL (RULE OF LAW)
I (ISSUE)
HL (HOLDING AND DECISION, relates to the RULE OF LAW behind the decision)
HR (HOLDING AND DECISION, gives the RATIONALE or reasoning behind the decision)
HA (HOLDING AND DECISION, applies the general principle(s) of law to the facts of the case to arrive at the decision)

Remember that a particular passage may well contain information necessary to more than one part of your brief, in which case you simply note that in the margin. If you are using the color-coded underlining method instead of marginal notation, simply make asterisks or checks in the margin next to the passage in question in the colors that indicate the additional sections of the brief where it might be utilized.

The economy of utilizing "shorthand" in marking cases for briefing can be maintained in the actual brief writing process itself by utilizing "law student shorthand" within the brief. There are many commonly used words and phrases for which abbreviations can be substituted in your briefs (and in your class notes also). You can develop abbreviations that are personal to you and which will save you a lot of time. A reference list of briefing abbreviations can be found on page x of this book.

C. Use Both the Briefing Process and the Brief as a Learning Tool

Now that you have a format and the tools for briefing cases efficiently, the most important thing is to make the time spent in briefing profitable to you and to make the most advantageous use of the briefs you create. Of course, the briefs are invaluable for classroom reference when you are called upon to explain or analyze a particular case. However, they are also useful in reviewing for exams. A quick glance at the fact summary should bring the case to mind, and a rereading of the rule of law should enable you to go over the underlying legal concept in your mind, how it was applied in that particular case, and how it might apply in other factual settings.

As to the value to be derived from engaging in the briefing process itself, there is an immediate benefit that arises from being forced to sift through the essential facts and reasoning from the court's opinion and to succinctly express them in your own words in your brief. The process ensures that you understand the case and the point that it illustrates, and that means you will be ready to absorb further analysis and information brought forth in class. It also ensures you will have something to say when called upon in class. The briefing process helps develop a mental agility for getting to the *gist* of a case and for identifying, expounding on, and applying the legal concepts and issues found there. The briefing process is the mental process on which you must rely in taking law school examinations; it is also the mental process upon which lawyers rely in serving their clients and in making a living.

Abbreviations for Briefs

acceptance	acp	offer	O
affirmed	aff	offeree	OE
answer	ans	offeror	OR
assumption of risk	a/r	ordinance	ord
attorney	atty	pain and suffering	p/s
beyond a reasonable doubt	b/r/d	parol evidence	p/e
bona fide purchaser	BFP	plaintiff	P
breach of contract	br/k	prima facie	p/f
cause of action	c/a	probable cause	p/c
common law	c/l	proximate cause	px/c
Constitution	Con	real property	r/p
constitutional	con	reasonable doubt	r/d
contract	K	reasonable man	r/m
contributory negligence	c/n	rebuttable presumption	rb/p
cross	x	remanded	rem
cross-complaint	x/c	res ipsa loquitur	RIL
cross-examination	x/ex	respondeat superior	r/s
cruel and unusual punishment	c/u/p	Restatement	RS
defendant	D	reversed	rev
dismissed	dis	Rule Against Perpetuities	RAP
double jeopardy	d/j	search and seizure	s/s
due process	d/p	search warrant	s/w
equal protection	e/p	self-defense	s/d
equity	eq	specific performance	s/p
evidence	ev	statute	S
exclude	exc	statute of frauds	S/F
exclusionary rule	exc/r	statute of limitations	S/L
felony	f/n	summary judgment	s/j
freedom of speech	f/s	tenancy at will	t/w
good faith	g/f	tenancy in common	t/c
habeas corpus	h/c	tenant	t
hearsay	hr	third party	TP
husband	H	third party beneficiary	TPB
injunction	inj	transferred intent	TI
in loco parentis	ILP	unconscionable	uncon
inter vivos	I/v	unconstitutional	unconst
joint tenancy	j/t	undue influence	u/e
judgment	judgt	Uniform Commercial Code	UCC
jurisdiction	jur	unilateral	uni
last clear chance	LCC	vendee	VE
long-arm statute	LAS	vendor	VR
majority view	maj	versus	v
meeting of minds	MOM	void for vagueness	VFV
minority view	min	weight of authority	w/a
Miranda rule	Mir/r	weight of the evidence	w/e
Miranda warnings	Mir/w	wife	W
negligence	neg	with	w/
notice	ntc	within	w/i
nuisance	nus	without	w/o
obligation	ob	without prejudice	w/o/p
obscene	obs	wrongful death	wr/d

Table of Cases

CHAPTER 1

An Overview of Procedure

Quick Reference Rules of Law

Hawkins v. Masters Farms, Inc.

Representative of estate (P) v. Tractor driver (D)

2003 WL 21555767 (D. Kan. 2003)

NATURE OF CASE: Motion to dismiss for lack of subject matter jurisdiction.

FACT SUMMARY: James Creal was killed when his automobile was struck by a tractor owned by Masters Farms, Inc. (D). Creal's estate (P) brought suit against Masters Farms, Inc. (D) in federal court alleging diversity subject matter jurisdiction. Masters Farms, Inc. (D) moved to dismiss on grounds of incomplete diversity among the parties.

🏛 RULE OF LAW
For purposes of determining diversity jurisdiction, a person is a "citizen" of the state in which he or she is "domiciled," which for adults is established by physical presence in a place in connection with the intent to remain there.

FACTS: On December 8, 2000, James Creal was killed in an automobile accident just south of Troy, Kansas, when his car was struck by a tractor driven by Masters (D), a citizen of Kansas. At the time of his death, James Creal was living in Kansas with his wife and her children. James Creal had lived in Missouri most of his life, while Mrs. Creal had resided in Kansas the majority of her life. When Mrs. Creal moved into an apartment in Troy, Kansas, in March 2000, James Creal brought his clothes, furniture, and many other items and moved to the new apartment. The Creals were married in July 2000. In November, the Creals moved into a house in Troy, Kansas. His death certificate listed Kansas as his residence. The representatives of James Creal (P) brought suit against Masters (D) in the federal district court for Kansas, alleging the existence of diversity jurisdiction under 28 U.S.C. § 1332. Masters (D) moved to dismiss, disputing that there was complete diversity among the parties.

ISSUE: For purposes of determining diversity jurisdiction, is a person a "citizen" of the state in which he or she is "domiciled," which for adults is established by physical presence in a place in connection with the intent to remain there?

HOLDING AND DECISION: (Van Bebber, J.) Yes. For purposes of determining diversity jurisdiction, a person is a "citizen" of the state in which he or she is "domiciled," which for adults is established by physical presence in a place in connection with the intent to remain there. Here, at the time of his death, Creal had not only established a physical presence in the State of Kansas, but also displayed intent to remain there. Although he lived the majority of his life in Missouri, he had been living in Kansas with his wife of five months for nearly one year at the time he died. Among other things, he had moved household items into the Kansas home; he contributed to household costs; and he purchased a new bedroom set with his wife. Any non-specific so-called "floating intention" of Creal to return to his former Missouri domicile would be insufficient to overcome the evidence that he was domiciled in Kansas at the time of his death. Masters's (D) motion to dismiss is granted.

▶ ANALYSIS

In *Hawkins*, the court noted that the party seeking to invoke federal jurisdiction bears the burden of proving that jurisdiction is proper. Because federal courts are courts of limited jurisdiction, the presumption is against federal jurisdiction.

Quicknotes

DIVERSITY OF CITIZENSHIP Parties are citizens of different states, or one party is an alien; a factor, along with a statutorily set dollar value of the matter in controversy, that allows a federal district court to exercise its authority to hear a lawsuit based on diversity jurisdiction.

DIVERSITY JURISDICTION The authority of a federal court to hear and determine cases involving parties who are of different states and an amount in controversy greater than a statutorily set amount.

FEDERAL JURISDICTION The authority of federal courts to hear and determine cases of a particular nature derived from the United States Constitution and rules promulgated by Congress pursuant thereto.

Bridges v. Diesel Service, Inc.

Disabled employee (P) v. Employer (D)

1994 U.S. Dist. LEXIS 9429 (E.D. Pa. 1994)

NATURE OF CASE: Motion for sanctions pursuant to Fed. R. Civ. P. 11.

FACT SUMMARY: Bridges (P) commenced this action against Diesel Service Inc. (D) under the Americans with Disabilities Act (ADA) alleging that his employer dismissed him from his job as a result of a disability.

🏛 RULE OF LAW
Fed. R. Civ. P. 11 imposes an obligation on counsel and client to stop, think, investigate, and research before filing papers either to initiate the suit or to conduct the litigation.

FACTS: Bridges (P) commenced this action against Diesel Service Inc. (D) under the Americans with Disabilities Act (ADA) alleging that his employer dismissed him from his job as a result of a disability. By an order dated June 29, 1994, the court dismissed Bridges's (P) complaint without prejudice for failure to exhaust administrative remedies. In particular, Bridges (P) did not file a charge with the Equal Employment Opportunity Commission (EEOC) until after commencement of this action. Diesel Service, Inc. (D) then moved for sanctions pursuant to Fed. R. Civ. P. 11.

ISSUE: Does Fed. R. Civ. P. 11 impose an obligation on counsel and client to stop, think, investigate, and research before filing papers either to initiate the suit or to conduct the litigation?

HOLDING AND DECISION: (Huyett, J.) Yes. Fed. R. Civ. P. 11 imposes an obligation on counsel and client to stop, think, investigate, and research before filing papers either to initiate the suit or to conduct the litigation. The court is not convinced that Plaintiff's lawyer displayed a competent level of legal research. A brief review of case law would have revealed the EEOC filing requirement. Further, an award of sanctions for failure to exhaust administrative remedies is not unprecedented. However, the court will not grant sanctions. The prime goal of Rule 11 sanctions is deterrence of improper conduct. In this case, monetary sanctions are not necessary to deter future misconduct, since plaintiff's counsel immediately acknowledged his error and attempted to rectify the situation. Motion is denied.

▶ ANALYSIS

It is possible that the court treated plaintiff's counsel with lenience in this case, since the action was brought under the Americans with Disabilities Act. As the court states in its decision, "The Court is aware of the need to avoid 'chilling' Title VII litigation." Generally, Fed. R. Civ. P. 11 sanctions are awarded where the complaint filed asserts patently unmeritorious or frivolous allegations.

■=■

Quicknotes

ADMINISTRATIVE REMEDIES Relief sought before an administrative body as opposed to a court.

FED. R. CIV. P. 11 Sets forth the requirement that every pleading or written paper be signed by at least one attorney of record; the representations made by the attorney to the court upon the signing of such document; and the sanctions for violation of the provision.

■=■

Bell v. Novick Transfer Co.

Automobile passenger (P) v. Trucking company (D)

17 F.R.D. 279 (D. Md. 1955)

NATURE OF CASE: Motion to dismiss for failure to state a claim.

FACT SUMMARY: Bell (P) filed a tort complaint in federal court after removal that stated only that Novick Transfer Co.'s (D) agent drove a truck that negligently collided with the car in which Bell (P) was riding, causing injury to Bell (P).

🏛 RULE OF LAW
A complaint that alleges only that a defendant negligently drove a motor vehicle and thereby injured the plaintiff is sufficient under Fed. R. Civ. P. 8.

FACTS: After Bell's (P) tort action arising out of an automobile-truck accident was removed to federal court, Bell (P) filed a complaint there that alleged only that an agent of Novick Transfer Co. (Novick) (D) drove a truck negligently so as to collide with a car in which Bell (P) was riding, causing injury to Bell (P). Novick (D) moved to dismiss the complaint for failure to state a cause of action.

ISSUE: Is a complaint that alleges only that defendant negligently drove a motor vehicle and thereby injured the plaintiff sufficient under Fed. R. Civ. P. 8?

HOLDING AND DECISION: (Thompsen, J.) Yes. This tort action was originally filed in Court of Common Pleas of Baltimore City but was removed to federal court. After such a removal, the Federal Rules of Civil Procedure apply rather than the laws of the State of Maryland. Thus, while Maryland law might regard the complaint here as insufficient for failure to state a cause of action, the inquiry here is to be made in light of the Federal Rules of Civil Procedure. Rule 8 controls the sufficiency of complaints and requires only "a short and plain statement of the claim showing the pleader is entitled to relief." The complaint in this case contains such a statement and sufficiently states a cause of action under Rule 8. A complaint that alleges only that a defendant negligently drove a motor vehicle and thereby injured the plaintiff is sufficient under Rule 8. Motion is overruled.

▶ ANALYSIS

A complaint is designed to apprise the defendant of the claim against which he is to defend. The argument against sufficiency in this case is that the defendant is not told what negligent acts he has allegedly committed, other than the general allegation of "negligence," giving rise to liability. However, the policy of granting everyone access to the courts militates toward permitting generalized allegations and forcing the defendant to move for a more particularized statement under Fed. R. Civ. P. 12(e).

■■■

Quicknotes

FED. R. CIV. P. 8 Sets forth the general rules of pleading a claim for relief.

MOTION TO DISMISS Motion to terminate a trial based on the adequacy of the pleadings.

REMOVAL Petition by a defendant to move the case to another court.

■■■

Fisher v. Ciba Specialty Chemicals Corp.

Property owner (P) v. Chemicals manufacturing plant owner (D)

245 F.R.D. 539 (S.D. Ala. 2007)

NATURE OF CASE: Motion to sever, pursuant to Fed. R. Civ. P. 20 and 21, in action alleging diminution of property value as the result of environmental contamination.

FACT SUMMARY: Ciba Specialty Chemicals Corp. (Ciba) (D) moved to sever, pursuant to Fed. R. Civ. P. 20 and 21, claims brought by five property owners (P) alleging that Ciba's (D) chemicals manufacturing plant contaminated and reduced the value of their property. Ciba (D) asserted inefficiency and prejudice as the primary grounds for its motion, which the property owner (P) opposed.

🏛 **RULE OF LAW**
Under Fed. R. Civ. P. 20 and 21, a cause of action based on multiple individual claims will not be severed into separate trials where it is anticipated that, although there will be some individual-specific evidence, there will be substantial overlapping background evidence for all plaintiffs' claims; the same roster of experts will be called; and any potential prejudice to the defendant can be mitigated through limiting instructions.

FACTS: Five individual property owners (P) joined together and brought suit against Ciba Specialty Chemicals Corp. (Ciba) (D), alleging that Ciba's (D) chemicals manufacturing plant contaminated and reduced the value of their property with widespread environmental pollutants, including DDT. Ciba (D) moved, pursuant to Fed. R. Civ. P. 20 and 21, to sever the action into five separate trials. Ciba (D) argued that (1) the property owners' claims did not arise from the same transaction or occurrence; (2) they would rely on individualized evidence to prove their claims; (3) Ciba (D) would invoke individual-specific defenses; and (4) a common trial would be prejudicial to Ciba (D). The property owners (P) opposed the motion, arguing that severing their essentially identical claims would cause great inefficiency, and undue delay and undue expense, while also burdening the court with presiding over a largely similar trial five times in a row. The district court considered the motion.

ISSUE: Under Fed. R. Civ. P. 20 and 21, will a cause of action based on multiple individual claims be severed into separate trials where it is anticipated that, although there will be some individual-specific evidence, there will be substantial overlapping background evidence for all plaintiffs' claims; the same roster of experts will be called; and any potential prejudice to the defendant can be mitigated through limiting instructions?

HOLDING AND DECISION: (Steele, J.) No. Under Fed. R. Civ. P. 20 and 21, a cause of action based on multiple individual claims will not be severed into separate trials where it is anticipated that, although there will be some individual-specific evidence, there will be substantial overlapping background evidence for all plaintiffs' claims; the same roster of experts will be called; and any potential prejudice to the defendant can be mitigated through limiting instructions. Whether to grant the motion is within the court's discretion. Factors considered in determining whether to sever include whether the claims arise from the same transaction or occurrence, whether they present some common question of law or fact, whether severance would facilitate settlement or judicial economy, and the relative prejudice to each side if the motion is granted or denied. The commonality of law and fact issues need not be absolute; only some law or fact questions need to be common to all parties. Under the circumstances of the case, holding a single trial will present both efficiencies and inefficiencies. However, the efficiencies outweigh the inefficiencies. First, it is anticipated that there will be substantial overlapping background evidence for all plaintiffs' claims concerning the environmental history and activities of the Ciba (D) plant, and the interactions of Ciba (D) with the media, government regulators, and alleged co-conspirators. Second, it is probable that the same roster of nine expert witnesses, all of whom live out of state, will be called to testify with respect to each plaintiff's claims. To require these nine experts (as well as out-of-state counsel) to travel to the court five times in quick succession (or to sit and wait in a hotel for days on end) to testify in five different trials would be financially foolhardy and needlessly wasteful of the parties' economic resources, potentially even rendering these trials cost-prohibitive. Moreover, if these nine experts would be testifying to substantially similar, partially overlapping opinions in each of these five trials, the attendant drag on the efficient administration of justice would be considerable, as the court would be subjected to something akin to a judicial *Groundhog Day*. Additionally, Ciba's (D) claims of extreme prejudice must be rejected. Ciba (D) asserts that it will be prejudiced by the holding of a single trial because: (1) a multiplicity of plaintiff-specific facts will confuse the jury; (2) to the extent that one plaintiff's claims are stronger than the others', evidence as to that plaintiff may unfairly taint the jury as to the other plaintiffs' claims; and (3) consolidation for trial will allow plaintiffs to bolster their individually weak cases by a suggestion that contamination is widespread. As to jury

Continued on next page.

confusion, federal juries are routinely asked to parse facts that are relevant to particular claims or particular parties and are able to do so without difficulty so long as counsel presents the evidence in a cogent, orderly fashion that makes clear which evidence attaches to which particular claims or defenses. As to any "tainting," limiting instructions may be drafted to circumscribe the uses for which particular evidence may be considered, as well as pattern charges stressing that the claims and defenses of each party must be considered separately and independently from those of each other party. Finally, it is anticipated that the plaintiffs will each make the case that contamination from Ciba's (D) plant is widespread, so that this "suggestion" will be before the jury in plaintiffs' evidentiary submission at trial, irrespective of whether severance is granted. For all these reasons, Ciba's (D) motion to sever is denied.

▶ *ANALYSIS*

Even if a court has found under Fed. R. Civ. P. 23 at the class certification stage that common issues do not predominate over individual-specific issues, such a finding, and a ruling against the plaintiffs based on it in no way suggests (much less mandates) a like outcome with respect to a motion under Fed. R. Civ. P. 20. That is because there is no predomination prerequisite for joinder of multiple plaintiffs' claims, and Fed. R. Civ. P. 20 contemplates a much lower threshold for allowing plaintiffs' claims to proceed to trial together than is required by Fed. R. Civ. P. 23 for class certification. As this case illustrates, the touchstone of the Fed. R. Civ. P. 20 joinder/severance analysis is whether the interests of efficiency and judicial economy would be advanced by allowing the claims to travel together, and whether any party would be prejudiced if they did.

■▬■

Quicknotes

SEVERANCE Dividing or separating; setting aside one or more claims in a lawsuit to be tried separately.

■▬■

Gordon v. T.G.R. Logistics, Inc.

Automobile accident victim (P) v. Corporation (D)

2017 WL 1947537 (D. Wyo. 2017)

NATURE OF CASE: Consideration of defendant's motion to compel production of plaintiff's Facebook account history for several years prior to the accident giving rise to the accident.

FACT SUMMARY: Gordon (P) suffered severe physical injuries when her vehicle was struck by a tractor-trailer unit owned by T.G.R. Logistics (D). Gordon (P) filed claims for both physical and emotional injuries.

🏛 RULE OF LAW

When determining the scope of permissible discovery pursuant to Fed. R. Civ. P. 26(b)(1), courts must determine if the information sought is privileged, relevant to a claim or defense, and proportional to the case.

FACTS: Gordon (P) suffered severe physical injuries when her vehicle was struck by a tractor-trailer unit owned by T.G.R. Logistics (D). Gordon's (P) claimed injuries included physical injuries, a traumatic brain injury, posttraumatic stress disorder, and depression. During discovery, T.G.R. Logistics (D) served a discovery request upon Gordon (P) for her entire Facebook account history, including the years prior to the accident. After Gordon (P) objected to the request, T.G.R. Logistics (D) filed a motion to compel the discovery.

ISSUE: When determining the scope of permissible discovery pursuant to Fed. R. Civ. P. 26(b)(1), must courts determine if the information sought is privileged, relevant to a claim or defense, and proportional to the case?

HOLDING AND DECISION: (Carman, J.) Yes. When determining the scope of permissible discovery pursuant to Fed. R. Civ. P. 26(b)(1), courts must determine if the information sought is privileged, relevant to a claim or defense, and proportional to the case. In this case, only the latter two prongs of the analysis are at issue. Social media presents significant issues regarding relevance and proportionality. Individuals now place vast troves of personal information online and that information may be relevant to the litigation. Production of such information may also not be expensive. However, simply because the production of the information may be easy or uncomplicated does not mean that the production is not burdensome. Here, T.G.R. Logistics (D) is correct that the production of the account history would not be expensive. The information sought could also lead to Gordon (P) having to explain every post where she expressed angst or emotional distress, including such instances that are personal or embarrassing. T.G.R.

Logistics (D) counters by now offering to reduce its request to only three years prior to the accident, as well as all post-accident history. This is too broad a request. Granting access to the account prior to the accident would likely produce only minimal relevant information while exposing Gordon's (P) private posts unnecessarily. This would exceed the limits of proportionality. Gordon (P) must, however, produce all post-accident history as it relates to her emotional turmoil, mental disability, or other events that relate to emotional distress or her physical injuries. She should also produce any history or photos that show her level of activity since the date of the accident. Defendant's motion to compel is thus denied in part and granted in part.

▶ ANALYSIS

In any personal injury claim, defendants will scour a plaintiff's social media accounts for both evidence of injuries or emotional distress prior to the accident date, as well as any evidence that the plaintiff's claimed damages are not as bad as claimed. Courts rely on the two elements discussed in this case—relevance and proportionality—to fashion the appropriate scope of discovery. Depending on the severity of the claimed injuries, these disputes over the scope of discovery become paramount during the early stages of the litigation.

■=■

Quicknotes

DISCOVERY Pretrial procedure during which one party makes certain information available to the other.

RELEVANCE The admissibility of evidence based on whether it has any tendency to prove or disprove a matter at issue in the case.

■=■

Houchens v. American Home Assurance Co.

Spouse of decedent (P) v. Life insurance company (D)

927 F.2d 163 (4th Cir. 1991)

NATURE OF CASE: Appeal of dismissal of action for damages for breach of contract.

FACT SUMMARY: On American Home Assurance Co.'s (D) summary judgment motion, the court dismissed Houchens's (P) suit for payment on two accidental death policies because of insufficient evidence that Houchens's (P) husband died accidentally.

🏛 RULE OF LAW
Under Fed. R. Civ. P. 56, a federal court must enter summary judgment if after complete discovery a party fails to show that the evidence, viewed in the light most favorable to that party, is sufficient to establish the existence of an essential element on which that party has the burden of proof.

FACTS: Houchens's (P) husband disappeared in Thailand in August 1980, and was not heard from since. Under Virginia law, a person who is missing for seven years is presumed dead. In 1988, Houchens (P) had her husband declared legally dead. Houchens (P) attempted to collect on two life insurance policies issued by American (D), under which the proceeds would be paid only upon proof that the insured's death was accidental. American Home Assurance Co. (American) (D) refused to pay and Houchens (P) sued in federal court for breach of contract. American (D) moved for summary judgment, arguing there was no evidence that the insured had died or that he had died accidentally. The district court granted the motion and dismissed the case, and Houchens (P) appealed.

ISSUE: Under Fed. R. Civ. P. 56, must a federal court enter summary judgment if a party fails to show that the evidence, viewed in the light most favorable to that party, is sufficient to establish the existence of an essential element on which that party has the burden of proof?

HOLDING AND DECISION: (Ervin, J.) Yes. Under Fed. R. Civ. P. 56, a federal court must enter summary judgment if a party fails to show that the evidence, viewed in the light most favorable to that party, is sufficient to establish the existence of an essential element on which that party has the burden of proof. Under Rule 56(c), a summary judgment motion must be granted where there is "no genuine issue as to any material fact." Here, Houchens (P) is entitled to the Virginia presumption that her husband is dead. However, for recovery on the policy it still must be shown that her husband's death was accidental. The meager circumstances surrounding his disappearance do not provide sufficient evidence to allow a reasonable jury to conclude that he died accidentally.

Under Virginia law, Houchens (D) had the burden of proof as to accident, a necessary element of her case. She had insufficient evidence to meet this burden. Thus, as there was no genuine issue as to a material fact, the summary judgment motion was properly granted. Affirmed.

▶ ANALYSIS

Houchens (P) cited two cases where the issue was the same and a summary judgment motion by the insurance company defendant was denied. In *Valley National Bank of Arizona v. J.C. Penney Ins. Co.*, Ariz. Ct. App., 129 Ariz. 108, 628 P.2d 991 (1981), the insured disappeared, and his skeletal remains were later found with bullet casings nearby. In *Martin v. Insurance Co. of America*, 1 Wash. App. 218, 460 P.2d 682 (1969), the insured disappeared in fog and snow on a steep and wooded mountainside after having last been seen, asking for directions, without a compass at the 3,000-foot level. In each of these cases, the court found that there was a genuine issue of material fact because there was sufficient evidence, unlike in the *Houchens* case, for a jury to find that the insured died accidentally.

■▬■▬■

Quicknotes

BURDEN OF PROOF The duty of a party to introduce evidence to support a fact that is in dispute in an action.

FED. R. CIV. P. 56(C) Provides a court arrive at a pre-verdict disposition on the case at bar when one party fails to prove an essential element of its case.

SUMMARY JUDGMENT Judgment rendered by a court in response to a motion by one of the parties, claiming that the lack of a question of material fact in respect to an issue warrants disposition of the issue without consideration by the jury.

■▬■▬■

Norton v. Snapper Power Equipment

Gardener (P) v. Lawn mower manufacturer (D)

806 F.2d 1545 (11th Cir. 1987)

NATURE OF CASE: Appeal from judgment notwithstanding the verdict denying damages for personal injuries.

FACT SUMMARY: In Norton's (P) suit for damages against Snapper Power Equipment (Snapper) (D), Snapper (D) moved for and was granted a judgment notwithstanding the verdict, contending that since a reconstruction of Norton's (P) accident with a Snapper (D) riding mower was impossible, the jury could not determine whether a blade-stopping device would have eliminated or lessened Norton's (P) injury.

🏛 RULE OF LAW
A judgment notwithstanding the verdict should be granted only where the evidence so strongly points in favor of a moving party that reasonable people could not arrive at a contrary verdict.

FACTS: Norton (P), a commercial gardener, was injured while riding a lawn mower manufactured by Snapper Power Equipment (Snapper) (D). Norton (P) sued Snapper (D) for damages based on strict liability. At the close of Norton's (P) case, and against the close of all evidence, Snapper (D) moved for a directed verdict. The court left the strict liability claim for the jury, and the jury returned a verdict for Norton (P), holding Snapper (D) liable for 80 percent of the injuries. After dismissing the jury, the court indicated that it would enter a judgment notwithstanding the verdict based on Snapper's (D) contention that since a reconstruction of Norton's (P) accident with the mower was impossible, the jury could not determine whether a blade-stopping device would have eliminated or lessened Norton's (P) injury. Norton (P) appealed.

ISSUE: Should a judgment notwithstanding the verdict be granted only where the evidence so strongly points in favor of a moving party that reasonable people could not arrive at a contrary verdict?

HOLDING AND DECISION: (Clark, J.) Yes. A judgment notwithstanding the verdict should be granted only where the evidence so strongly points in favor of a moving party that reasonable people could not arrive at a contrary verdict. The issues here were whether the failure to install "dead man" devices rendered the mower defective, and if the mower was defective, whether the lack of a "dead man" control caused the injury. Snapper (D) claims that there was little or no evidence to support the jury's verdict. The jury is, however, permitted to reconstruct the series of events by drawing an inference upon an inference.

The causation evidence here, although circumstantial, was far more impressive than Snapper (D) contends, and Snapper (D) was given every opportunity to point out the weaknesses in Norton's (P) proof but was unpersuasive to the jury. Reversed and remanded.

▶ ANALYSIS

Within ten days of an adverse verdict, the loser may move for a judgment notwithstanding the verdict. This motion asserts that even if all the winner's evidence is true, the loser is entitled to a verdict as a matter of law. A motion for a new trial may be based either on an error of law or an erroneous charge.

Quicknotes

DIRECTED VERDICT A verdict ordered by the court in a jury trial.

JUDGMENT NOTWITHSTANDING THE VERDICT (JUDGMENT N.O.V.) A judgment entered by the trial judge reversing a jury verdict if the jury's determination has no basis in law or fact.

STRICT LIABILITY Liability for all injuries proximately caused by a party's conducting of certain inherently dangerous activities without regard to negligence or fault.

Ison v. Thomas

Accident victim (P) v. Car driver (D)

Ky. Ct. App., 2007 WL 1194374 (2007)

NATURE OF CASE: Appeal from dismissal on summary judgment of a claim for personal injuries.

FACT SUMMARY: Ison's (P) claim against Thomas (D) for personal injuries was dismissed on the grounds that he had previously prevailed against Thomas (D) on a claim for property damages and was precluded from raising the personal injury claim under the rule against splitting one's cause of action.

🏛 RULE OF LAW
Where a plaintiff brings one action after another, and the claims in the subsequent action could have been brought in the prior action, the rule against splitting one's cause of action is not inapplicable if the plaintiff prevails in the prior action.

FACTS: Thomas (D) was found liable to Ison (P) for property damages arising from a car accident, and a jury awarded Ison (P) $5,000. Subsequently, Ison (P) brought suit against Thomas (D) for personal injuries arising from the same accident. Ison's (P) claim was dismissed on summary judgment under the rule against splitting one's cause of action. The trial court held that Ison's (P) personal injury claim was part of the same cause of action as his property damage claim and so had merged with the prior judgment. Ison (P) appealed, claiming that the trial court had misapplied the rule against splitting one's cause of action. The state's intermediate appellate court granted review.

ISSUE: Where a plaintiff brings one action after another, and the claims in the subsequent action could have been brought in the prior action, is the rule against splitting one's cause of action inapplicable if the plaintiff prevails in the prior action?

HOLDING AND DECISION: (Abramson, J.) No. Where a plaintiff brings one action after another, and the claims in the subsequent action could have been brought in the prior action, the rule against splitting one's cause of action is not inapplicable if the plaintiff prevails in the prior action. The rule against splitting one's cause of action is an aspect of the doctrine of res judicata. When a matter is in litigation, parties are required to bring forward their whole case; and the plea of res judicata applies not only to the points upon which the court was required by the parties to form an opinion and pronounce judgment, but to every point that properly belonged to the subject of litigation, and that the parties, exercising reasonable diligence, might have brought forward at the time. If the plaintiff prevails on his initial claim, other claims arising from the same transaction are said to merge with his judgment, and if the plaintiff loses initially, that judgment is said to bar any such subsequent claim. Although Thomas (D) did not raise res judicata as an affirmative defense in his answer, but raised it in his motion for summary judgment, that does not automatically waive this defense, provided Ison (P) was not prejudiced. Because the defense was raised before either party had expended much on discovery, Ison (P) was not prejudiced thereby. In sum, all claims against a single defendant arising from a single negligent incident must be brought in a single action. Ison (P) improperly split his claim for property damages from his claim for personal injury damages, where both claims arose against a single defendant as a result of a single accident. The damages claims should have been brought together, and because they were not, the trial court correctly ruled that the subsequent action is barred. Affirmed.

▌ ANALYSIS

The decision in this case echoes the Restatement (Second) Judgments, § 24, which provides that "[w]hen a valid and final judgment rendered in an action extinguishes the plaintiff's claim pursuant to the rules of merger or bar ... the claim extinguished includes all rights of the plaintiff to remedies against the defendant with respect to all or any part of the transaction, or series of connected transactions, out of which the action arose." The example used by the Restatement to illustrate this point is on all fours with the case at bar: "A and B, driving their respective cars, have a collision injuring A and damaging his car. The occurrence is single, and so is A's claim. If A obtains a judgment against B on the ground of negligence for the damage to the car, he is prevented by the doctrine of merger from subsequently maintaining an action for the harm to his person."

Quicknotes

CAUSE OF ACTION A fact or set of facts the occurrence of which entitles a party to seek judicial relief.

RES JUDICATA The rule of law that a final judgment by a court precludes subsequent litigation between the parties regarding the same cause of action.

Reise v. Board of Regents of the University of Wisconsin

Law school faculty applicant (P) v. State university (D)

957 F.2d 293 (7th Cir. 1992)

NATURE OF CASE: Appeal from order to submit to a mental examination.

FACT SUMMARY: E. H. Reise (P), who claimed he was discriminated against in his application to become a law school faculty member at the Law School of the University of Wisconsin at Madison (D), and that he suffered $4 million in damages from the resulting mental anguish, emotional distress, and illness, contended that it was erroneous to order him to submit to a mental examination.

RULE OF LAW

An interlocutory discovery order requiring a mental examination is not appealable prior to a final decision.

FACTS: E. H. Reise (P), a white male who graduated in the top of his class at the Law School of the University of Wisconsin at Madison (Law School) (D), applied for a faculty position at the Law School (D). When his application was denied, he brought suit, claiming that the denial was discriminatory, as in recent years the Law School (D) had been unwilling to consider anyone, no matter how skilled, who was not black, female, or otherwise eligible for preferential treatment. According to Reise (P), only one of the last 13 appointments to the faculty has been a white male. The Law School (D) countered that all the persons it hired were better lawyers and scholars than Reise (P). Reise (P) sought $4 million in damages from mental anguish, emotional distress, and illness that allegedly resulted from the Law School's (D) decision not to hire him. The trial court ordered that he submit to a mental examination under Fed. R. Civ. P. 35. Reise (P) objected on the grounds that an examination would reveal nothing of value, since he was over his distress and was not seeking damages on account of his current mental condition. Reise (P) appealed the order, and the U.S. Court of Appeals for the Seventh Circuit granted review.

ISSUE: Is an interlocutory discovery order requiring a mental examination appealable prior to a final decision?

HOLDING AND DECISION: (Easterbrook, J.) No. An interlocutory discovery order requiring a mental examination is not appealable prior to a final decision. Discovery orders, including orders to submit to an examination, are readily reviewable after final decision. A party aggrieved by the order assures eventual review by refusing to comply. The district judge then imposes sanctions under Fed. R. Civ. P. 37(b)(2). If Reise (P) were not to comply with the trial court's order, it is most likely that the court would impose a sanction striking Reise's (P) claim for damages on account of mental and physical distress. If Reise (P) then prevailed on the merits but did not obtain damages because of the order striking his claim, he could obtain full review on appeal: if the district judge abused his discretion in requiring Reise (P) to submit to an examination, the case would be remanded for further proceedings. Because almost all interlocutory appeals from discovery orders would end in affirmance (the district court possesses discretion, and review is deferential), the costs of delay via appeal, and the costs to the judicial system of entertaining these appeals, exceed in the aggregate the costs of the few erroneous discovery orders that might be corrected were appeals available. Further, requiring the complaining party to take some risk winnows weak claims, since only persons who have substantial objections to the examination and believe their legal positions strong will follow a path that could end in defeat. Among those who take the risk by balking at the order, some will lose on the merits, and their discovery disputes will become moot. Most of the remaining cases will end in affirmance, given deferential review. The number of retrials entailed by the procedure is small, the number of appeals avoided large. For all these reasons, the order is not appealable, and it is dismissed for lack of jurisdiction.

ANALYSIS

A "final" decision usually means the order ending the litigation, and, thus, an examination ordered under Fed. R. Civ. P. 35 does not meet that definition. Although the travail and expense of discovery and trial cannot be reversed at the end of the case, this alone has never been thought sufficient to allow pre-trial appeals. Indeed, even orders to produce information over strong objections based on privilege are not appealable, despite the claim that once the cat is out of the bag the privilege is gone.

Quicknotes

DISCOVERY Pretrial procedure during which one party makes certain information available to the other.

INTERLOCUTORY APPEAL The appeal of an issue that does not resolve the disposition of the case but is essential to a determination of the parties' legal rights.

Quick Reference Rules of Law

Pennoyer v. Neff

Purchaser of property (D) v. Real property owner (P)

95 U.S. 714 (1877)

NATURE OF CASE: Action to recover possession of land.

FACT SUMMARY: Neff (P) attacked the validity of a sheriff's sale of his property to satisfy a personal judgment obtained against him where service was by publication.

🏛 RULE OF LAW
Where the object of an action is to determine the personal rights and obligations of the parties, service by publication against a nonresident is ineffective to confer jurisdiction upon the court.

FACTS: Neff (P) owned real property in Oregon. Mitchell brought suit in Oregon to recover legal fees allegedly owed him by Neff (P). Neff (P), a nonresident, was served by publication and Mitchell obtained a default judgment. The court ordered Neff's (P) land sold at a sheriff's sale to satisfy the judgment. Pennoyer (D) purchased the property. Neff (P) subsequently learned of the sale and brought suit in Oregon to recover possession of the property. Neff (P) alleged that the court ordering the sale had never acquired in personam jurisdiction over him. Therefore, the court could not adjudicate the personal rights between Neff (P) and Mitchell, and the default judgment had been improperly entered.

ISSUE: Where an action involves the adjudication of personal rights and obligations of the parties, is service by publication against a nonresident sufficient to confer jurisdiction?

HOLDING AND DECISION: (Field, J.) No. Substituted service of process in actions against nonresidents of a state is effective only in proceedings in rem. Where an action involves the determination of personal rights and obligations of the parties, service by publication is ineffective to confer jurisdiction over the nonresident defendant. No state can exercise direct jurisdiction and authority over persons or property outside of its boundaries. The validity of every judgment depends upon the jurisdiction of the court rendering judgment. Thus, Mitchell could not obtain a personal judgment against Neff (P) without first obtaining in personam jurisdiction. Substituted service by publication is ineffective to confer personal jurisdiction over a nonresident. The sale was therefore void. A different result could have been reached if Mitchell had first obtained in rem jurisdiction by seizing the property at the time suit was commenced. Affirmed.

▶ ANALYSIS

Although no state can exercise direct jurisdiction and authority over people or property outside the state, the state may exercise jurisdiction over persons and property inside the state in ways that will affect persons and property outside the state. *Pennoyer v. Neff* established that every state had the power to regulate the way in which property within the state is acquired, enjoyed, and transferred. But a state cannot bring a person or property outside the state into its jurisdiction simply by using substituted service.

Quicknotes

IN PERSONAM JURISDICTION The jurisdiction of a court over a person as opposed to his interest in property.

IN REM JURISDICTION A court's authority over a thing so that its judgment is binding in respect to the rights and interests of all parties in that thing.

SERVICE OF PROCESS The communication of reasonable notice of a court proceeding to a defendant in order to provide him with an opportunity to be heard.

International Shoe Co. v. Washington

Delaware corporation (D) v. State (P)

326 U.S. 310 (1945)

NATURE OF CASE: Proceedings to recover unemployment contributions.

FACT SUMMARY: A state statute authorized the mailing of notice of assessment of delinquent contributions for unemployment compensation to nonresident employers. International Shoe Co. (International) (D) was a nonresident corporation. Notice of assessment was served on one of its salespersons within the state and was mailed to International's (D) office.

⚖ RULE OF LAW

For a state to subject a nonresident defendant to in personam jurisdiction, due process requires that the nonresident defendant have certain minimum contacts with the state such that the maintenance of the suit does not offend traditional notions of fair play and substantial justice.

FACTS: A Washington statute set up a scheme of unemployment compensation, which required contributions by employers. The statute authorized the commissioner, Washington (P), to issue an order and notice of assessment of delinquent contributions by mailing the notice to nonresident employers. International Shoe Co. (International) (D) was a Delaware corporation having its principal place of business in Missouri. International (D) employed 11 to 13 salespersons under the supervision of managers in Missouri. These salespeople resided in Washington, did most of their work there, and had no authority to enter into contracts or make collections. International (D) did not have an office in Washington and made no contracts there. Notice of assessment was served upon one of International's (D) Washington salespersons and a copy of the notice was sent by registered mail to International's (D) Missouri address.

ISSUE: For a state to subject a nonresident defendant to in personam jurisdiction, does due process require that the nonresident have certain minimum contacts with the state, such that the maintenance of the suit does not offend notions of fair play and substantial justice?

HOLDING AND DECISION: (Stone, C.J.) Yes. Historically the jurisdiction of courts to render judgment in personam is grounded on their power over the defendant's person, and the defendant's presence within the territorial jurisdiction of a court was necessary to a valid judgment. But now, due process requires only that in order to subject a defendant to a judgment in personam, if he is not present within the territorial jurisdiction, he has certain minimum contacts with the territory such that the mainte-

nance of the suit does not offend traditional notions of fair play and substantial justice. The contacts must be such as to make it reasonable, in the context of our federal system, to require a defendant corporation to defend the suit brought there. An estimate of the inconveniences that would result to the corporation from a trial away from its "home" is relevant. To require a corporation to defend a suit away from home where its contact has been casual or its activities isolated has been thought to lay too unreasonable a burden on the corporation. However, even single or occasional acts may, because of their nature, quality, and circumstances, be deemed sufficient to render a corporation liable to suit. Hence, the criteria to determine whether jurisdiction is justified are not simply mechanical or quantitative. Satisfaction of due process depends on the quality and nature of the activity in relation to the fair and orderly administration of the laws. In this case International's (D) activities were neither irregular nor casual. Rather, they were systematic and continuous. The obligation sued upon here arose out of these activities. They were sufficient to establish sufficient contacts or ties to make it reasonable to permit Washington (P) to enforce the obligations International (D) incurred there. Affirmed.

DISSENT: (Black, J.) The United States Constitution leaves to each state the power to tax and to open the doors of its courts for its citizens to sue corporations who do business in the state. It is a judicial deprivation to condition the exercise of this power on this court's notion of "fair play."

▶ ANALYSIS

Before this decision three theories had evolved to provide for suits by and against foreign corporations. The first was the consent theory. It rested on the proposition that since a foreign corporation could not carry on its business within a state without the permission of that state, the state could require a corporation to appoint an agent to receive service of process within the state. However, it soon became established law that a foreign corporation could not be prevented by a state from carrying on interstate commerce within its borders. The presence doctrine required that the corporation was "doing business" and "present" in the state. The third theory used either the present or consent doctrine, and it was necessary to determine whether the corporation was doing business within the state either to

Continued on next page.

decide whether its consent could properly be implied or to discover whether the corporation was present.

■■■■

Quicknotes

CONSENT JURISDICTION The forum having jurisdiction over a lawsuit as agreed upon by the parties prior to litigation.

IN PERSONAM JURISDICTION The jurisdiction of a court over a person as opposed to his interest in property.

MINIMUM CONTACTS The minimum degree of contact necessary in order to sustain a cause of action within a particular forum, consistent with the requirements of due process.

■■■■

McGee v. International Life Insurance Co.

Beneficiary (P) v. Insurance company (D)

355 U.S. 220 (1957)

NATURE OF CASE: Suit to enforce payment of life insurance proceeds.

FACT SUMMARY: McGee (P) was the beneficiary of a life insurance policy on a California resident who had purchased the policy from an insurer who was subsequently bought by International Life Insurance Co. (D). McGee obtained a judgment for the proceeds in California and attempted to enforce the judgment in Texas.

🏛 RULE OF LAW
Due process requires only that in order to subject a nonresident defendant to the personal jurisdiction of the forum, the suit be based on a contract that has substantial connection with the forum.

FACTS: Lowell Franklin, a resident of California, purchased a life insurance policy from an insurer. The reinsurer, International Life Insurance Co. (D), mailed a reinsurance certificate to the California resident offering to insure him. Franklin accepted this offer and paid all premiums by mail from his California home to the reinsurer's Texas office. The insured died, and the beneficiary, McGee (P), notified the insurer (D) of the death. The insurer (D) refused to make payment, and McGee (P) sued the insurer in California, obtaining a judgment.

ISSUE: Does due process require only that in order to subject a nonresident defendant to the personal jurisdiction of the forum, the suit be based on a contract that has substantial connection with the forum?

HOLDING AND DECISION: (Black, J.) Yes. Due process requires only that in order to subject a nonresident defendant to the personal jurisdiction of the forum, the suit be based on a contract that has substantial connection with the forum. Here, the insurance contract was delivered to California, and the premiums were payable there. The beneficiary and policyholders are California residents. It cannot be denied that California has a manifest interest in providing effective means of redress for its residents when their insurers refuse to pay claims. These residents would be at a severe disadvantage if forced to follow the insurance company to a distant state in order to hold it legally accountable.

▌ *ANALYSIS*

The fact of solicitation of the policy in California was a key element of this decision. That solicitation, albeit a single incident, could reasonably be thought to have put International Life Insurance Co. (D) on notice that it might be sued in California. If, on the other hand, the insured had taken out the policy in Texas and then moved to California, where he was the sole policyholder, this foreseeability argument would be greatly diluted. However, if the insured was one of a number of California policyholders, the exercise of personal jurisdiction there could be expected.

■=■

Quicknotes

FULL FAITH AND CREDIT DOCTRINE A judgment by a court of one state shall be given the same effect in another state.

MINIMUM CONTACTS The minimum degree of contact necessary in order to sustain a cause of action within a particular forum, consistent with the requirements of due process.

■=■

Hanson v. Denckla

Will legatees (P) v. Trust beneficiaries (D)

357 U.S. 235 (1958)

NATURE OF CASE: Appeal from disposition of property in a trust.

FACT SUMMARY: Mrs. Donner, mother of three daughters, established a trust in Delaware and later moved to Florida where she died.

🏛 RULE OF LAW
For there to be "minimal contacts" sufficient to support in personam jurisdiction, it is essential that there be some act by which the defendant purposefully avails itself of the privilege of conducting activities within the forum state, thus invoking the benefits and protections of its laws.

FACTS: Mrs. Donner established a trust in Delaware and later moved to Florida where she died. A will contest ensued among her three daughters: if Florida could acquire jurisdiction over the Delaware trust, two daughters would get the entire estate; if the Delaware courts had jurisdiction, all three daughters would share equally.

ISSUE: For there to be "minimal contacts" sufficient to support in personam jurisdiction, is it essential that there be some act by which the defendant purposefully avails itself of the privilege of conducting activities within the forum state, thus invoking the benefits and protections of its laws?

HOLDING AND DECISION: (Warren, C.J.) Yes. For there to be "minimal contacts" sufficient to support in personam jurisdiction, it is essential that there be some act by which the defendant purposefully avails itself of the privilege of conducting activities with the forum state, thus invoking the benefits and protections of its laws. In this case, no such contacts could be found. The Delaware trustee had no office in Florida and conducted no business there. No trust assets were ever held in Florida or administered there, and there was no solicitation of business in that state either in person or by mail. Consequently, this suit was not one to enforce an obligation that arose from a privilege exercised in Florida. However minimal the burden of defending in a foreign tribunal, a defendant may not be called upon to do so unless he or she has had the minimum contacts with that state that are a prerequisite to its exercise of power over him or her. Florida lacked jurisdiction.

▶ ANALYSIS

The case really revolves around the validity of the inter vivos trust. The trust was created in Delaware, and the corpus remains there. The fact that some Florida residents are beneficiaries thereunder, or that they wish to defeat the trust, is not a compelling state interest. It certainly is not a more substantial interest than is Delaware's right to construe the validity of a trust created under its laws and the corpus of which is within its jurisdiction. The fact that the settlor was a Florida resident is immaterial. She was not a resident when the trust was created, nor was she attempting to have the trust set aside.

Quicknotes

IN PERSONAM JURISDICTION The jurisdiction of a court over a person as opposed to his interest in property.

INTER VIVOS TRUST Property that is held by one person for the benefit of another and which is created by an instrument that takes effect during the life of the grantor.

MINIMUM CONTACTS The minimum degree of contact necessary in order to sustain a cause of action within a particular forum, consistent with the requirements of due process.

RESIDUARY CLAUSE (OF WILL) A clause contained in a will disposing of the assets remaining following distribution of the estate.

Shaffer v. Heitner

Corporation (D) v. Shareholder (P)

433 U.S. 186 (1977)

NATURE OF CASE: Appeal from a finding of state jurisdiction.

FACT SUMMARY: Heitner (P) brought a derivative suit against Greyhound (D) directors for antitrust losses it had sustained in Oregon. The suit was brought in Delaware, Greyhound's (D) state of incorporation.

🏛 RULE OF LAW
Jurisdiction cannot be founded on property within a state unless there are sufficient contacts within the meaning of the test developed in *International Shoe Co. v. Washington*.

FACTS: Heitner (P) owned one share of Greyhound (D) stock. Greyhound (D) had been subjected to a large antitrust judgment in Oregon. Heitner (P), a nonresident of Delaware, brought a derivative suit in Delaware, the state of Greyhound's (D) incorporation. Jurisdiction was based on sequestration of Greyhound (D) stock that was deemed to be located within the state of incorporation. The Delaware sequestration statute allowed property within the state to be seized ex parte to compel the owner to submit to the in personam jurisdiction of the court. None of the stock was actually in Delaware, but a freeze order was placed on the corporate books. Greyhound (D) made a special appearance to challenge the court's jurisdiction to hear the matter. Greyhound (D) argued that the sequestration statute was unconstitutional under the line of case's beginning with *Snidatch v. Family Finance Corp.*, 395 U.S. 337 (1969). Greyhound (D) also argued that there were insufficient contacts with Delaware to justify an exercise of jurisdiction. The Delaware courts found that the sequestration statute was valid since it was not a per se seizure of the property and was merely invoked to compel out-of-state residents to defend actions within the state. Little or no consideration was given to the "contact" argument based on a finding that the presence of the stock within the state conferred quasi in rem jurisdiction.

ISSUE: May a state assume jurisdiction over an issue merely because defendant's property happens to be within the state?

HOLDING AND DECISION: (Marshall, J.) No. Mere presence of property within a state is insufficient to confer jurisdiction on a court absent independent contacts within the meaning of *International Shoe Co. v. Washington*, 326 U.S. 310 (1945), which would make acceptance constitutional. We expressly disapprove that line of cases represented by *Harris v. Balk*, 198 U.S. 215 (1905), which permits jurisdiction merely because the property happens to be within the state. If sufficient contacts do not exist to assume jurisdiction absent the presence of property within the state, it cannot be invoked on the basis of property within the court's jurisdiction. We base this decision on the fundamental concepts of justice and fair play required under the Due Process and Equal Protection Clauses of the Fourteenth Amendment. Here, the stock is not the subject of the controversy. There is no claim to ownership of it or injury caused by it. The defendants do not reside in Delaware or have any contacts there. The injury occurred in Oregon. No activities complained of were done within the forum. Finally, Heitner (P) is not even a Delaware resident. Jurisdiction was improperly granted. Reversed.

CONCURRENCE: (Powell, J.) I would only disagree as to cases involving property permanently within the state, e.g., real property. Such property should confer jurisdiction.

CONCURRENCE: (Stevens, J.) I concur in the result since purchase of stock in the marketplace should not confer in rem jurisdiction in the state of incorporation. I also concur with Mr. Justice Powell's statements.

CONCURRENCE AND DISSENT: (Brennan, J.) A state may exercise jurisdiction over a party only on the basis of the minimum contacts among the parties, the contested transaction, and the forum state. In this case, however, the assertion of jurisdiction was based on the presence of property, in the form of capital stock, in Delaware. This is quasi in rem jurisdiction and is not based upon minimum contacts. However, even under the minimum contacts analysis that the majority requires today, jurisdiction should not be denied in this case. The State of Delaware has a strong interest in adjudicating claims as to corporations chartered by it. It must provide restitution for its corporations, it has a regulatory interest, and an interest in providing a convenient forum for the entity that is a creature of its law. Thus, jurisdiction should attach.

▶ ANALYSIS

While the corporation could be sued in its state of incorporation under the dissent's theory, the suit is against the directors and neither the site of the wrong nor the residence of a defendant is in Delaware. The decision will have a major impact only in cases such as this one, where the

Continued on next page.

state really has no reason to want to adjudicate the issue. Of course, real property would still be treated as an exception.

▰▰▰

Quicknotes

EX PARTE A proceeding commenced by one party without providing any opposing parties with notice or which is uncontested by an adverse party.

IN REM JURISDICTION A court's authority over a thing so that its judgment is binding in respect to the rights and interests of all parties in that thing.

QUASI IN REM JURISDICTION A court's authority over the defendant's property within a specified geographical area.

▰▰▰

World-Wide Volkswagen Corp. v. Woodson

Automobile distributor (P) v. Court (D)

444 U.S. 286 (1980)

NATURE OF CASE: Petition for a writ prohibiting the exercise of in personam jurisdiction.

FACT SUMMARY: World-Wide Volkswagen Corp. (P) sought a writ of prohibition to keep district court Judge Woodson (D) from exercising in personam jurisdiction over it, alleging it did not have sufficient "contacts" with the forum state of Oklahoma to render it subject to such jurisdiction.

🏛 RULE OF LAW
A state court may exercise personal jurisdiction over a nonresident defendant only so long as there exist sufficient "minimum contacts" between him and the forum state such that maintenance of the suit does not offend "traditional notions of fair play and substantial justice."

FACTS: World-Wide Volkswagen Corp. (World-Wide) (P) was the regional distributor of Audi automobile for the tri-state area of New York, New Jersey, and Connecticut. It was the distributor of the particular Audi that the Robinsons purchased from a New York dealer and drove to Oklahoma, where three family members were severely burned when another car struck their Audi in the rear. The Robinsons brought a products-liability action in an Oklahoma district court, suing the New York dealership and World-Wide (a New York corporation) (P). Claiming that no evidence showed it had any connection with Oklahoma whatsoever, World-Wide (P) sought a writ of prohibition to keep district court Judge Woodson (D) from exercising in personam jurisdiction. World-Wide (P) argued that a lack of sufficient contacts with the forum state made assertion of such jurisdiction improper under the Due Process Clause. The Oklahoma Supreme Court denied the writ, noting that World-Wide (P) could foresee that the automobiles it sold would be taken into other states, including Oklahoma. The United States Supreme Court granted certiorari.

ISSUE: Must a defendant have "minimum contacts" with the forum state before it can exercise in personam jurisdiction over him?

HOLDING AND DECISION: (White, J.) Yes. Under the Due Process Clause, the exercise of in personam jurisdiction over a defendant is not constitutional unless he has sufficient "minimum contacts" with the forum state so that maintenance of the suit does not offend "traditional notions of fair play and substantial justice." Here, World-Wide (P) had no "contacts, ties, or relations" with Oklahoma, so personal jurisdiction could not be exercised. As for the notion that it was foreseeable that cars sold in New York would wind up in Oklahoma, the foreseeability that is critical to due process analysis is not the mere likelihood that a product will find its way into the forum state. Rather, it is that the defendant's conduct and connection with the forum state are such that he should reasonably anticipate being hauled into court there. Such conduct and connection are simply missing in this case. Reversed.

DISSENT: (Brennan, J.) The automobile is designed specifically to facilitate travel from place to place, and the sale of one purposefully injects it into the stream of interstate commerce. Thus, this case is not unlike those where in personam jurisdiction is properly exercised over one who purposefully places his product into the stream of interstate commerce with the expectation it will be purchased by consumers in other states. Furthermore, a large part of the value of automobiles is the extensive, nationwide network of highways. State maintenance of such roads contributes to the value of World-Wide's (P) business. World-Wide (P) also participates in a network of related dealerships with nationwide service facilities. Having such facilities in Oklahoma also adds to the value of World-Wide's (P) business. Thus, it has the required minimum contacts with Oklahoma to render this exercise of personal jurisdiction constitutional.

▶ ANALYSIS

Over the years, modern transportation and communication have made foreign-state suits much less of a burden to defendants. This resulted in a relaxing of the due process limits placed on state jurisdiction down to the "minimum contacts" concept. However, even if there were no inconvenience to the defendant, a state could not exercise personal jurisdiction over him if he had no "contacts, ties, or relations." This is true even if that state had a strong interest in applying its law to the controversy, and it was the most convenient location for litigation, etc. The reason is that the Due Process Clause serves two distinct functions: the first is as a guarantor against inconvenient litigation but the second is as a guardian of interstate federalism. It is in this second capacity that the Due Process Clause would prevent assumption of jurisdiction in the aforementioned instance by recognizing the "territorial limitations on the power of the respective states."

■▬■▬■

Continued on next page.

Quicknotes

DUE PROCESS CLAUSE Clauses, found in the Fifth and Fourteenth Amendments to the United States Constitution, providing that no person shall be deprived of "life, liberty, or property, without due process of law."

IN PERSONAM JURISDICTION The jurisdiction of a court over a person as opposed to his interest in property.

MINIMUM CONTACTS The minimum degree of contact necessary in order to sustain a cause of action within a particular forum, consistent with the requirements of due process.

J. McIntyre Machinery, Ltd. v. Nicastro

Product manufacturer (D) v. Injured worker (P)

564 U.S. 873 (2011)

NATURE OF CASE: Appeal of judgment by state supreme court.

FACT SUMMARY: A person who was injured when he used a piece of heavy machinery sued the foreign manufacturer in New Jersey state court. The company disputed the state's jurisdiction.

> **RULE OF LAW**
> In products liability cases, the "stream-of-commerce" doctrine cannot displace the general rule that the exercise of judicial power is not lawful unless the defendant purposefully avails itself of the privilege of conducting activities within the forum state, thus invoking the benefits and protections of its laws.

FACTS: Robert Nicastro (P) injured his hand while using a metal-shearing machine that was manufactured by J. McIntyre Machinery, Ltd. (J. McIntyre) (D). The machine was manufactured in England, where J. McIntyre (D) is incorporated and operates, and the injury occurred in New Jersey. Nicastro (P) filed suit in New Jersey. The New Jersey Supreme Court found that it had jurisdiction over J. McIntyre (D) because J. McIntyre (D) machines were sold in the United States, the company attended annual conventions for the scrap recycling industry to advertise, four machines were identified in New Jersey, and J. McIntyre (D) guided advertising and sales efforts for the U.S. distributor. J. McIntyre (D) appealed.

ISSUE: In products liability cases, can the "stream-of-commerce" doctrine displace the general rule that the exercise of judicial power is not lawful unless the defendant purposefully avails itself of the privilege of conducting activities within the forum state, thus invoking the benefits and protections of its laws?

HOLDING AND DECISION: (Kennedy, J.) No. In products liability cases, the "stream-of-commerce" doctrine cannot displace the general rule that the exercise of judicial power is not lawful unless the defendant purposefully avails itself of the privilege of conducting activities within the forum state, thus invoking the benefits and protections of its laws. The Supreme Court of New Jersey held that New Jersey's courts can exercise jurisdiction over a foreign manufacturer of a product as long as the manufacturer knows or reasonably should know that its products are distributed through a nationwide distribution system that might lead to those products being sold in any of the 50 states. That rule is from *Asahi Metal Industry Co. v. Superior Court of Cal., Solano County*, 480 U.S. 102 (1987). Based on that test, the court concluded that the British

manufacturer of scrap metal machines was subject to New Jersey jurisdiction, even though the company had at no time advertised in, sent goods to, or in any way targeted the state. Those who live or operate primarily outside a state have a due process right not to be subjected to judgment in its courts, as a general rule. Where the individual or corporation explicitly consents to jurisdiction, is present in a state at the time a suit starts, is a citizen or has a domicile within the state, or is incorporated in the state, jurisdiction is proper, because all of those situations indicate an intent to submit to the laws of the state. The stream-of-commerce exception to the general rule refers to the movement of goods from manufacturers through distributors to consumers, and advocates of the exception argue that the placement of goods into the stream of commerce with the expectation that they will be purchased by consumers indicates purposeful availment. But the exception only holds where the activities manifest an intention to submit to the power of the sovereign. In this case, J. McIntyre (D) directed marketing and sales efforts at the United States, but not directly to New Jersey, and because of that, a federal court might have jurisdiction, but a New Jersey state court does not. It is J. McIntyre's (D) purposeful contacts with New Jersey, not with the United States, that are relevant. Because J. McIntyre has not engaged in conduct purposefully directed at New Jersey, New Jersey state courts did not have jurisdiction to hear the case. Reversed.

CONCURRENCE: (Breyer, J.) The judgment is correct, but it is determined by precedent. There is no reason to construct new general rules that limit jurisdiction, since on the basis of existing precedent, the case can be decided. No precedent finds that a single isolated sale, even if accompanied by the sales here, is sufficient. Nicastro (P) failed to meet his burden of showing that it was constitutionally proper to exercise jurisdiction over petitioner J. McIntyre (D).

DISSENT: (Ginsburg, J.) J. McIntyre (D) wanted to establish a market for its product in the United States and took steps to do so. Where in the United States buyers of the product live or operate is irrelevant to the manufacturer. The company simply wants to sell its product in the United States. Under *International Shoe Co. v. Washington*, 326 U.S. 310 (1945), personal jurisdiction is established.

▍ *ANALYSIS*

The absence of a majority opinion makes it difficult to identify a reliable rule. Three justices voted to reverse on

Continued on next page.

the basis of a new rule that limits jurisdiction more severely than precedent; three others voted to reverse on the basis of precedent, with making a new rule; and three others voted to affirm on the basis of precedent.

Quicknotes

FORUM STATE The state in which a court, or other location in which a legal remedy may be sought, is located.

PURPOSEFUL AVAILMENT An element in determining whether a defendant had the required minimum contacts in a forum necessary in order for a court to exercise jurisdiction over the party, whereby the court determines whether the defendant intentionally conducted activities in the forum and thus knows, or could reasonably expect, that such conduct could give rise to litigation in that forum.

Abdouch v. Lopez

Former book owner (P) v. Bookseller (D)

Neb. Sup. Ct., 285 Neb. 718, 829 N.W.2d 662 (2013)

NATURE OF CASE: Appeal from dismissal for lack of jurisdiction of action for infringement of privacy rights.

FACT SUMMARY: Helen Abdouch (P), a resident of Nebraska, brought suit in Nebraska, contending that Ken Lopez (D) and his company, Ken Lopez Bookseller (KLB) (D), residents of Massachusetts, violated her rights of privacy by using an inscription in Abdouch's (P) stolen copy of a book to advertise on the KLB (D) rare books website. Lopez (D) and KLB (D) claimed there were insufficient contacts with Nebraska to give that state's courts jurisdiction over the case.

RULE OF LAW
Contacts with a state that are created by an interactive website are not sufficient to support jurisdiction for an intentional tort cause of action where the website's content is not aimed at the state or its residents, and where the website's owner otherwise has minimal contacts with the state.

FACTS: Helen Abdouch (P), a Nebraska resident, had been the executive secretary of the Nebraska presidential campaign of John F. Kennedy (JFK). In 1963, Abdouch (P) received a copy of Richard Yates's book, *Revolutionary Road*. Yates, who had been JFK's press secretary, had inscribed the book to Abdouch (P). At some point, Abdouch's (P) inscribed copy of the book was stolen. In 2009, Ken Lopez (D) and his rare books company, Ken Lopez Bookseller (KLB) (D), residents of Massachusetts, obtained the book and sold it to a non-Nebraska resident. Abdouch (P) learned in 2011 that Lopez (D) had been using the inscription to advertise on the KLB (D) rare books. A picture of the inscription, an accompanying advertisement, and the word "SOLD" had been on the website for over three years. Abdouch (P) brought suit in Nebraska state court alleging that Lopez (D) and KLB (D) violated her privacy rights by using the inscription to advertise on the Internet. Lopez (D) and KLB (D) never exhibited at, or attended a book fair in Nebraska. KLB had an active mailing list for its catalogs of approximately 1,000 individuals and entities. Only two individuals on that list were located in Nebraska. Those two individuals had solicited contact with KLB (D) and had requested to be placed on KLB's (D) mailing list; KLB (D) had not solicited them. Also, neither of these two individuals had any connection to the claims at issue in Abdouch's (P) lawsuit. KLB's (D) total sales for 2009 through 2011 were approximately $3.9 million. In 2009, KLB (D) sold three books to a single Nebraska customer, earning a total of $76. In 2010, KLB

(D) sold three books to two Nebraska customers for $239.87. In 2011, two books were sold to a Nebraska customer for $299. All these sales were initiated by the customers through the KLB's (D) website. Lopez (D) and KLB (D) had no other contacts with Nebraska. Accordingly, they moved to dismiss for lack of jurisdiction, and the trial court granted their motion, finding insufficient contacts with Nebraska to support jurisdiction. The state's highest court granted review.

ISSUE: Are contacts with a state that are created by an interactive website sufficient to support jurisdiction for an intentional tort cause of action where the website's content is not aimed at the state or its residents, and where the website's owner otherwise has minimal contacts with the state?

HOLDING AND DECISION: (McCormack, J.) No. Contacts with a state that are created by an interactive website are not sufficient to support jurisdiction for an intentional tort cause of action where the website's content is not aimed at the state or its residents, and where the website's owner otherwise has minimal contacts with the state. The state's long-arm statute extends jurisdiction over nonresidents having any contact with or maintaining any relation to the state as far as the U.S. Constitution permits. Thus, the issue is whether Lopez (D) and KLB (D) had sufficient contacts with Nebraska so that the exercise of personal jurisdiction would not offend federal principles of due process. The case presents an issue of first impression in the state. However, other courts confronted with the issue of Internet jurisdiction have adopted the sliding scale test set forth in *Zippo Mfg. Co. v. Zippo Dot Com, Inc.*, 952 F. Supp. 1119 (W.D. Pa. 1997). Under that test, at one end of the spectrum, are situations where a defendant clearly does business over the Internet. At the other end of the spectrum are situations where the defendant has simply posted information on the Internet that is accessible to users in foreign jurisdictions. The middle ground is occupied by interactive websites where a user can exchange information with the host computer. Here, KLB's (D) website is interactive. However, beyond the minimal website sales to Nebraska residents and mailing catalogs to two Nebraska residents, Lopez's (D) and KLB's (D) contacts with Nebraska are nonexistent. They do not own, lease, or rent land in Nebraska. They have never advertised directly in Nebraska, participated in book fairs in Nebraska, or attended meetings in Nebraska, and neither has paid sales tax in Nebraska. Further, under federal law, when a plain-

Continued on next page.

tiff's claims are for intentional torts, the inquiry focuses on whether the conduct underlying the claims was purposely directed at the forum state. Here, Abdouch's (P) cause of action is an intentional tort, but there is no evidence that Lopez (D) and KLB (D) purposefully directed the advertisement at Nebraska, nor is there evidence that Lopez and KLB intended to invade Abdouch's (P) privacy in the state. Rather, the limited Internet sales appear to be random, fortuitous, and attenuated contacts with Nebraska—and thus the contacts from the website are unrelated to Abdouch's (P) cause of action. Under the effects test formulated by the United States Supreme Court in *Calder v. Jones*, 465 U.S. 783 (1984), a defendant's tortious acts can serve as a source of personal jurisdiction only where the plaintiff makes a prima facie showing that the defendant's acts (1) were intentional, (2) were uniquely or expressly aimed at the forum state, and (3) caused harm, the brunt of which was suffered—and which the defendant knew was likely to be suffered—in the forum state. Abdouch (P) contends that she can prevail under this test, but the evidence is to the contrary. Lopez (D) and KLB's (D) placement of the advertisement online was directed at the entire world, without expressly aiming it at Nebraska, and there is no evidence suggesting that Nebraska residents were targeted with the advertisement. Although the advertisement does mention "Abdouch was the executive secretary of the Nebraska (John F.) Kennedy organization," the advertisement does not expressly direct its offer of sale to Nebraska. The mere mention of Nebraska was incidental and was not included for the purposes of having the consequences felt in Nebraska. Also, Lopez (D) did not know that Abdouch (P) was a resident of Nebraska. He assumed that she had passed away and thus had no way of knowing that the brunt of harm would be suffered in Nebraska. For all these reasons, Abdouch's (P) complaint fails to plead facts to demonstrate that Lopez (D) and KLB (D) had sufficient minimum contacts with Nebraska such that they could have anticipated being hauled into a Nebraska court for their online advertisement. Affirmed.

▶ ANALYSIS

Applying the *Calder* effects test in the context of Internet intentional tort cases, the federal circuit courts have rejected the argument that posting defamatory or invasive material to the Internet is sufficient to confer personal jurisdiction. The circuits typically construe the test narrowly, so that, absent additional contacts, mere effects in the forum state are insufficient to confer personal jurisdiction. Where an Internet posting is aimed at the world generally and is not targeted or aimed at the state or its residents, the courts have consistently held that such postings by themselves are insufficient to confer jurisdiction.

Quicknotes

INTENTIONAL TORT A legal wrong resulting in a breach of duty, which is intentionally or purposefully committed by the wrongdoer.

JURISDICTION The authority of a court to hear and declare judgment in respect to a particular matter.

LONG-ARM STATUTE A state statute conferring personal jurisdiction to state courts over a defendant not residing in the state, when the cause of action arises as a result of activities conducted within the state or affecting state residents.

Goodyear Dunlop Tires Operations, S.A. v. Brown

Foreign subsidiaries of U.S. corporation (D) v. Decedents' parents (P)

564 U.S. 915 (2011)

NATURE OF CASE: Appeal of state court's assertion of jurisdiction.

FACTS SUMMARY: The parents of two American boys killed in a bus accident in France brought suit in North Carolina, where the boys lived, against the tire company.

RULE OF LAW

A state may not exercise general personal jurisdiction over a foreign subsidiary of a U.S. corporation where the subsidiary lacks continuous and systematic business contacts with the state.

FACTS: The parents (P) of two American boys who were killed in a bus accident in France brought suit in North Carolina state court against Goodyear Tire and Rubber Company (D) and three Goodyear subsidiaries (D) operating in Turkey, France, and Luxembourg. The parents (P) claimed that the accident resulted from a defective tire manufactured at the Turkish subsidiary's plant. Although Goodyear USA (D) operates in North Carolina, the three foreign subsidiaries (D) have no place of business, employees, or bank accounts in the state and neither solicit nor do business in the state. A small percentage of the subsidiaries' (D) tires were distributed in North Carolina by other Goodyear USA (D) affiliates, however. The subsidiaries (D) moved to dismiss the claims against them for lack of personal jurisdiction. The trial court denied the motion, and the North Carolina Court of Appeals affirmed, holding that the court had general jurisdiction over the subsidiaries (D) because their tires had reached the state through "the stream of commerce."

ISSUE: May a state exercise general personal jurisdiction over a foreign subsidiary of a U.S. corporation where the subsidiary lacks continuous and systematic business contacts with the state?

HOLDING AND DECISION: (Ginsburg, J.) No. A state may not exercise general personal jurisdiction over a foreign subsidiary of a U.S. corporation where the subsidiary lacks continuous and systematic business contacts with the state. As stated in *International Shoe Co. v. Washington*, 326 U. S. 310, 316 (1945), and its progeny, a distinction exists between general and specific personal jurisdiction. General personal jurisdiction arises from a defendant's "continuous and systematic" affiliation with a state and permits a state to exercise personal jurisdiction over the defendant for any claim, regardless of whether the claim itself has any connection to the defendant's activities in the state. Specific personal jurisdiction arises from a connection between the state and the underlying claim and permits a state to exercise jurisdiction only with respect to that claim. In this case, the North Carolina courts conflated the two types of jurisdiction, improperly using the isolated presence of the subsidiaries' products in the state as a result of others' actions to justify jurisdiction over the subsidiaries for claims having nothing to do with those products. Reversed.

ANALYSIS

Key to this case is the distinction between two types of personal jurisdiction: general and specific. General jurisdiction is all-purpose, in the sense that it allows any claim to be brought against a defendant as long as the defendant has "systematic and continuous" contacts with that forum. Specific jurisdiction exists where there is a connection between a forum and a particular controversy, and it is limited to that controversy. In this case, only general jurisdiction was in issue: The site of the accident and the factory where the tires were made were both outside of North Carolina, so there was no connection between the state and the controversy, and specific jurisdiction was therefore not properly at issue. As to whether general jurisdiction existed, the Court focused on the "stream of commerce," and reached the conclusion that jurisdiction did not exist.

Quicknotes

GENERAL JURISDICTION Refers to the authority of a court to hear and determine all cases of a particular type.

PERSONAL JURISDICTION The court's authority over a person or parties to a lawsuit.

Daimler AG v. Bauman

Foreign corporation (D) v. Foreign residents (P)

571 U.S. 117 (2014)

NATURE OF CASE: Appeal from reversal of dismissal, for lack of personal jurisdiction, of action asserting claims under the Alien Tort Statute and the Torture Victim Protection Act of 1991, as well as under state and foreign law.

FACT SUMMARY: Argentinian residents (P) brought suit against Daimler AG (Daimler) (D) in U.S. federal district court asserting various claims under the Alien Tort Statute and the Torture Victim Protection Act of 1991, as well as under state and foreign law, claiming that MB Argentina, an Argentinian subsidiary of Daimler (D), collaborated with state security forces during Argentina's 1976–1983 "Dirty War" to kidnap, detain, torture, and kill certain MB Argentina workers, among them, plaintiffs or persons closely related to the plaintiffs. Daimler (D) moved to dismiss for lack of personal jurisdiction, as none of MB Argentina's alleged actions occurred in the United States, because Daimler (D) had insufficient presence in the United States, and because jurisdiction could not be predicated on the presence in the United States of its indirect subsidiary, MBUSA.

RULE OF LAW

Notwithstanding significant contacts that may be imputed to a foreign corporation, the corporation is not subject to general jurisdiction in a state where the corporation is not at "home," i.e., where it is incorporated or has its principal place of business.

FACTS: Residents of Argentina (P) filed suit against Daimler AG (Daimler) (D) in California federal district court, alleging that MB Argentina, an Argentinian subsidiary of Daimler, collaborated with state security forces during Argentina's 1976–1983 "Dirty War" to kidnap, detain, torture, and kill certain MB Argentina workers, among them, plaintiffs or persons closely related to plaintiffs. Based on those allegations, plaintiffs asserted claims under the Alien Tort Statute and the Torture Victim Protection Act of 1991, as well as under California and Argentina law. Personal jurisdiction over Daimler (D) was predicated on the California contacts of MBUSA, an indirect Daimler (D) subsidiary, one incorporated in Delaware with its principal place of business in New Jersey. MBUSA, as an independent contractor, distributes vehicles manufactured by Daimler (D) to independent dealerships throughout the United States, including California. Daimler (D) moved to dismiss the action for want of personal jurisdiction. Opposing that motion, plaintiffs argued that jurisdiction over Daimler (D) could be founded on the California contacts of MBUSA. The district court granted Daimler's (D) motion to dismiss, finding that Daimler (D) itself has insufficient contacts with California to support jurisdiction, and that MBUSA did not act as Daimler's (D) agent. Reversing, the court of appeals held that MBUSA, which it assumed to fall within the California courts' all-purpose jurisdiction, was Daimler's (D) "agent" for jurisdictional purposes, so that Daimler (D), too, should generally be answerable to suit in California. The United States Supreme Court granted certiorari.

ISSUE: Notwithstanding significant contacts that may be imputed to a foreign corporation, is the corporation subject to general jurisdiction in a state where the corporation is not at "home," i.e., where it is incorporated or has its principal place of business?

HOLDING AND DECISION: (Ginsburg, J.) No. Notwithstanding significant contacts that may be imputed to a foreign corporation, the corporation is not subject to general jurisdiction in a state where the corporation is not at "home," i.e., where it is incorporated or has its principal place of business. Since *International Shoe* [*v. Washington*, 326 U.S. 310 (1945)], specific jurisdiction has become the centerpiece of modern jurisdiction theory. This Court's general jurisdiction opinions, in contrast, have been few. As is evident from these post-*International Shoe* decisions, while specific jurisdiction has been cut loose from *Pennoyer's* sway (*Pennoyer* [*v. Neff*, 95 U.S. 714 (1877)], held that a tribunal's jurisdiction over persons reaches no farther than the geographic bounds of the forum), general jurisdiction has not been stretched beyond limits traditionally recognized. As the Court has increasingly focused on the relationship among the defendant, the forum, and the litigation, i.e., the attributes of specific jurisdiction, general jurisdiction has come to occupy a less dominant place in the contemporary scheme. Taking these trends into account, even assuming, arguendo, that MBUSA qualifies as at home in California, Daimler's (D) affiliations with California are not sufficient to subject it to the general jurisdiction of California courts. Assuming MBUSA is at home in California and that MBUSA's contacts are imputable to Daimler (D), nevertheless there would still be no basis to subject Daimler (D) to general jurisdiction in California. The paradigm all-purpose forums for general jurisdiction are a corporation's place of incorporation and principal place of business. Plaintiffs' reasoning, however, would reach well beyond these exemplar bases to approve the exercise of general jurisdiction in every state in which a

Continued on next page.

corporation "engages in a substantial, continuous, and systematic course of business." Instead, the proper inquiry is whether a foreign corporation's affiliations with the state are so continuous and systematic as to render it essentially at home in the forum state. Neither Daimler (D) nor MBUSA is incorporated in California, nor does either entity have its principal place of business there. If Daimler's (D) California activities sufficed to allow adjudication of this Argentina-rooted case in California, the same global reach would presumably be available in every other state in which MBUSA's sales are sizable. The Court has never before sanctioned a view of general jurisdiction so grasping. The court of appeals, therefore, had no warrant to conclude that Daimler (D), even with MBUSA's contacts attributed to it, was at home in California, and hence subject to suit there on claims by foreign plaintiffs having nothing to do with anything that occurred or had its principal impact in California. Finally, the transnational context of this dispute bears attention. It is significant that the court of appeals paid little heed to the risks to international comity posed by its expansive view of general jurisdiction, which are not embraced by other nations. For these reasons, the exercise of personal jurisdiction over Daimler (D) would be inappropriate. Reversed.

CONCURRENCE: (Sotomayor, J.) The result of the Court's decision is correct, but not its approach. Here, Daimler (D) has conceded that California courts may exercise general jurisdiction over MBUSA on the basis of its contacts with California, and the Court assumes that MBUSA's contacts may be attributed to Daimler (D) for the purpose of deciding whether Daimler (D) is also subject to general jurisdiction. However, the Court errs in holding that these contacts are insufficient to permit the exercise of general jurisdiction over Daimler (D)—not because the contacts are too few, but because Daimler's (D) contacts with other forums are too many. In other words, the Court does not dispute that the presence of multiple offices, the direct distribution of thousands of products accounting for billions of dollars in sales, and continuous interaction with customers throughout a state would be enough to support the exercise of general jurisdiction over some businesses. Daimler (D) is just not one of those businesses, the Court concludes, because its California contacts must be viewed in the context of its extensive "nationwide and worldwide" operations. Such an approach is wrong, as it ignores the lodestar of our personal jurisdiction jurisprudence: A state may subject a defendant to the burden of suit if the defendant has sufficiently taken advantage of the state's laws and protections through its contacts in the state; whether the defendant has contacts elsewhere is immaterial. The Court instead should have reached the conclusion that exercising jurisdiction over Daimler (D) in this case was inappropriate because, no matter how extensive Daimler's (D) contacts with California, that state's exercise of jurisdiction would be unreasonable given the case involves foreign plaintiffs

suing a foreign defendant based on foreign conduct and given a more appropriate forum is available.

▶ ANALYSIS

Arguably, the majority's approach will result in several injustices. For example, it could result in small businesses being treated unfairly in comparison to national and multinational conglomerates: whereas a larger company will often be immunized from general jurisdiction in a state on account of its extensive contacts outside the forum, a small business will not be. The approach could also ostensibly create the incongruous result that an individual defendant whose only contact with a forum state is a one-time visit will be subject to general jurisdiction if served with process during that visit, but a large corporation that owns property, employs workers, and does billions of dollars' worth of business in the state will not be, simply because the corporation has similar contacts elsewhere (though the visiting individual surely does as well). Finally, the majority's approach could significantly shift the risk of loss from multinational corporations to the individuals harmed by their actions, since such corporations would be immunized from suit in any state, even if—and possibly because—the corporation has a massive presence in multiple states.

◼▬◼

Quicknotes

GENERAL JURISDICTION Refers to the authority of a court to hear and determine all cases of a particular type.

PERSONAL JURISDICTION The court's authority over a person or parties to a lawsuit.

◼▬◼

Bristol-Myers Squibb Co. v. Superior Court

Corporation (D) v. Class of individuals (P)

137 S. Ct. 1773 (2017)

NATURE OF CASE: Appeal from the California Supreme Court's decision in favor of the plaintiffs.

FACT SUMMARY: More than 600 plaintiffs alleged they suffered physical injuries caused by a drug, Plavix, manufactured by Bristol-Myers Squibb (BMS) (D), including 592 residents of other states.

🏛 **RULE OF LAW**

For a state court to exercise specific jurisdiction over a claim, the lawsuit must arise out of or relate to the defendant's contacts with the state.

FACTS: More than 600 plaintiffs alleged they suffered physical injuries caused by a drug, Plavix, a blood thinning pharmaceutical, manufactured by Bristol-Myers Squibb (BMS) (D). The cases were all filed in California Superior Court. The plaintiffs included 86 residents of California and 592 residents of thirty-three other states. BMS (D) is incorporated in Delaware and headquartered in New York. BMS (D) does have 400 employees working in California, including 250 sales representatives. Between 2007 and 2012, BMS (D) took in over $900 million in sales from Plavix. Significantly, the 592 residents of the other states did not allege they obtained Plavix in California or from a source in California. They did not claim they were injured in California nor did they receive any medical treatment in the state. After initial proceedings at the lower court levels, the California Supreme Court eventually decided that the California courts had specific jurisdiction over the claims filed by the nonresidents. BMS (D) appealed to the United States Supreme Court.

ISSUE: For a state court to exercise specific jurisdiction over a claim, must the lawsuit arise out of or relate to the defendant's contacts with the state?

HOLDING AND DECISION: (Alito, J.) Yes. For a state court to exercise specific jurisdiction over a claim, the lawsuit must arise out of or relate to the defendant's contacts with the state. A state court with general jurisdiction may adjudicate any claim made against a defendant, even if all the claims arise in a different state. General jurisdiction typically applies when a corporation has its headquarters in a particular state. Conversely, specific jurisdiction over a claim only arises when there is a connection between the state and the underlying case, usually via an activity or occurrence that takes place within the state. When assessing personal jurisdiction, courts must consider several factors. These include the interests of the forum state and of the plaintiff in proceeding with the cause in the plaintiff's forum of choice, but the main concern is the burden upon the defendant. Personal jurisdiction is limited by the territorial limitations of the state. Here, the California Supreme Court improperly concluded that its courts had jurisdiction over the claims of the nonresidents simply because their claims were similar to that of the state residents. This appears to be a form of general jurisdiction that is not supported by any prior decisions of this Court. Here, there are no connections between California and the claims of the nonresidents. Those plaintiffs did not purchase the drug in California, did not take the drug there, and were not treated for any injuries in the state. Accordingly, there are no facts present to establish specific jurisdiction over the claims of the nonresidents. Reversed.

DISSENT: (Sotomayor, J.) The majority's decision will make it difficult for class actions to proceed in one particular state court. Defendant corporations will now be forced to litigate separate claims in multiple jurisdictions. Clearly BMS (D) availed itself of the protections of the state of California by employing 400 people in the state and selling over $900 million dollars of the product in the state. The claims of the nonresidents also relate to BMS's (D) in-state activities. The nonresidents' claims are materially identical to the actions of BMS (D) in California.

▶ **ANALYSIS**

It is not yet apparent whether this decision has had a significant impact on the filing of class action lawsuits across the country. The decision clearly limits, if not bars, the ability of nonresident plaintiffs to file claims in a jurisdiction where specific jurisdiction will not be present over their claims.

■▬■

Quicknotes

CLASS ACTION A suit commenced by a representative on behalf of an ascertainable group that is too large to appear in court, shares a commonality of interests, and will benefit from a successful result.

PERSONAL JURISDICTION The court's authority over a person or parties to a lawsuit.

■▬■

Burnham v. Superior Court

Husband and father (P) v. Court (D)

495 U.S. 604 (1990)

NATURE OF CASE: Appeal from denial of motion to quash service of process in dissolution action on the grounds that the court lacked personal jurisdiction.

FACT SUMMARY: Dennis Burnham (P) and his wife were living in New Jersey when they decided to separate. Mrs. Burnham moved with the children to California, filed for divorce in that state and served Mr. Burnham (P) while he was visiting.

> 🏛 **RULE OF LAW**
> State courts have jurisdiction over nonresidents who are physically present in the state.

FACTS: Dennis Burnham (P) and his wife were living in New Jersey when they decided to separate. Mrs. Burnham moved with the children to California and filed for divorce in that state. Mr. Burnham (P) visited his children in January of 1988, at which time he was served with a California court summons and a copy of his wife's divorce petition. He made a special appearance in the California Superior Court (D) moving to quash the service of process on the ground that the Court (D) lacked personal jurisdiction over him because his only contacts with California were a few short visits to the state for the purpose of conducting business and visiting his children. The Superior Court (D) denied the motion, and the California Court of Appeals denied mandamus relief. The court held it to be a valid jurisdictional predicate for in personam jurisdiction that Mr. Burnham (P) was present in the forum state and personally served with process. The United States Supreme Court granted certiorari.

ISSUE: Do state courts have jurisdiction over nonresidents who are physically present in the state?

HOLDING AND DECISION: (Scalia, J.) Yes. State courts have jurisdiction over nonresidents who are physically present in the state. Jurisdiction based on physical presence alone constitutes due process because it is one of the continuing traditions of our legal system that define the due process standard of traditional notions of fair play and substantial justice. That standard was developed by analogy to physical presence, and it would be perverse to say it could now be turned against that touchstone of jurisdiction. Affirmed.

CONCURRENCE: (Brennan, J.) History is an important factor in establishing whether a jurisdictional rule satisfies due process requirements, but it is not the only factor such that all traditional rules of jurisdiction are, ipso facto, forever constitutional.

CONCURRENCE: (Stevens, J.) It is sufficient to note that the historical evidence and consensus identified by Justice Scalia, the considerations of fairness identified by Justice Brennan, and the common sense displayed by Justice White, all combine to demonstrate that this is, indeed, a very easy case.

▶ ANALYSIS

In a footnote to the above case, Justice Scalia explained that in *Helicopteros Nacionales de Columbia v. Hall*, 466 U.S. at 414 (1984), the Supreme Court held that due process is not offended by a state's subjecting a corporation to its jurisdiction when there are sufficient contacts between the state and the foreign corporation. However, the only holding supporting that statement involved regular service of summons upon a corporate president while in the forum state acting in that capacity. See *Perkins v. Benguet Consolidated Mining Co.*, 342 U.S. 437 (1952). It may be whatever special rule exists permitting continuous and systematic contacts to support jurisdiction with respect to matters unrelated to activity in the forum applied only to corporations, which have never fitted comfortably within a jurisdictional regime based primarily upon de facto power over the defendant's person.

■=■

Quicknotes

PERSONAL JURISDICTION The court's authority over a person or parties to a lawsuit.

SERVICE OF PROCESS The communication of reasonable notice of a court proceeding to a defendant in order to provide him with an opportunity to be heard.

■=■

Carnival Cruise Lines, Inc. v. Shute

Cruise company (D) v. Customers (P)

499 U.S. 585 (1991)

NATURE OF CASE: Review of denial of defense motion for summary judgment in personal injury action.

FACT SUMMARY: Shute (P), an injured cruise ship passenger, filed suit in her home state despite a stipulation in her passenger ticket requiring all suits to be filed in Florida.

🏛 RULE OF LAW
Reasonable forum-selection clauses contained in passenger tickets are presumptively valid.

FACTS: The Shutes (P), residents of Washington State, purchased passage for a seven-day cruise on a ship owned by Carnival Cruise Lines, Inc. (Carnival Cruise) (D). The cruise tickets they received contained a forum-selection clause setting the State of Florida as the forum where any disputes arising from the cruise would be litigated. Carnival Cruise (D) had its principal place of business in Florida, and many of its cruises departed from there. During the cruise, Mrs. Shute (P) was injured in a slip-and-fall accident. The Shutes (P) filed a negligence action in Washington. Carnival Cruise (D) moved for summary judgment, contending that the forum clause in the Shutes's (P) ticket required them to bring their suit in a Florida court. The U.S. Court of Appeals for the Ninth Circuit denied its motion on the ground that the clause was not a product of negotiation, and the United States Supreme Court granted certiorari.

ISSUE: Are reasonable forum-selection clauses contained in passenger tickets presumptively valid?

HOLDING AND DECISION: (Blackmun, J.) Yes. Reasonable forum-selection clauses contained in passenger tickets are presumptively valid. They are permissible because a cruise line has a special interest in limiting the fora in which it potentially could be subject to suit. Such a clause also dispels any confusion about where a suit must be brought, thereby sparing litigants and courts the time and expense of litigating the issue. Finally, the passengers themselves benefit from forum clauses because fares are reduced commensurate with the money saved by the cruise line in limiting the fora where it may be sued. Since in this case there is no bad-faith motive apparent in Carnival Cruise's (D) forum provision, and the Shutes (P) have conceded that they had notice of the provision, the Ninth Circuit erred in refusing to enforce the clause. Reversed.

DISSENT: (Stevens, J.) The prevailing rule is that forum-selection clauses are not enforceable if they were not freely bargained for, create additional expense for one party, or deny one party a remedy.

▶ ANALYSIS

Besides forum-selection clauses, a contract may contain a choice of law clause, stipulating which jurisdiction's substantive law will govern, or an arbitration clause, requiring parties to use arbitration as their exclusive forum. The most extreme example of a contract provision limiting a defendant's right to appeal or to even raise a defense to an action is the "cognovit." A cognovit note is written authority of a debtor for entry of a judgment against him if the obligation set forth in the note is not paid when due. Such agreements are prohibited in many states.

Quicknotes

COGNOVIT NOTE A note signed by a debtor authorizing an attorney to enter judgment against him if payment is not made thereon.

FORUM-SELECTION CLAUSE Provision contained in a contract setting forth the particular forum in which the parties would resolve a matter if a dispute were to arise.

Mullane v. Central Hanover Bank & Trust Co.

Guardian of trust beneficiaries (P) v. Bank (D)

339 U.S. 306 (1950)

NATURE OF CASE: Constitutional challenge of the sufficiency of the notice provision of the New York Banking Law relating to beneficiaries of common-trust funds.

FACT SUMMARY: Central Hanover Bank & Trust Co. (D) pooled a number of small trust funds, and beneficiaries (some of whom lived out of state) were notified by publication in a local newspaper.

🏛 RULE OF LAW
In order to satisfy due process challenges, notice must be by means calculated to inform the desired parties, and, where they reside outside of the state and their names and addresses are available, notice by publication is insufficient.

FACTS: A New York statute allowed corporate trustees to pool the assets of numerous small trusts administered by them. This allowed more efficient and economical administration of the funds. Each participating trust shared ratably in the common fund, but the trustees held complete control of all assets. A periodic accounting of profits, losses, and assets were to be submitted to the courts for approval. Beneficiaries were to be notified of the accounting so that they might object to any irregularities in the administration of the common fund. Once approved by the court, their claims would be barred. A guardian would be appointed to protect the interests of principal and income beneficiaries. Central Hanover Bank & Trust Co. (D) established a common fund by consolidating the corpus of 113 separate trusts under their control. Notice of the common fund was sent to all interested parties along with the relevant portions of the statute. Notice of accountings was by publication in a local New York newspaper. Mullane (P) was the appointed guardian for all parties known and unknown who had an interest in the trust's income. He objected to the sufficiency of the statutory notice provisions claiming that they violated the Due Process Clause of the Fourteenth Amendment. Notice by publication was not a reasonable method of informing interested parties that their rights were being affected, especially with regard to out-of-state beneficiaries. Mullane's (P) objections were overruled in state courts and Mullane (P) brought the present federal appeal.

ISSUE: Is notice by publication sufficient to satisfy due process challenges where the parties to be informed reside out of state and an alternative means, better calculated to give actual notice, is available?

HOLDING AND DECISION: (Jackson, J.) No. The purpose of a notice requirement is to inform parties that their rights are being affected. Therefore, the method chosen should, if at all possible, be reasonably designed to accomplish this end. Notice in a New York legal paper is not reasonably calculated to provide out-of-state residents with the desired information. While the state has a right to discharge trustees of their liabilities through the acceptance of their accounting, it must also provide beneficiaries with adequate notice so that their rights to contest the accounting are not lost. In cases where the identity or whereabouts of beneficiaries or future interest holders is unknown, then publication is the most viable alternate means available for giving notice. Publication is only a supplemental method of giving notice. However, the Court will approve its use where alternative methods are not reasonably possible or practical. Where alternative methods, better calculated to give actual notice, are available, publication is an impermissible means of providing notice. Notice to known beneficiaries via publication is inadequate, not because it in fact fails to inform everyone, but, because under the circumstances, it is not readily calculated to reach those who could easily be informed by other means at hand. Since publication to known beneficiaries is ineffective, the statutory requirement violates the Due Process Clause of the Fourteenth Amendment. These parties have, at least potentially, been deprived of property without due process of law. With respect to remote future interest holders and unknown parties, publication is permissible. Reversed and remanded.

▶ ANALYSIS

Ineffective notice provisions violate procedural due process rights. As in all due process challenges, there must be a legitimate state interest and the means selected must be reasonably adapted to accomplish the state's purpose. While in *Mullane* the state's ends were permissible, the method of giving notice was unreasonable as it pertained to known parties. As has been previously stated, publication is only a supplementary method for giving notice. It is normally used in conjunction with other means when personal service by hand is unavailable or impractical. *Mullane* has been applied to condemnation cases where a known owner of property was never personally served. *Schroeder v. City of New York*, 371 U.S. 208 (1962). Factors considered by the Court involve the nature of the action, whether the party's whereabouts or identity are known or unknown, whether he is a resident and whether or not he has attempted to avoid personal service. If an attempt to avoid service is made, then constructive service by publi-

Continued on next page.

cation in conjunction with substitute service by mail is permitted. Finally, foreign corporations are generally required to appoint resident agents authorized to accept service of process.

∎▬∎

Quicknotes

DUE PROCESS The constitutional mandate requiring the courts to protect and enforce individuals' rights and liberties consistent with prevailing principles of fairness and justice and prohibiting the federal and state governments from such activities that deprive its citizens of life, liberty, or property interest.

NOTICE Communication of information to a person by one authorized or by an otherwise proper source.

∎▬∎

Gibbons v. Brown

Automobile passenger (D) v. Fellow passenger (P)

Fla. Dist. Ct. App., 716 So. 2d 868 (1998)

NATURE OF CASE: Appeal from dismissal of a personal-injury action.

FACT SUMMARY: Mrs. Brown (P) filed a suit against Gibbons (D), a Texas resident, in Florida two years after Gibbons (D) had sued Mr. Brown in a Florida case involving the same auto accident.

🏛 RULE OF LAW
A prior decision to file a lawsuit in a state does not qualify as sufficient activity in the state to confer personal jurisdiction.

FACTS: Mr. Brown was driving a car in Canada, in which Mrs. Brown (P) and Gibbons (D) were passengers. After a collision, Gibbons (D), a Texas resident, sued Mr. Brown in Florida. Two years later, Mrs. Brown (P) filed suit against Gibbons (D) in Florida for allegedly causing the accident by giving faulty directions. The trial court dismissed the action based on a lack of personal jurisdiction over Gibbons (D). Mrs. Brown (P) appealed.

ISSUE: Does a prior decision to file a lawsuit in a state qualify as sufficient activity in the state to confer personal jurisdiction?

HOLDING AND DECISION: (Per curiam) No. A prior decision to file a lawsuit in a state does not qualify as sufficient activity in the state to confer personal jurisdiction. Obtaining personal jurisdiction over a nonresident defendant requires a two-pronged showing. First, there must be sufficient jurisdictional facts to bring the defendant within the long-arm statute. Then, there must be sufficient minimum contacts between the defendant and forum state such that jurisdiction would not violate due process. Florida requires that nonresident defendants engage in substantial and not isolated activity within the state in order to be subject to personal jurisdiction. There is no doubt that when an out-of-state plaintiff brings an action in Florida, she is subject to jurisdiction in subsequent actions regarding the same subject matter. However, in the present case, there were two years separating Gibbons's (D) suit against Mr. Brown and Mrs. Brown's (P) current action. Additionally, Mrs. Brown (P) was not a party to the first suit. Given these facts, and the lack of any other contact between Gibbons (D) and Florida, the grounds for personal jurisdiction do not meet the state's requirements. Complaint dismissal ordered.

▶ ANALYSIS

The court acknowledged that Florida does not allow jurisdiction to the full range allowed by the United States Constitution. Thus, in the present case, it is possible that another state would have allowed the case against Gibbons (D) to proceed. However, the court never reached the issue of whether the minimum contacts required by due process had been met.

Quicknotes

LONG-ARM STATUTE A state statute conferring personal jurisdiction to state courts over a defendant not residing in the state, when the cause of action arises as a result of activities conducted within the state or affecting state residents.

PERSONAL JURISDICTION The court's authority over a person or parties to a lawsuit.

PROCEDURAL DUE PROCESS The constitutional mandate that if the state or federal government acts so as to deny a citizen of a life, liberty, or property interest the individual is first entitled to notice and the right to be heard.

Thompson v. Greyhound Lines, Inc.

Passenger (P) v. Bus line (D)

2012 WL 6213792 (S.D. Ala. 2012)

NATURE OF CASE: Motion to dismiss on the grounds, inter alia, of improper venue.

FACT SUMMARY: Thompson (P) brought suit in federal court in Alabama against Greyhound Lines, Inc. (Greyhound) (D) on several state-law claims arising from his having fallen asleep on a bus and missing a court appearance in Mississippi because the bus driver did not wake him and took him back to Alabama. Greyhound (D) moved to dismiss on grounds, inter alia, of improper venue.

RULE OF LAW

Where venue is improper in a federal district, but would be proper in a different district, a case will be transferred to the proper district instead of being dismissed where doing so serves the interests of justice.

FACTS: Thompson (P) on March 14 bought from Greyhound Lines, Inc. (Greyhound) (D) in Pensacola, Florida, a one-way ticket to Tunica, Mississippi, to arrive at 5:05 p.m. on March 15. A Greyhound (D) bus delivered Thompson (P) from Pensacola to Mobile, Alabama, just after midnight on March 15. Seven hours later, Greyhound (D) personnel directed Thompson (P) to board a Colonial Trailways (D) bus. The driver, Reeves (D)—a Florida resident—announced that the bus was traveling only to Jackson, Mississippi, and would thereafter return to Mobile. Reeves (D) also announced that his bus was scheduled to arrive in Jackson at 12:05 p.m. and that a bus would depart Jackson at 12:30 p.m., arriving in Tunica at 5:05 p.m. Thompson (P), upon hearing this, decided it was time for a nap. Thompson (P) awoke at 2:30 p.m., finding himself heading back to Mobile. Reeves (D) refused to change course. Thompson (P) then remained in Mobile for over nine hours before his brother sent him a pre-paid ticket back to Pensacola. Because of these events, Thompson (P) "missed his court-date and was found guilty in absentia." He sued Greyhound (D), Colonial Trailways (D), and Reeves (D) on several state law causes of action, basing subject matter jurisdiction on diversity of citizenship. Greyhound (D) moved to dismiss on grounds of improper venue, as well as for failure to state a claim.

ISSUE: Where venue is improper in a federal district, but would be proper in a different district, will a case be transferred to the proper district instead of being dismissed where doing so serves the interests of justice?

HOLDING AND DECISION: (Steele, J.) Yes. Where venue is improper in a federal district, but would

be proper in a different district, a case will be transferred to the proper district instead of being dismissed where doing so serves the interests of justice. As a threshold matter, challenges to venue should be considered before motions to dismiss for failure to state a claim. Thus, it is proper to consider Greyhound's (D) motion to dismiss for improper venue. A plaintiff has the burden of showing that venue in the forum is proper, but where there has been no evidentiary hearing, the plaintiff need present only prima facie showing that venue is proper. Thompson (P) has failed to make such a showing. Venue can be established in a judicial district in which any defendant resides, if all defendants are residents of the state in which the district is located. Because Reeves (D) was a Florida resident, venue is improper under 28 U.S.C. § 1391(b)(1). Under 28 U.S.C. § 1391(b)(2), venue is also proper in a judicial district in which a substantial part of the events or omissions giving rise to the claim occurred. Here, the only event that occurred in this District was that Thompson (P) changed buses here, and that event did not "directly give rise to a claim." The mere fact that Thompson (P) passed through this District and changed buses here is not a "part of the events or omissions giving rise to the claim," much less a "substantial" part. Accordingly, venue is not proper under § 1391(b)(2). However, a substantial part of the events or omissions giving rise to Thompson's (P) claims certainly occurred in the Southern District of Mississippi. Where a case has been improperly filed in the wrong district, the court in that district has the discretion to dismiss the case, or, if the interests of justice would be served, to transfer the case to the proper district, provided that district has jurisdiction over the matter. Here, the Southern District of Mississippi would have specific personal jurisdiction since the key events giving rise to Thompson's (P) claims occurred there. Generally, the interests of justice favor transferring a case to the appropriate judicial district rather than dismissing it. Because Greyhound (D) has failed to articulate any reasons why dismissal should be preferred over transferring the case, the case should be transferred to the Southern District of Mississippi. Greyhound's (D) motion to dismiss is, therefore, denied.

▶ ANALYSIS

Although the court here notes that the transferee court must have personal jurisdiction over the parties, the court must also have subject matter jurisdiction. Thompson's (P) action in the Southern District of Mississippi was dis-

Continued on next page.

missed because that court determined that Thompson (P) was a Florida citizen at the time he filed that action. Because Reeves (D) was also a Florida citizen, the court lacked diversity jurisdiction under 28 U.S.C. § 1332, and no federal question was asserted under 28 U.S.C. § 1331. Thus, the defendants were able to prevail without ever reaching the issue of whether Thompson (P) failed to state a claim.

Quicknotes

DIVERSITY OF CITIZENSHIP Parties are citizens of different states, or one party is an alien; a factor, along with a statutorily set dollar value of the matter in controversy, that allows a federal district court to exercise its authority to hear a lawsuit based on diversity jurisdiction.

DIVERSITY JURISDICTION The authority of a federal court to hear and determine cases involving parties who are of different states and an amount in controversy greater than a statutorily set amount.

PERSONAL JURISDICTION The court's authority over a person or parties to a lawsuit.

SUBJECT MATTER JURISDICTION The authority of the court to hear and decide actions involving a particular type of issue or subject.

VENUE The specific geographic location over which a court has jurisdiction to hear a suit.

Piper Aircraft v. Reyno

Aircraft company (D) v. Crash victims' representative (P)

454 U.S. 235 (1981)

NATURE OF CASE: Appeal from dismissal on the basis of forum non conveniens.

FACT SUMMARY: Reyno (P), the representative of five victims of an air crash, brought suit in California even though the location of the crash and the homes of the victims were in Scotland.

🏛 RULE OF LAW

A plaintiff may not defeat a motion to dismiss for forum non conveniens merely by showing that the substantive law that would be applied in the alternative forum is less favorable to her than that of the present forum.

FACTS: Reyno (P) was the representative of five air crash victims' estates and brought suit for wrongful death in United States district court in California, even though the accident occurred and all the victims resided in Scotland. Piper Aircraft (D) moved to dismiss for forum non conveniens, contending that Scotland was the proper forum. Reyno (P) opposed the motion on the basis that the Scottish laws were less advantageous to her position than American laws. The district court granted the motion, while the court of appeals reversed. The United States Supreme Court granted certiorari.

ISSUE: May a plaintiff defeat a motion to dismiss for forum non conveniens merely on the basis that the laws of the alternative forum are less advantageous?

HOLDING AND DECISION: (Marshall, J.) No. A plaintiff may not defeat a motion to dismiss for forum non conveniens merely by showing that the substantive law of the alternative forum is less advantageous than that of the present forum. In this case, all the evidence, witnesses, and interests were in Scotland. Thus, the most convenient forum was there. As a result, the motion was properly granted. Reversed.

▶ ANALYSIS

The Court in this case specifically noted that under some circumstances, the fact that the chosen state's laws are less attractive to the defendant could be used to defeat a motion to dismiss for forum non conveniens. If the state chosen by the plaintiff has the only adequate remedy for the wrong alleged, then the motion may be denied.

Quicknotes

FORUM NON CONVENIENS An equitable doctrine permitting a court to refrain from hearing and determining a case when the matter may be more properly and fairly heard in another forum.

MOTION TO DISMISS Motion to terminate a trial based on the adequacy of the pleadings.

Atlantic Marine Construction Co. v. United States District Court

Party to a contract containing a forum-selection clause (P) v. Federal district court (D)

571 U.S. 49 (2013)

NATURE OF CASE: Appeal from affirmance of denial of motions to dismiss or to transfer an action involving a contract containing a forum-selection clause.

FACT SUMMARY: Notwithstanding that Atlantic Marine Construction Co. (Atlantic Marine) (P) and J-Crew Management, Inc. (J-Crew) had a contract that contained a forum-selection clause providing that all disputes between the parties would be litigated in Virginia, J-Crew brought suit in the District Court for the Western District of Texas (District Court) (D). The District Court denied Atlantic Marine's (P) motions to either dismiss the action or transfer it to a district court in Virginia, finding that Atlantic Marine (P) had not carried its burden under 28 U.S.C. § 1404(a) for a transfer, which it concluded was the only mechanism for enforcing a forum-selection clause that points to a federal district. Atlantic Marine (P) challenged the District Court's (D) rulings.

> ## 🏛 RULE OF LAW
> A forum-selection clause may be enforced in a civil action by a motion to transfer under 28 U.S.C. § 1404(a), but not under 28 U.S.C. § 1406(a) or Fed. R. Civ. P. 12(b)(3).

FACTS: Atlantic Marine Construction Co. (Atlantic Marine) (P), a Virginia corporation, entered a subcontract with J-Crew Management, Inc. (J-Crew), a Texas corporation, for work on a construction project. The subcontract included a forum-selection clause, which stated that all disputes between the parties would be litigated in Virginia. When a dispute arose, however, J-Crew filed suit in the Western District of Texas. Atlantic Marine (P) moved to dismiss, arguing that the forum-selection clause rendered venue "wrong" under 28 U.S.C. § 1406(a) and "improper" under Fed. R. Civ. P. 12(b)(3). In the alternative, Atlantic Marine (P) moved to transfer the case to the Eastern District of Virginia under 28 U.S.C. § 1404(a). The District Court for the Western District of Texas (D) denied both motions. It concluded that § 1404(a) is the exclusive mechanism for enforcing a forum-selection clause that points to another federal forum; that Atlantic Marine (P) bore the burden of establishing that a transfer would be appropriate under § 1404(a); and that the court would consider both public- and private-interest factors, only one of which was the forum-selection clause. After weighing those factors, the court held that Atlantic Marine (P) had not carried its burden. The court of appeals affirmed, agreeing with the District Court (D) that § 1404(a) is the exclusive mechanism for enforcing a forum-selection clause that points to

another federal forum; that dismissal under Rule 12(b)(3) would be the correct mechanism for enforcing a forum-selection clause that pointed to a nonfederal forum; and that the District Court (D) had not abused its discretion in refusing to transfer the case after conducting the balance-of-interests analysis required by § 1404(a). The United States Supreme Court granted certiorari.

ISSUE: May a forum-selection clause be enforced in a civil action by a motion to transfer under 28 U.S.C. § 1404(a), but not under 28 U.S.C. § 1406(a) or Fed. R. Civ. P. 12(b)(3)?

HOLDING AND DECISION: (Alito, J.) Yes. A forum-selection clause may be enforced in a civil action by a motion to transfer under 28 U.S.C. § 1404(a), but not under 28 U.S.C. § 1406(a) or Fed. R. Civ. P. 12(b)(3). Section 1406(a) and Rule 12(b)(3) allow dismissal only when venue is "wrong" or "improper." Whether venue is "wrong" or "improper" depends exclusively on whether the court in which the case was brought satisfies the requirements of federal venue laws. 28 U.S.C. § 1391, which governs venue generally, states that "[e]xcept as otherwise provided by law ... this section shall govern the venue of all civil actions brought in" federal district courts. Section 1391(a)(1). It then defines districts in which venue is proper in § 1391(b). If a case falls within one of § 1391(b)'s districts, venue is proper; if it does not, venue is improper, and the case must be dismissed or transferred under § 1406(a). Whether the parties' contract contains a forum-selection clause has no bearing on whether a case falls into one of the specified districts. Although a forum-selection clause does not render venue in a court "wrong" or "improper" under § 1406(a) or Rule 12(b)(3), the clause may be enforced through a motion to transfer under § 1404(a), which permits transfer to any other district where venue is proper or to any district to which the parties have agreed by contract or stipulation. Section 1404(a), however, governs transfer only within the federal court system. When a forum-selection clause points to a state or foreign forum, the clause may be enforced through the doctrine of forum non conveniens. Section 1404(a) is a codification of that doctrine for the subset of cases in which the transferee forum is another federal court. For all other cases, parties may still invoke the residual forum non conveniens doctrine. Because both § 1404(a) and the forum non conveniens doctrine from which it derives entail the same balancing-of-interests standard, courts should evaluate a forum-selection clause pointing to a

Continued on next page.

nonfederal forum in the same way that they evaluate a forum-selection clause pointing to a federal forum. Although the court of appeals correctly identified § 1404(a) as the appropriate provision to enforce the forum-selection clause in this case, it erred in failing to make the adjustments required in a § 1404(a) analysis when the transfer motion is premised on a forum-selection clause. When the parties have agreed to a valid forum-selection clause, a district court should ordinarily transfer the case to the forum specified in that clause, as only under extraordinary circumstances unrelated to the convenience of the parties should a § 1404(a) motion be denied. Although no such exceptional factors appear to be present in this case, the case is remanded for the lower court to make that determination. Reversed and remanded.

▶ ANALYSIS

In the typical case not involving a forum-selection clause, a district court considering a § 1404(a) motion (or a forum non conveniens motion) must evaluate both the convenience of the parties and various public-interest considerations. Ordinarily, the district court would weigh the relevant factors and decide whether, on balance, a transfer would serve "the convenience of parties and witnesses" and otherwise promote "the interest of justice." The Court here noted that this calculus changes when the parties' contract contains a valid forum-selection clause. The Court reasoned that when parties have contracted in advance to litigate disputes in a particular forum, courts should not unnecessarily disrupt the parties' settled expectations, since a forum-selection clause may have figured centrally in the parties' negotiations and may have affected how they set monetary and other contractual terms; it may, in fact, have been a critical factor in their agreement to do business together in the first place. Thus, the Court concluded that in all but the most unusual cases, "the interest of justice" is served by holding parties to their bargain.

■▬■

Quicknotes

FORUM NON CONVENIENS An equitable doctrine permitting a court to refrain from hearing and determining a case when the matter may be more properly and fairly heard in another forum.

FORUM-SELECTION CLAUSE Provision contained in a contract setting forth the particular forum in which the parties would resolve a matter if a dispute were to arise.

■▬■

Subject Matter Jurisdiction of the Federal Courts

Quick Reference Rules of Law

Louisville & Nashville Railroad v. Mottley

Railroad company (D) v. Injured passengers (P)

211 U.S. 149 (1908)

NATURE OF CASE: Appeal of a decision overruling a demurrer in an action for specific performance of a contract.

FACT SUMMARY: Mottley (P) was injured on a train owned by Louisville & Nashville Railroad (D), which granted Mottley (P) a lifetime free pass, which he sought to enforce.

🏛 RULE OF LAW
Alleging an anticipated constitutional defense in the complaint does not give a federal court jurisdiction if there is no diversity of citizenship between the litigants.

FACTS: In 1871, Mottley (P) and his wife were injured while riding on the Louisville & Nashville Railroad (D). The Mottleys (P) released their claims for damages against the Louisville & Nashville Railroad (D) upon receiving a contract granting free transportation during the remainder of their lives. In 1907, the Louisville & Nashville Railroad (D) refused to renew the Mottleys' (P) passes, relying upon an act of Congress that forbade the giving of free passes or free transportation. The Mottleys (P) filed an action in a Circuit Court of the United States for the Western District of Kentucky. The Mottleys (P) and the Louisville & Nashville Railroad (D) were both citizens of Kentucky. Therefore, the Mottleys (P) attempted to establish federal jurisdiction by claiming that the Louisville & Nashville Railroad (D) would raise a constitutional defense in their answer, thus raising a federal question. The Louisville & Nashville Railroad (D) filed a demurrer to the complaint for failing to state a cause of action. The demurrer was denied. On appeal, the Supreme Court did not look at the issue raised by the litigants, but on their own motion raised the issue of whether the federal courts had jurisdiction to hear the case.

ISSUE: Does an allegation in the complaint that a constitutional defense will be raised in the answer raise a federal question that would give a federal court jurisdiction if no diversity of citizenship is alleged?

HOLDING AND DECISION: (Moody, J.) No. The Supreme Court reversed the lower court's ruling and remitted the case to that court with instructions to dismiss the suit for want of jurisdiction. Neither party to the litigation alleged that the federal court had jurisdiction in this case, and neither party challenged the jurisdiction of the federal court to hear the case. Because the jurisdiction of the circuit court is defined and limited by statute, the Supreme Court stated that it is their duty to see that such

jurisdiction is not exceeded. Both parties to the litigation were citizens of Kentucky and so there was no diversity of citizenship. The only way that the federal court could have jurisdiction in this case would be if there was a federal question involved. Mottley (P) did allege in his complaint that the Louisville & Nashville Railroad (D) based their refusal to renew the free pass on a federal statute. Mottley (P) then attempted to allege information that would defeat the defense of the Louisville & Nashville Railroad (D). This is not sufficient. The plaintiff's complaint must be based upon the federal laws of the Constitution to confer jurisdiction on the federal courts. Mottley's (P) cause of action was not based on any federal laws or constitutional privileges; it was based on a contract. Even though it is evident that a federal question will be brought up at the trial, plaintiff's cause of action must be based on a federal statute or the constitution in order to have a federal question that would grant jurisdiction to the federal courts. Reversed and remanded.

▶ ANALYSIS

If Mottley (P) could have alleged that he was basing his action on a federal right, it would have been enough to have given the federal court jurisdiction. The federal court would have had to exercise jurisdiction at least long enough to determine whether there actually was such a right. If the federal court ultimately concludes that the claimed federal right does not exist, the complaint would be dismissed for failure to state a claim upon which relief can be granted rather than for lack of jurisdiction. The court has the power to determine the issue of subject matter jurisdiction on its own motion as it did in this case. Subject matter jurisdiction can be challenged at any stage of the proceeding.

■■■■

Quicknotes

DIVERSITY OF CITIZENSHIP Parties are citizens of different states, or one party is an alien; a factor, along with a statutorily set dollar value of the matter in controversy, that allows a federal district court to exercise its authority to hear a lawsuit based on diversity jurisdiction.

DIVERSITY JURISDICTION The authority of a federal court to hear and determine cases involving parties who are of different states and an amount in controversy greater than a statutorily set amount.

Continued on next page.

FEDERAL QUESTION The authority of the federal courts to hear and determine in the first instance matters pertaining to the federal Constitution, federal law, or treaties of the United States.

SUBJECT MATTER JURISDICTION The authority of the court to hear and decide actions involving a particular type of issue or subject.

Redner v. Sanders

[Parties not identified.]

2000 WL 1161080 (S.D.N.Y. 2000)

NATURE OF CASE: Motion to dismiss for lack of diversity jurisdiction.

FACT SUMMARY: When plaintiff claimed he was a "resident" of France, defendants argued that only plaintiff's "citizenship" in France would satisfy federal diversity jurisdictional requirements.

🏛 RULE OF LAW

For purposes of diversity jurisdiction under 28 U.S.C. § 1332(a)(2), the controversy must be between citizens of a state and citizens or subjects of a foreign state, not merely "residents."

FACTS: Plaintiff filed a complaint in federal court, alleging that he was at all times mentioned "a citizen of the United States residing in France," and that defendants are residents of the State of New York. Defendants moved to dismiss for lack of subject matter jurisdiction, arguing that mere residency in a foreign country does not equate with citizenship of a foreign country as required by 28 U.S.C. § 1332(a)(2).

ISSUE: For purposes of diversity jurisdiction under 28 U.S.C. § 1332(a)(2), must the controversy be between citizens of a state and citizens or subjects of a foreign state, not merely "residents?"

HOLDING AND DECISION: (Griesa, J.) Yes. For purposes of diversity jurisdiction under 28 U.S.C. § 1332(a)(2), the controversy must be between citizens of a state and citizens or subjects of a foreign state, not merely "residents." Here, plaintiff's complaint speaks of his "residing" in France, whereas the statute speaks of citizenship. The two are not synonymous. It appears in fact that defendants are citizens of the State of New York. However, for jurisdiction to exist under (a)(2), plaintiff would need to be a citizen of a foreign state, not merely a resident, and the complaint itself actually alleges that plaintiff is a citizen of the United States. Thus, the case does not involve an action between citizens of the United States and a citizen of a foreign state. Accordingly, there is no jurisdiction under § 1332(a)(2). Motion granted, and suit dismissed.

▶ ANALYSIS

In *Redner*, the court noted that plaintiff's affidavit was entirely lacking in details what his living in France involved. Plaintiff provided no information about exactly where he lived, what kind of a residence he had, whether he had any family in France, or what professional activities he carried out in France.

■■■

Quicknotes

28 U.S.C. § 1332 Provides for original jurisdiction in federal district court for all civil actions between citizens of different states.

■■■

Hertz Corp. v. Friend

Rental car company (D) v. Employees (P)

559 U.S. 77 (2010)

NATURE OF CASE: Appeal from state supreme court.

FACT SUMMARY: [Hertz Corp. (D) tried to remove a class action against it to federal court on the basis of diversity jurisdiction. The employees (P) objected, arguing that because Hertz (D) derived more revenue from California than any other, and because the plurality of its business activities occurred there, California was its principal place of business.]

> ## RULE OF LAW
> The phrase "principal place of business" in the federal diversity jurisdiction statute refers to the place where the corporation's high-level officers direct, control, and coordinate corporation's activities.

FACTS: [California-based employees (P) of Hertz Corp. (D) claimed in a class action that Hertz (D) violated California's wage and hours laws. Hertz (D) tried to remove to federal court on the basis of diversity jurisdiction. The federal diversity jurisdiction statute provides that "a corporation shall be deemed to be a citizen of any state by which it has been incorporated and of the state where it has its principal place of business." The employees (P) objected, arguing that because Hertz (D) derived more revenue from California than any other, and because the plurality of its business activities occurred there, California was its principal place of business.]

ISSUE: Does the phrase "principal place of business" in the federal diversity jurisdiction statute refer to the place where the corporation's high-level officers direct, control, and coordinate corporation's activities?

HOLDING AND DECISION: (Breyer, J.) Yes. The phrase "principal place of business" in the federal diversity jurisdiction statute refers to the place where the corporation's high-level officers direct, control, and coordinate corporation's activities. Some courts refer to this test as the "nerve center" test. Normally, this would be where the corporation maintains its headquarters, provided headquarters is not simply an office where the corporation holds its board meetings. This interpretation is supported by the statute's language. The statute uses the word "place" in the singular form of the word, not the plural. It is also supported by its advancement of administrative simplicity, which demands that courts be provided straightforward rules under which they can readily assure themselves of their power to hear a case. And it is supported by the statute's legislative history, which suggests that the words "principal place of business" should be interpreted to be no more complex than the initial test put forth by the Judicial Conference, the "half of gross income" test, a test the Conference rejected as too impractical to apply. A "nerve center" test offers greater simplicity. There may be no perfect test that satisfies all administrative and purposive criteria, but some complication must be accepted in view of the necessity of having a clearer rule.

► ANALYSIS

Remember that the nerve center is a single place within a state and not a measure of corporate activity statewide. In the Court's view, this aspect of the nerve center test makes it relatively easy to apply, will promote greater predictability, and is consistent with legislative history suggesting that determining corporate citizenship should not be a complex and impractical task. *Hertz* should promote predictability and uniformity in determining corporate citizenship, particularly in circuits that previously applied multifactor tests or compared corporate activity within multiple states to determine a company's principal place of business.

Quicknotes

DIVERSITY JURISDICTION The authority of a federal court to hear and determine cases involving a statutory sum and in which the parties are citizens of different states, or in which one party is an alien.

In re Ameriquest Mortgage Co. Mortgage Lending Practices Litigation

Real estate appraiser (D) v. Mortgager (P)

2007 U.S. Dist. LEXIS 70805 (N.D. Ill. 2007)

NATURE OF CASE: Motion to dismiss state law claims that were based on the court's supplemental jurisdiction.

FACT SUMMARY: Barbara Skanes (P) claimed that house appraiser Douglas Trevino (D) inflated the value of Skanes's (P) property to increase the loan amount for which she could qualify and increase Ameriquest's (D) potential profit.

RULE OF LAW

Supplemental jurisdiction is proper where there is a sufficient nexus between state and federal claims, and statutory discretionary factors do not weigh in favor of a decision to decline to exercise supplemental jurisdiction.

FACTS: Barbara Skanes (P) claimed that house appraiser Douglas Trevino (D) inflated the value of Skanes's (P) property to increase the loan amount for which she could qualify and to increase Ameriquest's (D) potential profit. She filed a federal claim under the Truth in Lending Act, seeking rescission of the mortgage and statutory damages. She also claimed that at the time of her closing Ameriquest (D) gave her improper and misleading disclosures of her right to cancel her mortgage. In the second and third counts of her claim, she alleged state law fraud claims against Ameriquest (D) and Trevino (D). Trevino (D) moved to dismiss the state law claims.

ISSUE: Is supplemental jurisdiction proper where there is a sufficient nexus between state and federal claims, and statutory discretionary factors do not weigh in favor of a decision to decline to exercise supplemental jurisdiction?

HOLDING AND DECISION: (Aspen, J.) Yes. Supplemental jurisdiction is proper where there is a sufficient nexus between state and federal claims, and statutory discretionary factors do not weigh in favor of a decision to decline to exercise supplemental jurisdiction. Where a court already has jurisdiction over some federal claim, it also has supplemental jurisdiction over state claims that are factually connected to the federal claim. The factual connection is sufficient as long as the facts are common and operative. To determine whether the federal and state law claims are connected by common and operative facts, the facts necessary to prove the federal claim are compared with those necessary to the success of the state claim. In this case, Skanes (P) explicitly connected her federal and state claims. She did not fully know of her right to cancel her mortgage, she paid too much during the life of the loan because the mortgage was overstated, and she has not been able to refinance the mortgage due to the over-statement. The connection is operative, in that if the court were to dismiss the state law claims, it may not be able to grant the rescission of the mortgage under the federal Truth in Lending Act (TILA). Because the court cannot conclude that the resolution of one of her state claims will have no effect on the resolution on her federal claims, supplemental jurisdiction is proper. In addition, there is no reason to choose not to exercise that jurisdiction under discretionary powers. Motion to dismiss denied.

ANALYSIS

In this case, the court says that the factual bases for the federal and state claims are essentially the same, and the resolution of one claim impacts the other. But the connection between the facts need not be as tight as they are in this case to support a finding that supplemental jurisdiction is proper.

■■■

Quicknotes

SUPPLEMENTAL JURISDICTION A doctrine granting authority to a federal court to hear a claim that does not invoke diversity jurisdiction if it arises from the same transaction or occurrence as the primary action.

■■■

Szendrey-Ramos v. First Bancorp

Employee (P) v. Employer (D)

512 F. Supp. 2d 81 (D.P.R. 2007)

NATURE OF CASE: Motion to dismiss employment discrimination claim.

FACT SUMMARY: A bank's general counsel was fired after finding that some bank officials violated the bank's code of ethics. She sued under Title VII of the 1964 Civil Rights Act for discrimination and retaliation, and under Puerto Rican law for wrongful discharge, defamation, tortious interference with contract, and violations of the Puerto Rican constitution.

RULE OF LAW

A court may decline to exercise supplemental jurisdiction where (1) the state law claims raise complex or novel issues, or (2) the state law claims substantially predominate over the federal claim.

FACTS: Carmen Szendrey-Ramos (P) was general counsel for First Bancorp (D) in Puerto Rico. When an outside law firm sent Szendrey (P) a report alleging possible ethical and legal violations by bank officials, Szendrey (P) conducted an investigation. Szendrey (P) found that there were some violations of the bank's (D) code of ethics. The bank (D) fired Szendrey (P), blaming her for some of the events she had investigated. She sued under the federal Title VII of the 1964 Civil Rights Act for discrimination and retaliation, and under Puerto Rican law for wrongful discharge, defamation, tortious interference with contract, and violations of the Puerto Rican constitution.

ISSUE: May a court decline to exercise supplemental jurisdiction where (1) the state law claims raise complex or novel issues, or (2) the state law claims substantially predominate over the federal claim?

HOLDING AND DECISION: (Casellas, J.) Yes. A court may decline to exercise supplemental jurisdiction where (1) the state law claims raise complex or novel issues, or (2) the state law claims substantially predominate over the federal claim. Here, the state law claims exceed the federal claims in number and scope. Some of the state claims mimic the federal claims, but most—including wrongful discharge, tortious interference with contracts, and defamation—are distinct and have their own elements of proof, which is not necessary to establish the Title VII claims. The predominance of the state claims over the federal claims is enough to decline to exercise supplemental jurisdiction. But Puerto Rican law claims require a more probing analysis of Szendrey's (P) performance as general counsel, and any shortcomings she may have had, and this leads to another reason for declining to exercise supplemental jurisdiction, which is the presence of complex or novel issues of state law. The interpretation of the relevant Puerto Rico laws is usually the province of the Puerto Rico Supreme Court. The laws at issue in this case are silent on the issue of a lawyer's claim against her former client, and the possibility of divulging confidential information in order to pursue such a claim, and Puerto Rican courts have not yet addressed the issue. Therefore, the Puerto Rico law claims will be dismissed without prejudice, so they may be refiled in Puerto Rican courts.

▶ *ANALYSIS*

Note that the court could have declined to exercise supplemental jurisdiction on the basis of the predominance of the Puerto Rican claims alone. But the court considered it significant that neither Puerto Rican statutes nor Puerto Rican courts had addressed the issues underlying the non-federal claims. Given that the Puerto Rican claims presented issues of first impression, the federal court declined to exercise jurisdiction on that point as well.

Quicknotes

SUPPLEMENTAL JURISDICTION A doctrine granting authority to a federal court to hear a claim that does not invoke diversity jurisdiction if it arises from the same transaction or occurrence as the primary action.

Caterpillar, Inc. v. Lewis

Manufacturer (D) v. Injured person (P)

519 U.S. 61 (1996)

NATURE OF CASE: Appeal of judgment vacating verdict for the defense in personal-injury case.

FACT SUMMARY: A federal district court denied a motion to remand a case to state court even though the case lacked complete diversity and later entered judgment after the nondiverse defendant had settled out of the case.

🏛 RULE OF LAW
A district court's error in failing to remand a case improperly removed does not prevent adjudication if the jurisdictional requirements are satisfied at the time of judgment.

FACTS: Lewis (P) filed a personal-injury claim in state court. The case was removed to federal district court at Caterpillar Inc.'s (D) request although there was not complete diversity of citizenship among the parties. After the removal, Lewis (P) moved to remand the case to state court for lack of federal jurisdiction. The district court denied the motion. Subsequently, the nondiverse defendant settled out of the case. At trial, Caterpillar (D) prevailed. Lewis (P) appealed, claiming that the district court did not have jurisdiction at the time of removal. The court of appeals agreed and vacated the judgment. Caterpillar (D) appealed.

ISSUE: Does a district court's error in failing to remand a case improperly removed prevent adjudication if the jurisdictional requirements are satisfied at the time of judgment?

HOLDING AND DECISION: (Ginsburg, J.) No. A district court's error in failing to remand a case improperly removed does not prevent adjudication if the jurisdictional requirements are satisfied at the time of judgment. The lack of subject matter jurisdiction at the time of removal is not fatal to later adjudication of the case. The only issue is whether the jurisdictional requirements are met at the time the judgment is entered. In the present case, allowing removal when there was not complete diversity was a mistake by the district court. However, when judgment was entered, complete diversity did exist. Thus, there was sufficient subject matter jurisdiction to adjudicate the case. Reversed and remanded.

▌ *ANALYSIS*

In the present case, the nondiverse defendant settled out of the litigation prior to judgment. It would present a more difficult question if the nondiverse defendant had not been dismissed from the case by the district court. In such circumstances, the federal court would be acting without any subject matter jurisdiction.

Quicknotes

DIVERSITY OF CITIZENSHIP Parties are citizens of different states, or one party is an alien; a factor, along with a statutorily set dollar value of the matter in controversy, that allows a federal district court to exercise its authority to hear a lawsuit based on diversity jurisdiction.

DIVERSITY JURISDICTION The authority of a federal court to hear and determine cases involving parties who are of different states and an amount in controversy greater than a statutorily set amount.

SUBJECT MATTER JURISDICTION A court's ability to adjudicate a specific category of cases based on the subject matter of the dispute.

CHAPTER 4

State Law in Federal Courts: Erie and its Entailments

Quick Reference Rules of Law

Erie Railroad v. Tompkins

Railroad company (D) v. Pedestrian (P)

304 U.S. 64 (1938)

NATURE OF CASE: Action to recover damages for personal injury allegedly caused by negligent conduct.

FACT SUMMARY: In a personal-injury suit, a federal district court trial judge refused to apply applicable state law because such law was "general" (judge-made) and not embodied in any statute.

🏛 RULE OF LAW

Although the 1789 Rules of Decision Act left federal courts unfettered to apply their own rules of procedure in common-law actions brought in federal court, state law governs substantive issues. State law includes not only statutory law, but case law as well.

FACTS: Tompkins (P) was walking in a right of way parallel to some railroad tracks when an Erie Railroad (Erie) (D) train came by. Tompkins (P) was struck and injured by what he would, at trial, claim to be an open door extending from one of the rail cars. Under Pennsylvania case law (the applicable law since the accident occurred there), state courts would have treated Tompkins (P) as a trespasser in denying him recovery for other than wanton or willful misconduct on Erie's (D) part. Under "general" law, recognized in federal courts, Tompkins (P) would have been regarded as a licensee and would only have been obligated to show ordinary negligence. Because Erie (D) was a New York corporation, Tompkins (P) brought suit in a federal district court in New York, where he won a judgment for $30,000. Upon appeal to a federal circuit court, the decision was affirmed.

ISSUE: Was the trial court in error in refusing to recognize state case law as the proper rule of decision in deciding the substantive issue of liability?

HOLDING AND DECISION: (Brandeis, J.) Yes. The trial court was in error in refusing to recognize state case law as the proper rule of decision in deciding the substantive issue of liability. Although the 1789 Rules of Decision Act left federal courts unfettered to apply their own rules of procedure in common-law actions brought in federal court, state law governs substantive issues. State law includes not only statutory law, but case law as well. The Court's opinion is in four parts: (1) *Swift v. Tyson*, 41 U.S. (16 Pet.) 1 (1842), which held that federal courts exercising jurisdiction on the ground of diversity of citizenship need not, in matters of general jurisprudence, apply the unwritten law of the state as declared by its highest court, is overruled. Section 34 of the Federal Judiciary Act of 1789, c. 20, 28 U.S. § 725 requires that federal courts in all matters, except those where some federal law is controlling,

apply as their rules of decision the law of the state, unwritten as well as written. Up to this time, federal courts had assumed the power to make "general law" decisions even though Congress was powerless to enact "general law" statutes. (2) *Swift* had numerous political and social defects. The hoped-for uniformity among state courts had not occurred; there was no satisfactory way to distinguish between local and general law. On the other hand, *Swift* introduced grave discrimination by noncitizens against citizens. The privilege of selecting the court for resolving disputes rested with the noncitizen who could pick the more favorable forum. The resulting far-reaching discrimination was due to the broad province accorded "general law" in which many matters of seemingly local concern were included. Furthermore, local citizens could move out of the state and bring suit in a federal court if they were disposed to do so; corporations, similarly, could simply reincorporate in another state. More than statutory relief is involved here; the unconstitutionality of *Swift* is clear. (3) Except in matters governed by the federal Constitution or by acts of Congress, the law to be applied in any case is the law of the state. There is no federal common law. The federal courts have no power derived from the Constitution or by Congress to declare substantive rules of common law applicable in a state whether they are "local" or "general" in nature. (4) The federal district court was bound to follow the Pennsylvania case law, which would have denied recovery to Tompkins (P). Reversed.

CONCURRENCE: (Reed, J.) It is unnecessary to go beyond interpreting the meaning of "laws" in the Rules of Decision Act. Article III and the Necessary and Proper Clause of Article I of the Constitution, might provide Congress with the power to declare rules of substantive law for federal courts to follow.

▌ ANALYSIS

Erie can fairly be characterized as the most significant and sweeping decision on civil procedure ever handed down by the United States Supreme Court. As interpreted in subsequent decisions, *Erie* held that while federal courts may apply their own rules of procedure, issues of substantive law must be decided in accord with the applicable state law: usually the state in which the federal court sits. Note, however, how later Supreme Court decisions have made inroads into the broad doctrine enunciated here.

Continued on next page.

Quicknotes

DIVERSITY OF CITIZENSHIP Parties are citizens of different states, or one party is an alien; a factor, along with a statutorily set dollar value of the matter in controversy, that allows a federal district court to exercise its authority to hear a lawsuit based on diversity jurisdiction.

DIVERSITY JURISDICTION The authority of a federal court to hear and determine cases involving parties who are of different states and an amount in controversy greater than a statutorily set amount.

FEDERAL JURISDICTION The authority of federal courts to hear and determine cases of a particular nature derived from the United States Constitution and rules promulgated by Congress pursuant thereto.

SUBJECT MATTER JURISDICTION The authority of the court to hear and decide actions involving a particular type of issue or subject.

Guaranty Trust Co. v. York

Trustee (D) v. Note holder (P)

326 U.S. 99 (1945)

NATURE OF CASE: Class action alleging fraud and misrepresentation.

FACT SUMMARY: York (P), barred from filing suit in state court because of the state statute of limitations, brought an equity action in federal court based upon diversity of citizenship jurisdiction.

🏛 RULE OF LAW

Where a state statute that would completely bar recovery in state court has significant effect on the outcome-determination of the action, even though the suit is brought in equity, the federal court is bound by the state law.

FACTS: York (P) sued Guaranty Trust Co. (D) in a federal diversity action. New York substantive law governed. Guaranty Trust (D) asserted the defense of the statute of limitations. York (P) argued that the statute of limitations did not bar the suit because it was on the "equity side" of federal court. The federal court of appeals ruled the suit was not barred, and Guaranty Trust (D) appealed.

ISSUE: Does a state statute of limitations, which would bar a suit in state court, also act as a bar to the same action if the suit is brought in equity in federal court and jurisdiction being based on diversity of citizenship?

HOLDING AND DECISION: (Frankfurter, J.) Yes. A state statute of limitations, which would bar a suit in state court, may also act as a bar to the same action if the suit is brought in equity in federal court and jurisdiction is based on diversity of citizenship. *Erie Railroad Co. v. Tompkins*, 304 U.S. 64 (1938), overruled a particular way of looking at law after its inadequacies had been laid bare. The question is not whether a statute of limitations is deemed a matter of "procedure" in some sense. The question is whether such a statute concerns merely the manner and the means by which a right to recover, as recognized by the state, is enforced, or whether such statutory limitation is a matter of substance in the aspect that alone is relevant to the problem, namely, whether it significantly affects the result of a litigation for a federal court to disregard a law of a state that would be controlling in an action upon the same claim by the same parties in a state court. In essence, the intent of *Erie* was to insure that in all cases where a federal court is exercising jurisdiction solely because of the diversity of citizenship of the parties, the outcome of the litigation in the federal court should be substantially the same, so far as legal rules determine the outcome of a litigation, as it would be if tried in a state court. Reversed and remanded.

▶ ANALYSIS

While clarifying *Erie*, the legal foundation supporting *Guaranty Trust* may be undergoing a process of slow erosion by contemporary courts. *Hanna v. Plumer*, 380 U.S. 460 (1965), held that where state law conflicts with the Federal Rules of Civil Procedure, the latter prevails regardless of the effect on the outcome of the litigation. And in *Byrd v. Blue Ridge Electric Cooperative*, 356 U.S. 525 (1958), the Court suggested that some constitutional doctrines (there, the right to a jury trial in federal court) are so important as to be controlling over state law, regardless of whether application of such constitutional doctrines would result in an outcome different than that which would result under the law of the state in which the federal court sits.

Quicknotes

COMITY A rule pursuant to which courts in one state give deference to the statutes and judicial decisions of another.

DIVERSITY OF CITIZENSHIP Parties are citizens of different states, or one party is an alien; a factor, along with a statutorily set dollar value of the matter in controversy, that allows a federal district court to exercise its authority to hear a lawsuit based on diversity jurisdiction.

DIVERSITY JURISDICTION The authority of a federal court to hear and determine cases involving parties who are of different states and an amount in controversy greater than a statutorily set amount.

***ERIE* DOCTRINE** Federal courts must apply state substantive law and federal procedural law.

Byrd v. Blue Ridge Rural Electric Cooperative

Injured employee (P) v. Electric utility (D)

356 U.S. 525 (1958)

NATURE OF CASE: Negligence action for damages.

FACT SUMMARY: Byrd (P) was injured while connecting power lines for a subcontractor of Blue Ridge Electric Cooperative, Inc. (D).

🏛 RULE OF LAW
The *Erie* doctrine requires that federal courts in diversity cases must respect the definitions of rights and obligations created by state courts, but state laws cannot alter the essential characteristics and functions of the federal courts, and the jury function is such an essential function (provided for in the Seventh Amendment).

FACTS: Byrd (P) was injured while on a construction job for Blue Ridge Electric Cooperative, Inc. (Blue Ridge) (D) and sued Blue Ridge (D) in tort. Although Byrd (P) was employed by an independent contractor, Blue Ridge (D) argued that Byrd (P) was performing the same work as Blue Ridge's (D) regular employees and was therefore a "statutory" employee whose exclusive remedy was under the South Carolina workers' compensation legislation. Blue Ridge (D) contended that despite the *Erie* doctrine, [*Erie Railroad Co. v. Tompkins,* 304 U.S. 64 (1938)], South Carolina law could not be allowed to preclude his right to a jury.

ISSUE: Do *Erie* doctrine considerations require that all state determinations of rights be upheld regardless of their intrusions into federal determinations?

HOLDING AND DECISION: (Brennan, J.) No. The *Erie* doctrine requires that federal courts in diversity cases must respect the definitions of rights and obligations created by state courts, but state laws cannot alter the essential characteristics and functions of the federal courts, and the jury function is such an essential function (provided for in the Seventh Amendment). The South Carolina determination here that immunity is a question of law to be tried by a judge is merely a determination of the form and mode of enforcing immunity. It does not involve any essential relationship or determination of right created by the state. Of course, the *Erie* doctrine will reach even such form and mode determinations where no affirmative countervailing considerations can be found. Here, however, the Seventh Amendment makes the jury function an essential factor in the federal process protected by the Constitution. Reversed and remanded.

▶ ANALYSIS

This case points up a major retreat by the Court in its interpretation of the *Erie* doctrine. The *Guaranty Trust* case, 326 U.S. 99 (1945), had stated that the *Erie* doctrine required that federal courts not tamper with state remedies for violations of state-created rights. In *Byrd,* the Court retreats, stating that questions of mere "form and mode" of remedy (i.e., trial by jury or judge) is not necessarily the province of the states where essential federal rights (i.e., Seventh Amendment) are involved. Note that the Court does not abandon the *Guaranty Trust* rationale, however (that the outcome of a case should not be affected by the choice of court in which it is filed). The Court expresses doubt that the permitting of trial by jury here will make any difference in the final determination of the case. Note the inconsistency of argument here since the Court first states that trial by jury is an essential right, and then states that it is really insignificant after all.

Quicknotes

ERIE DOCTRINE Federal courts must apply state substantive law and federal procedural law.

Hanna v. Plumer

Injured claimant (P) v. Executor of defendant (D)

380 U.S. 460 (1965)

NATURE OF CASE: Appeal of dismissal in federal diversity tort action.

FACT SUMMARY: Hanna (P) filed tort action in federal court in Massachusetts, where Plumer (D) resided, for an auto accident that occurred in South Carolina.

🏛 RULE OF LAW

The *Erie* doctrine mandates that federal courts are to apply state substantive law and federal procedural law, but, where matters fall roughly between the two and are rationally capable of classification as either, the Constitution grants the federal court system the power to regulate their practice and pleading (procedure).

FACTS: In this diversity suit for personal injuries, Plumer (D) represented the estate of one of the drivers involved. Massachusetts law provided that suits required personal service of process on the estate's executor. Process was instead served under Fed. R. Civ. P. 4[(e)(2)(B)], which allowed for the summons and complaint to be left with a competent adult at the defendant's residence. The federal circuit court agreed with the federal district court that the claim should be dismissed because of Hanna's (P) failure to comply with the state's method of serving process within the applicable limitations period. Hanna (P) appealed.

ISSUE: Does the *Erie* doctrine classification of "substantive law questions" extend to embrace questions involving both substantive and procedural considerations merely because such a question might have an effect on the determination of the substantive outcome of the case?

HOLDING AND DECISION: (Warren, C.J.) No. The *Erie* doctrine [*Erie Railroad Co. v. Tompkins*, 304 U.S. 64 (1938)], mandates that federal courts are to apply state substantive law and federal procedural law, and, where matters fall roughly between the two and are rationally capable of classification as either, the Constitution grants the federal court system the power to regulate their practice and pleading (procedure). It is well settled that the Enabling Act for the Federal Rules of Civil Procedure requires that a procedural effect of any rule on the outcome of a case be shown to actually "abridge, enlarge, or modify" the substantive law in a case for the *Erie* doctrine to come into play. Where, as here, the question only goes to procedural requirements (i.e., service of summons, a dismissal for improper service here would not alter the substantive right of Hanna [P] to serve Plumer [D] personally and refile or effect the substantive law of negligence in the

case), Article III and the Necessary and Proper Clause provide that the Congress has a right to provide rules for the federal court system such as Fed. R. Civ. P. 4[(e)(2) (B)]. "Outcome determination analysis was never intended to serve as a talisman" for the *Erie* doctrine. The judgment of the appellate court must be reversed.

CONCURRENCE: (Harlan, J.) I agree with the result of the Court and its rejection of the outcome-determination test. However, the Court was wrong in stating that anything arguably procedural is constitutionally placed within the province of the federal government to regulate. The test for "substantive" would be whether "the choice of rule would substantially affect those primary decisions respecting human conduct which our constitutional system leaves to state regulation."

▶ ANALYSIS

This case points a return to the basic rationales of *Erie R. Co. v. Tompkins*, 304 U.S. 64 (1938). First, the Court asserts that one important consideration in determining how a particular question should be classified (substantive or procedural) is the avoidance of "forum shopping" (the practice of choosing one forum such as federal, to file in, in order to gain the advantages of one), which permits jurisdictions to infringe on the substantive law-defining powers of each other. Second, the Court seeks to avoid inequitable administration of the laws that would result from allowing jurisdictional considerations to determine substantive rights. Justice Warren here, in rejecting the "outcome determination" test, asserts that any rule must be measured ultimately against the Federal Rules Enabling Act and the Constitution.

◼▤◼

Quicknotes

PROCEDURAL LAW Law relating to the process of carrying out a lawsuit and not to the substantive rights asserted by the parties.

SUBSTANTIVE LAW Law that pertains to the rights and interests of the parties and upon which a cause of action may be based.

◼▤◼

CHAPTER 5

Incentives to Litigate

Quick Reference Rules of Law

Troupe v. C & S Wholesale Grocers, Inc.

Slip and fall victim (P) v. Grocery store operator (D)

2009 WL 1938787 (M.D. Ga. 2009)

NATURE OF CASE: Motion to remand in action for negligence.

FACT SUMMARY: Troupe's (P) negligence case against C & S Wholesale Grocers, Inc. (C & S Wholesale) (D) was removed to federal court. Troupe (P) moved to remand the case to state court, claiming that her medical expenses were in the neighborhood of $14,000. C & S Wholesale (D) countered that if Troupe (P) prevailed, her recovery would be greater than $75,000—the minimum amount needed to establish amount-in-controversy jurisdiction.

RULE OF LAW
A case will not be remanded to state court where, if the plaintiff prevails on its claims, the plaintiff will recover more than the minimum amount in controversy needed to establish jurisdiction.

FACTS: After slipping and falling at C & S Wholesale Grocers, Inc.'s (C & S Wholesale's) (D) store, Troupe (P) brought suit in state court, asserting claims for negligence, and seeking damages for severe physical injuries and distress, punitive damages, special and general damages, and costs. Troupe's (P) medical records showed that she suffered severe pain that was not alleviated by pain medications and other interventions, including physical therapy, chiropractic manipulation, and spinal blocks, and that her condition remained unabated a year after the fall. The records also indicated that she lived alone, was self-employed, and owned her own house cleaning service. She had informed her physicians that her pain was exacerbated by lifting, bending, stooping, and prolonged standing—all of which were required in her profession as a house cleaner. She also told her physicians that she was forced to reduce the number of houses she could clean because of her back condition and that she had to discontinue personal activities such as exercising, which also aggravated her pain. C & S Wholesale (D) removed to federal court, asserting that if Troupe (P) prevailed, her recovery would be greater than $75,000—the amount needed to establish amount in controversy jurisdiction. Troupe (P), claiming her medical expenses were only around $14,000, moved to remand the case to state court.

ISSUE: Will a case be remanded to state court where, if the plaintiff prevails on its claims, the plaintiff will recover more than the minimum amount in controversy needed to establish jurisdiction?

HOLDING AND DECISION: (Royal, J.) No. A case will not be remanded to state court where, if the plaintiff prevails on its claims, the plaintiff will recover more than the minimum amount in controversy needed to establish jurisdiction. The issue presented is whether the court has original jurisdiction on the basis of the amount in controversy. Where, as here, the amount of damages is unspecified, the defendant only need show by a preponderance of the evidence that the amount of damages is likely to exceed the minimum amount in controversy necessary to establish subject matter jurisdiction. Here, the amount in controversy is not apparent from the face of the complaint, which only specified Troupe's (P) medical expenses. There is no way to determine from the complaint whether Troupe (P) has been so badly injured as to make an award of over $75,000 more likely than not. However, given the additional evidence presented in Troupe's (P) medical records, it is likely that if Troupe (P) proves the assertions she made to her physicians, she would be able to prevail on claims for unspecified damages for long-term medical expenses, loss of wages and earning capacity, mental and physical pain and suffering, and loss of enjoyment of life in addition to her specified claim for medical expenses and her claim for punitive damages. Accordingly, C & S Wholesale (D) has satisfied its burden of establishing that the special, general, and punitive damages in this case, if proven, will "more likely than not" exceed the minimum jurisdictional amount. Troupe's (P) motion to remand is denied.

ANALYSIS

The burden of proving any jurisdictional fact rests upon the party seeking to invoke the jurisdiction of the federal courts. Thus, in this case, C & S Wholesale (D) bore the burden of establishing that the requisite jurisdictional amount had been met. This burden may be a heavy one. Some circuits hold that when a plaintiff makes a specific demand for judgment for less than the jurisdictional amount, the defendant is required to prove to "a legal certainty" that the amount in controversy actually exceeds the jurisdictional minimum. Under this standard, a defendant may be permitted to remain in federal court only if she shows that the case is clearly worth more than the jurisdictional threshold. However, where a plaintiff has made an unspecified demand for damages in state court, as was the case here, a removing defendant must only prove the amount in controversy by a preponderance of the evidence. Thus, if the damages are unspecified in the complaint, the defendant's burden is only to prove that the actual damages will more likely than not exceed the mini-

Continued on next page.

mum jurisdictional amount. Here, C & S Wholesale (D) was able to meet this less stringent standard.

∎▬∎

Quicknotes

AMOUNT IN CONTROVERSY The value of a claim sought by a party to a lawsuit.

PREPONDERANCE OF THE EVIDENCE A standard of proof requiring the trier of fact to determine whether the fact sought to be established is more probable than not.

SUBJECT MATTER JURISDICTION The authority of the court to hear and decide actions involving a particular type of issue or subject.

∎▬∎

Lucy Webb Hayes Natl. Training School v. Geoghegan

Hospital (P) v. Patient (D)

281 F. Supp. 116 (D.D.C. 1967)

NATURE OF CASE: Motion to dismiss an action for an injunction to remove a trespasser.

FACT SUMMARY: Lucy Webb Hayes Natl. Training School, which ran the Sibley Memorial Hospital (collectively, the "Hospital") (P), sought an injunction to remove Geoghegan (D) from the Hospital (P). Geoghegan (D) moved to dismiss, asserting that money damages would adequately compensate the Hospital (P).

🏛 RULE OF LAW
An action for an injunction will not be dismissed where money damages are inadequate to satisfy the plaintiff's claims.

FACTS: Geoghegan (D) had been a patient for a long time at Sibley Memorial Hospital, a private hospital run by Lucy Webb Hayes Natl. Training School (collectively, the "Hospital") (P). The Hospital (P) determined at some point that Geoghegan (D) no longer needed to be hospitalized and that her medical needs could be met at a nursing facility. The Hospital (P) demanded that Geoghegan (D) depart the Hospital (P), but she refused. The Hospital (P) then brought suit seeking an injunction to have Geoghegan (D) removed as a trespasser. Geoghegan's (D) husband (D) wanted her to stay in the Hospital (P) for the remainder of her life and was willing to pay the Hospital (P) for her to stay. Accordingly, the Geoghegans (D) moved to dismiss on the grounds that money damages would be adequate to compensate the Hospital (P).

ISSUE: Will an action for an injunction be dismissed where money damages are an inadequate remedy?

HOLDING AND DECISION: (Holtzoff, J.) No. An action for an injunction will not be dismissed where money damages are an inadequate remedy. Here an action for damages would be an inadequate remedy. A private hospital has a right to accept or decline any patient, and it has a moral duty to reserve its accommodations for persons who actually need medical and hospital care. It would be a deviation from its purposes to act as a nursing home for aged persons who do not need constant medical care but who need nursing care, which can be provided in nursing homes and similar institutions. Hospitals have a duty not to permit their facilities to be diverted to the uses for which hospitals are not intended. It is also well established that equity will enjoin a continuing trespass where an action for damages would not be an adequate remedy. Because an action for damages would not solve the prob- lem faced by the Hospital (P), and is an inadequate remedy, the Geoghegans' (D) motion to dismiss is denied.

▶ ANALYSIS

Ordinarily, money damages are considered an adequate remedy for a single trespass, whereas such damages may not be considered an adequate remedy for continuous or multiple trespasses. If it is not clear that a legal remedy will be adequate, as was the case here, the court will explore policy considerations (here, the court looked at the public interest served by the Hospital (P)), which ordinarily do not come into play in a legal damages context.

Quicknotes

DAMAGES Monetary compensation that may be awarded by the court to a party who has sustained injury or loss to his person, property, or rights due to another party's unlawful act, omission, or negligence.

INJUNCTION A court order requiring a person to do, or prohibiting that person from doing, a specific act.

TRESPASSERS Persons present on the land of another without the knowledge or express permission of the owner, and to whom only a minimum duty of care is owed for injuries incurred while on the premises.

Winter v. Natural Resources Defense Council, Inc.

U.S. Navy (D) v. Environmental defense organization (P)

555 U.S. 7 (2008)

NATURE OF CASE: Challenge to a preliminary injunction.

FACT SUMMARY: The Natural Resources Defense Council (P) filed suit against the U.S. Navy (the Navy) (D) to stop the Navy (D) from using sonar in its training programs due to the effect sonar may have on marine mammals. A federal district court granted a preliminary injunction against the Navy (D), and the U.S. Court of Appeals for the Ninth Circuit upheld it.

🏛 RULE OF LAW
A plaintiff who seeks a preliminary injunction must establish he is likely to succeed on the merits, he is likely to suffer irreparable harm in the absence of preliminary relief, the balance of equities tips in his favor, and an injunction is in the public interest.

FACTS: The U.S. Navy (the Navy) (D) prepares for war through training exercises at sea. The exercises include training in the use of modern sonar to detect and track enemy submarines, and sonar has been part of the training for 40 years. Active sonar, which involves emitting pulses of sound underwater and then receiving the acoustic waves that echo off the target, is the most effective technology for identifying submerged submarines in torpedo range. But the Natural Resources Defense Council (the Council) (P) believes that active sonar harms marine mammals that share the waters with the Navy. Such harm can include permanent hearing loss, decompression sickness, and major behavioral disruptions. A federal law—the Marine Mammal Protection Act of 1972—prohibits harassing marine mammals, but the Secretary of Defense may exempt any action or category of actions from the law if such actions are necessary for national defense. The Navy (D) had been granted an exemption for the training that occurred in this case. Another federal law—the National Environmental Policy Act of 1969—requires federal agencies "to the fullest extent possible" to prepare an environmental impact statement for every major federal action significantly affecting the quality of the human environment, unless the agency determines that the proposed action will not have a significant impact on the environment, and bases that conclusion on a shorter environmental assessment (EA). The Navy (D) had concluded that the training exercises would not have a significant impact on the environment and issued an EA to that effect in 2007. The Council (P) then filed suit against the Navy (D) to stop the Navy (D) from using sonar in its training programs. A federal district court granted a preliminary

injunction against the Navy (D), and the U.S. Court of Appeals for the Ninth Circuit upheld it.

ISSUE: Must a plaintiff who seeks a preliminary injunction establish he is likely to succeed on the merits, he is likely to suffer irreparable harm in the absence of preliminary relief, the balance of equities tips in his favor, and an injunction is in the public interest?

HOLDING AND DECISION: (Roberts, C.J.) Yes. A plaintiff who seeks a preliminary injunction must establish he is likely to succeed on the merits, he is likely to suffer irreparable harm in the absence of preliminary relief, the balance of equities tips in his favor, and an injunction is in the public interest. First, the district court and the Ninth Circuit held that when a plaintiff demonstrates a strong likelihood of prevailing on the merits, a preliminary injunction may be entered based only on a "possibility" of irreparable harm. This "possibility" standard is too lenient. Irreparable injury must be likely, not merely possible, for an injunction to be justified. It is an extraordinary remedy that can only be awarded on a clear showing that the plaintiff is entitled to such relief. But even though the courts both stated the incorrect standard, it appears from the record that they found that the Council (P) had in fact established a "near certainty" of irreparable harm, so the statement of the incorrect standard did not cause harm. Second, even if the Council (P) had shown irreparable injury from the Navy's (D) training exercises, any injury is outweighed by the public interest and the Navy's (D) interest in effective, realistic training of its sailors. Consideration of these factors requires denial of the preliminary injunction. The threat posed by enemy submarines and the need for extensive sonar training to counter the threat is absolutely necessary. The seriousness of the possible harm to the ecological, scientific, and recreational interests advanced by the Council (P) is substantial, but the balance of equities and consideration of the overall public interest tip strongly in favor of the Navy (D). The most serious possible injury caused by the sonar would be to harm an unknown number of the marine mammals the Council (P) studies and observes, but forcing the Navy (D) to deploy an inadequately trained antisubmarine force jeopardizes the safety of the fleet. This is not a judgment on the underlying merits of the claims, but this judgment does make clear that it would be an abuse of discretion to enter a permanent injunction, after final decision on the merits, along the same lines as the preliminary injunction. Reversed, and the preliminary injunction is vacated.

Continued on next page.

DISSENT: (Ginsburg, J.) Equity jurisdiction allows for flexibility and courts must evaluate claims for equitable relief on a sliding scale, awarding relief based on a lower likelihood of harm when the likelihood of success is very high.

▶ ANALYSIS

It is unusual for the Supreme Court to hear a challenge to a preliminary injunction. Typically, it hears the merits of a petitioner's claims. But the Court made very clear that its belief in the overriding national security interest associated with the Navy's training program should lead the lower court to reject a permanent injunction after a decision on the merits as well, thus influencing a final judgment by the district court even if the district court finds that the Navy violated an environmental statute. This case also illustrates the Court's rejection of the Ninth Circuit's "mere possibility" test, which the United States government had been seeking for some time.

Quicknotes

IRREPARABLE HARM Such harm that because it is either too great, too small, or of a continuing character that it cannot be properly compensated in damages, and the remedy for which is typically injunctive relief.

PRELIMINARY INJUNCTION A judicial mandate issued to require or restrain a party from certain conduct; used to preserve a trial's subject matter or to prevent threatened injury.

Fuentes v. Shevin

Owner of chattels (P) v. Court (D)

407 U.S. 67 (1972)

NATURE OF CASE: Constitutional challenge to Florida's prejudgment replevin procedure on due process grounds.

FACT SUMMARY: Margarita Fuentes (P) had her stove and stereo picked up by the sheriff prior to the adjudication of a suit filed by Firestone Tire and Rubber Co. for nonpayment of the installment sales contract.

🏛 RULE OF LAW

Procedural due process requires that a party whose rights are being affected be given a meaningful opportunity to be heard; and in order that the party may enjoy that right, the party must be notified.

FACTS: Margarita Fuentes (Fuentes) (P) purchased a gas stove and service policy, and later a stereo, from Firestone Tire and Rubber Co. (Firestone). After a year, there arose a dispute between Fuentes (P) and Firestone over the servicing of the stove. Firestone filed an action for replevin of both the stove and the stereo, claiming Fuentes (P) had defaulted on her installment payments. Before she was served with the complaint, Firestone obtained a writ of replevin and the sheriff seized the stove and stereo. The prejudgment replevin statutes did not require a convincing showing that the goods were wrongfully detained before seizure. A person could merely file a complaint, post a bond, and request a writ. To obtain a hearing, the person whose property was seized had to initiate a suit for a hearing. Fuentes (P) attacked the prejudgment replevin statute as violative of due process. The state court upheld the legislation, and Fuentes (P) appealed.

ISSUE: Are these state statutes constitutionally defective in that they fail to provide for a hearing at a meaningful time?

HOLDING AND DECISION: (Stewart, J.) Yes. Procedural due process requires that a party whose rights are being affected be given a meaningful opportunity to be heard; and in order that the party may enjoy that right the party must be notified. The constitutional right to be heard is a basic aspect of the duty of government to follow a fair process of decision-making when it acts to deprive a person of his possessions. This right to be heard minimizes substantively unfair or mistaken deprivations of property, a danger that is especially great when the state seizes goods simply upon the application of and for the benefit of a private party. Without due process of law, there would be no safeguards to protect a person's property from governmental interference. The right to speak out in one's own defense before an impartial arbitrator is a fundamental right that must be protected. If the right to notice and a hearing is to serve its full purpose, then it is clear that it must be granted at a time when the deprivation can still be prevented. While return of possession and damages can be granted at a later hearing, nothing can undo the fact that a person's property was arbitrarily taken from him without procedural due process of law. That the hearing required by due process is subject to waiver, and is not fixed in form, does not affect its root requirement that an individual be given an opportunity for a hearing before he is deprived of any significant property interest, except for extraordinary situations where some valid governmental interest is at stake that justifies postponing the hearing until after the event. The statute's requirements of requesting a writ, posting bond, and stating in a conclusory fashion that the property is wrongfully held merely test the applicant's own belief in his rights. Since his private gain is at stake, the danger is all too great that his confidence in his cause will be misplaced. While possession may be reinstated by the posting of a counter-bond, it is well settled that a temporary, non-final deprivation of property is nonetheless violative of the Due Process Clause of the Fourteenth Amendment. Moreover, the Due Process Clause encompasses both the possessory rights to property and situations where the title is in dispute. Situations requiring a postponement of notice and hearing are truly unusual. They require an important governmental purpose, a special need for prompt action, and are initiated by and for the benefit of the government as opposed to a private individual (e.g., war effort, economic disaster, etc.). The contention that the parties waived their constitutional rights is also without merit, since waiver requires clear and explicit language indicating exactly the rights to be waived. For the above-mentioned reasons, both Florida's and Pennsylvania's prejudgment replevin statutes violate the Due Process Clause of the Fourteenth Amendment. Vacated and remanded.

▶ ANALYSIS

In California, Michigan, and a large number of other states, the writ of replevin is now referred to as claim and delivery. In California, this action is contained in § 511.010, et seq. of the Code of Civil Procedure. A hearing is required for the granting of a writ of possession (comparable to the prior writ of replevin) under the guidelines set out in § 512.010. Exceptions are made for property feloniously taken, credit cards, and property acquired in the normal course of trade

Continued on next page.

or business for commercial use. It must be alleged that the property is not necessary for the support of the defendant or his family and that there is a danger that the property will become unavailable to levy, its value will be substantially impaired, and it is necessary to protect the property (§ 512.020). At the hearing, the court will make its determination based on affidavits, pleadings, and other evidence on record. Upon showing of good cause, the court may admit additional evidence or continue the hearing until the new evidence can be obtained (§ 512.050). Finally, with regard to waiver of a hearing requirement, it appears that it is permissible if the parties are acting at arm's length and have equal bargaining power, *D.H. Overmeyer Co. v. Frick Co.*, 405 U.S. 174 (1972); however, if the consumer has no option but to buy on credit, the parties are not equal in bargaining power and the clause is unconscionable, *Kosches v. Nichols*, 327 N.Y.S. 2d 968 (1971). This is but another example of consumer protection. The businessman can waive his constitutional rights, but the consumer cannot.

■▬■

Quicknotes

GARNISHMENT Satisfaction of a debt by deducting payments directly from the debtor's wages before payments are paid to debtor by his employer; due process requires that the debtor be first given notice and an opportunity to be heard.

PROCEDURAL DUE PROCESS The constitutional mandate that if the state or federal government acts so as to deny a citizen of a life, liberty, or property interest the individual is first entitled to notice and the right to be heard.

REPLEVIN An action to recover personal property wrongfully taken.

■▬■

Buckhannon Board and Care Home, Inc. v. West Virginia Department of Health and Human Resources

Declaratory-relief complainant (P) v. State (D)

532 U.S. 598 (2001)

NATURE OF CASE: Appeal of denial of attorney's fees award.

FACT SUMMARY: Buckhannon Board and Care Home, Inc. (Buckhannon) (P) brought suit to declare provisions of a state statute invalid as violating a federal statute. When the state statute was amended to delete the attacked provisions, Buckhannon (P) sought attorney's fees under the federal statute even though its federal court suit was dismissed as moot.

> 🏛 **RULE OF LAW**
> An award of attorney's fees and costs to a "prevailing party" under federal statutes may be awarded only to a party who has secured a judgment on the merits or a court-ordered consent decree.

FACTS: Buckhannon Board and Care Home, Inc. (Buckhannon) (P), which operated care homes and assisted living facilities, ran afoul of a state regulation that required residents to be sufficiently ambulatory to get out of a burning building. After receiving a cease and desist order from the West Virginia Department of Health and Human Resources (D) requiring closure of its residential-care facilities, Buckhannon (P) brought suit against the latter, seeking declaratory and injunctive relief that the self-preservation requirement violated the Fair Housing Amendments Act of 1990. The West Virginia Legislature subsequently enacted legislation eliminating the self-preservation requirement, and the federal district court dismissed Buckhannon's (P) suit as moot. Buckhannon (P) thereupon requested attorney's fees as the "prevailing party" under the Fair Housing Amendments Act. The court denied the motion, the court of appeals affirmed, and Buckhannon (P) appealed.

ISSUE: May an award of attorney's fees and costs to a "prevailing party" under federal statutes be awarded only to a party who has secured a judgment on the merits or a court-ordered consent decree?

HOLDING AND DECISION: (Rehnquist, C.J.) Yes. An award of attorney's fees and costs to a "prevailing party" under federal statutes may be awarded only to a party who has secured a judgment on the merits or a court-ordered consent decree. In designating those parties eligible for an award of litigation costs, Congress employed the term "prevailing party," a legal term of art that indicates one who has been awarded some relief by the court. Enforceable judgments on the merits and court-ordered consent decrees create the "material alteration of the legal

relationship of the parties" necessary to permit an award of attorney's fees. However, the "catalyst theory," which would allow an award where there is no judicially sanctioned change in the relationship of the parties, should not give rise to an award of attorney's fees. A defendant's voluntary change in conduct, although perhaps accomplishing what the plaintiff sought to achieve by the lawsuit, lacks the necessary judicial imprimatur on the change. The legislative history on the issue is at best ambiguous as to the availability of the "catalyst" theory for awarding attorney's fees. Particularly in view of the "American Rule" that attorney's fees will not be awarded absent explicit statutory authority, such legislative history is clearly insufficient to alter the accepted meaning of the statutory term. Affirmed.

DISSENT: (Ginsburg, J.) To "prevail" so as to receive attorney's fees, it should not be a requirement that the court enter a judgment on the merits. Nor should there necessarily be any finding of wrongdoing. A court-approved settlement will do. The catalyst rule, as applied by the clear majority of federal circuits, is a key component of the fee-shifting statutes Congress adopted to advance enforcement of civil rights.

▶ **ANALYSIS**

In *Buckhannon*, the Supreme Court noted that, in addition to judgments on the merits, settlement agreements enforced through a consent decree may serve as the basis for an award of attorney's fees.

■■■

Quicknotes

AMERICAN RULE The rule that attorney's fees are not recoverable, unless expressly provided by law or pursuant to a contract.

CONSENT DECREE A decree issued by a court of equity ratifying an agreement between the parties to a lawsuit; an agreement by a defendant to cease illegal activity.

JUDGMENT ON THE MERITS A determination of the rights of the parties to litigation based on the presentation evidence, barring the party from initiating the same suit again.

■■■

Quick Reference Rules of Law

Haddle v. Garrison (S.D. Ga. 1996)

Employee (P) v. Employer (D)

Unpublished Opinion. Docket No. 96-00029-CV-1 (S.D. Ga. 1996)

NATURE OF CASE: Motion to dismiss for failure to state a claim.

FACT SUMMARY: Haddle (P) sued his former employer for allegedly conspiring to fire him to deter him from testifying at a federal criminal trial.

🏛 RULE OF LAW
A 42 U.S.C. § 1985(2) claim requires the plaintiff suffer actual injury, and discharge from at-will employment does not constitute actual injury.

FACTS: Haddle (P), a former employee at Healthmaster Home Health Care, Inc. (Healthmaster) (D), alleged that his employment was terminated in an attempt to deter his participation as a witness at a federal criminal trial. Haddle (P) filed suit in district court for violation of 42 U.S.C. § 1985(2). Healthmaster (D) and their officers (D) moved to dismiss for failure to state a claim upon which relief can be granted. They argued that because Haddle (P) was an at-will employee, there was no actual injury as required by 42 U.S.C. § 1985(2).

ISSUE: Does discharge from at-will employment constitute actual injury for purposes of 42 U.S.C. § 1985(2)?

HOLDING AND DECISION: (Alaimo, J.) No. A 42 U.S.C. § 1985(2) claim requires the plaintiff suffer actual injury, and discharge from at-will employment does not constitute actual injury. Section 1985(2) provides that one or more persons may not engage in a conspiracy to deter, intimidate, or threaten another from attending and testifying at a federal court proceeding and cause an injury. Fed. R. Civ. P. 12(b)(6) permits a defendant to move to dismiss a complaint where the plaintiff has failed to state a claim upon which relief can be granted. This motion attacks the legal sufficiency of the complaint. Consequently, a court must assume that all of the factual allegations of the complaint are true in deciding the motion. In the present case, the U.S. Court of Appeals for the Eleventh Circuit has already ruled that at-will employees have no constitutionally protected property interest in continued employment and thus suffer no actual injury under § 1985(2) when discharged. Accordingly, Haddle (P) has failed to state a federal claim, even if his allegations about the conspiracy to deter him from testifying are true. The motion to dismiss is granted.

▌ ANALYSIS

On appeal, the Eleventh Circuit affirmed this decision in per curiam decision, holding that precedent forecloses Michael A. Haddle's (P) arguments on appeal (unpublished opinion, Docket No. 96-8856 (11th Cir. 1997)). However, the Supreme Court eventually took up the case because it conflicted with the decisions in two other circuits. In the end, Haddle's (P) appeal was upheld and the dismissal reversed.

Quicknotes

FED. R. CIV. P. 12 Allows for successive motions to dismiss for failure to state a claim.

Haddle v. Garrison

[Parties not identified.]

Unpublished Opinion. Docket No. 96-8856 (11th Cir. 1997)

NATURE OF CASE: Appeal from dismissal of a 42 U.S.C. § 1985(2) claim for failure to state a claim.

FACT SUMMARY: [See the brief for *Haddle v. Garrison* (S.D. Ga. 1996) on page 68 in this *Casenote Legal Briefs* book.]

🏛 RULE OF LAW
An appeal from a dismissal for failure to state a claim will be denied where the appellant's arguments are foreclosed by prior precedent.

FACTS: [See the brief for *Haddle v. Garrison* (S.D. Ga. 1996) on page 68 in this *Casenote Legal Briefs* book.]

ISSUE: Will an appeal from a dismissal for failure to state a claim be denied where the appellant's arguments are foreclosed by prior precedent?

HOLDING AND DECISION: (Per curiam) Yes. An appeal from a dismissal for failure to state a claim will be denied where the appellant's arguments are foreclosed by prior precedent. Haddle's arguments on appeal are foreclosed by this court's decision in *Morast v. Lance*, 807 F.2d 926 (11th Cir. 1987). The judgment of the district court is therefore affirmed.

▶ ANALYSIS

In *Morast v. Lance*, 807 F.2d 926 (1987), the U.S. Court of Appeals for the Eleventh Circuit held that an at-will employee who is dismissed pursuant to a conspiracy proscribed by 42 U.S.C. § 1985(2) has no cause of action. The *Morast* court explained that to make out a cause of action under § 1985(2) the plaintiff must have suffered an actual injury. Because Morast was an at-will employee, he had no constitutionally protected interest in continued employment. Therefore, Morast's discharge did not constitute an actual injury under this statute. Relying on its decision in *Morast*, the court of appeals affirmed in this extremely short opinion. Haddle appealed again, and the United States Supreme Court granted certiorari to resolve a split among the circuits. The Supreme Court held that Haddle had suffered a harm that could support damages finding, and, accordingly, it reversed.

■=■

Haddle v. Garrison

Employee (P) v. Employer (D)

525 U.S. 121 (1998)

NATURE OF CASE: Appeal from dismissal of action under 42 U.S.C. § 1985(2).

FACT SUMMARY: Haddle (P) sued his former employer for allegedly conspiring to fire him to deter him from testifying at a federal criminal trial.

🏛 **RULE OF LAW**
A claim under Civil Rights Act of 1871, Rev. Stat. § 1980, 42 U.S.C. § 1985(2) does not require an injury to a constitutionally protected property interest.

FACTS: Healthmaster Home Health Care, Inc. (Healthmaster) (D) and officers Garrison (D) and Kelly (D) were indicted by a federal grand jury in 1995. Haddle (P), an employee, had cooperated with the investigation and was expected to appear as a witness at the resulting criminal trial. Garrison (D) and Kelly (D) allegedly conspired with the other officers at Healthmaster (D) to terminate Haddle (P) in retaliation. Haddle (P) filed suit in district court for violation of 42 U.S.C. § 1985(2). Healthmaster (D) and the officers (D) moved to dismiss for failure to state a claim upon which relief can be granted. The district court ruled that because Haddle (P) was an at-will employee, there was no actual injury as required by § 1985(2). The dismissal motion was granted and the U.S. Court of Appeals for the Eleventh Circuit affirmed. Since Eleventh Circuit's decision conflicted with the holdings in two other circuits, the United States Supreme Court granted certiorari.

ISSUE: Does a claim under 42 U.S.C.§ 1985(2) require an injury to a constitutionally protected property interest?

HOLDING AND DECISION: (Rehnquist, C.J.) No. A claim under Civil Rights Act of 1871, Rev. Stat. § 1980, 42 U.S.C. § 1985(2) does not require an injury to a constitutionally protected property interest. Section 1985 (2) provides that one or more persons may not engage in a conspiracy to deter, intimidate, or threaten another from attending and testifying at a federal court proceeding. The Eleventh Circuit held there was no injury to Haddle (P) because he had no property interest in at-will employment that could give rise to damages. However, nothing in the language of § 1985(2) or the remedial provisions establishes this requirement. The section is directed against intimidation or retaliation against witnesses, not the deprivation of property. The fact employment at will is not property does not mean the loss of this employment does not cause injury. Such harm has long been a compensable injury under tort law and is similar to intentional interference with contractual relations. Dismissal of Haddle's (P) complaint for failure to state a claim was in error. Reversed and remanded.

▶ **ANALYSIS**

The employment term for "at-will employees" is not definite, and when *Haddle* was decided, very few Supreme Court cases addressed the issue of at-will employment. In addition, amici in the case included the National Whistleblowers Association. The Court's reversal arguably could have caused a significant increase in the number of whistleblower cases filed in federal court.

■=■

Quicknotes

SUPPLEMENTAL JURISDICTION A doctrine granting authority to a federal court to hear a claim that does not invoke diversity jurisdiction if it arises from the same transaction or occurrence as the primary action.

■=■

Ashcroft v. Iqbal

Former U.S. Attorney General (D) v. Pakistani citizen (P)

556 U.S. 662 (2009)

NATURE OF CASE: Certiorari to determine complaint sufficiency in constitutional claim.

FACT SUMMARY: Javaid Iqbal (P), a Pakistani citizen, was arrested in the United States on criminal charges and detained by federal officials soon after the 9/11 terrorist attacks. He claimed his confinement conditions violated his constitutional rights. The federal official defendants moved to dismiss Iqbal's (P) complaint as facially insufficient.

🏛 RULE OF LAW
A well-pleaded complaint requires nonconclusory, plausible, factual pleadings.

FACTS: United States officials arrested Javaid Iqbal (P), a Pakistani citizen and Muslim, on criminal charges and detained him after the 9/11 terrorist attacks. Iqbal (P) filed a federal complaint alleging he was deprived of certain constitutional rights while confined. He alleged the deprivations occurred because of his race, religion, or national origin. He named former U.S. Attorney General John Ashcroft (D) and Federal Bureau of Investigation (FBI) Director Robert Mueller (D) in addition to several others. Ashcroft (D) and Mueller (D) moved to dismiss the complaint as facially insufficient and raised the defense of qualified immunity based on their official status at the time of the confinement. The district court denied the motion and Ashcroft (D) and Mueller (D) took an interlocutory appeal to the U.S. Court of Appeals for the Second Circuit. The Second Circuit affirmed, and the United States Supreme Court granted certiorari.

ISSUE: Does a well-pleaded complaint require nonconclusory, plausible, factual pleadings?

HOLDING AND DECISION: (Kennedy, J.) Yes. A well-pleaded complaint requires nonconclusory, plausible, factual pleadings. Iqbal's (P) complaint alleges the federal government had a policy of detaining Arab Muslims after the 9/11 attacks until the individuals were "cleared" by the FBI. Iqbal (P) claimed Ashcroft (D) was the "architect" of this policy and Mueller (D) was instrumental in its "adoption, promulgation, and implementation." This Court held in *Bell Atlantic Corp. v. Twombly*, 550 U.S. 544 (2007), that pleadings required factual content that allows the court to draw the reasonable inference that the defendant is liable for the alleged misconduct. The plausibility standard did not rise to a probability but requires more than conclusions of misconduct. *Twombly* supported the principles that a court accepts factual allegations as true but need not accept conclusory allegations as true. Fed. R.

Civ. P. 8 may now permit more flexibility, but it does not permit mere conclusions. Further, only a complaint that states a plausible claim survives a motion to dismiss. The courts may begin their analysis with determining which pleadings include factual allegations that will be entitled to a presumption of truth. Here, Iqbal (P) states only conclusory allegations that Ashcroft (D) was the principal architect and Mueller (D) was the principal implementer of the policies. These conclusory allegations are not entitled to a presumption of truth. Iqbal (P) fails to include factual allegations supporting his conclusions that Ashcroft (D) and Mueller (D) knew of the federal officials' behavior regarding his confinement. The consideration then becomes whether the complaint suggests an entitlement to relief. It does not. Iqbal (P) was plausibly held for reasons other than race, religion, or national origin. Detaining such suspects until cleared does not violate constitutional protections. Iqbal (P) argues *Twombly* should be limited to antitrust pleadings, but nothing supports this theory. *Twombly* is the pleading standard for all civil actions. Iqbal (P) finally argues Fed. R. Civ. P. 9(b) permits him "general" rather than "specific" pleading for an alleged constitutional violation. Rule 9(b) does not override the factual pleading requirements of Rule 8 but merely requires even greater specificity for the enumerated claims. Reversed and remanded.

DISSENT: (Souter, J.) Consistent with *Twombly*, nonconclusory allegations should be taken as true unless they are "sufficiently fantastic to defy reality." The key allegations here are not conclusory and the complaint was facially sufficient.

DISSENT: (Breyer, J.) The lower court expressly rejected minimally intrusive discovery in favor of dismissal. That would have been appropriate because the discovery could have been in anticipation of a summary judgment motion.

▶ ANALYSIS

Pleading requirements have become stricter so general notice is no longer sufficient. The defendant is not merely put on notice of the plaintiff's claim but is entitled to factual allegations informing it of the support for the claim. Some analysts were concerned about the future of litigation because of a fear that pleadings would have to be so specific that most plaintiffs would not be able to

Continued on next page.

proceed. Most courts, however, have required factual pleading for a long time and did not become more stringent after *Iqbal*. The rule stated in *Iqbal* is "plausibility" not "probability" so the allegations do not have to be proven on the face of the complaint, but the facts alleged must be plausible and permit a reasonable inference of defendant's misconduct.

◼◼◼

Quicknotes

INTERLOCUTORY APPEAL The appeal of an issue that does not resolve the disposition of the case but is essential to a determination of the parties' legal rights.

◼◼◼

Stradford v. Zurich Insurance Co.

Insured (P) v. Insurer (D)

2002 WL 31027517 (S.D.N.Y. 2002)

NATURE OF CASE: Motion to dismiss counter-claim.

FACT SUMMARY: When Dr. Stradford (P) sued his insurer, Zurich Insurance Company (Northern) (D), for property damage, Northern (P) counterclaimed for fraud, contending that Stradford (P) was fully aware the damage had occurred during a period in which the policy had lapsed for nonpayment of premiums. Stradford (P) moved to dismiss the fraud claim.

🏛 RULE OF LAW
Under Fed. R. Civ. P. 9(b), the time, place, and nature of alleged misrepresentations must be disclosed to a party accused of fraud.

FACTS: Dr. Stradford (P), a dentist, brought suit against his insurer, Zurich Insurance Company (Northern) (D), for water damage allegedly occurring to his property during a period that Northern (D) claimed was an interim period when the insurance had lapsed because of Stradford's (P) failure to make premium payments. Northern (D), accordingly, counterclaimed against Stradford (P), contending that Stradford (P), by making the claim and filing the suit, knowingly had devised a scheme and artifice to defraud the insurer and obtain money by false pretenses and representations. Stradford (P) moved to dismiss the counterclaim that was based in fraud for failure to state the fraud claim with sufficient particularity.

ISSUE: Under Fed. R. Civ. P. 9(b), must the time, place, and nature of alleged misrepresentations be disclosed to a party accused of fraud?

HOLDING AND DECISION: (Buchwald, J.) Yes. Under Fed. R. Civ. P. 9(b), the time, place, and nature of alleged misrepresentations must be disclosed to a party accused of fraud. Here, Northern's (D) counterclaims simply failed to identify the statement made by Stradford (P) that they claimed to be false. Thus, it is unclear from the face of the counterclaims whether Northern (D) was asserting that Stradford's (P) claimed losses were improperly inflated, that Stradford's (P) office never even flooded, or that the offices flooded, but not during the term of the insurance policy. In essence, Northern (D) claimed that Stradford (P) lied but failed to identify the lie. The primary purpose of Rule 9(b) is to afford a litigant accused of fraud fair notice of the claim and the factual ground upon which it is based. Here, Northern's (D) counterclaims failed to provide Stradford (P) with fair notice of precisely which statement, or which aspect of his claim, Northern (D) alleged to be false. The counterclaims were therefore insufficient under Rule 9(b) and must be dismissed. However, in accordance with the practice of the Second Circuit, Northern (D) is permitted to file an amended pleading, which it has done, which cures the defects found in the counterclaims by making it clear that it was alleging that Stradford's (P) office was flooded at a time when he had permitted the insurance policy to lapse, yet that he misrepresented the date of the loss to try to bring the loss within the coverage period. Defendant's request for permission to move for summary judgment is granted.

▶ ANALYSIS

Fed. R. Civ. P. 9(b) provides that in all averments of fraud or mistake, the circumstances constituting fraud or mistake shall be stated with particularity. Malice, intent, knowledge, and other condition of mind of a person may be averred generally.

Quicknotes

FED. R. CIV. P. 9(B) Sets forth the requirements for pleading fraud or mistake and requires the circumstances constituting fraud or mistake to be plead with particularity; malice, intent, knowledge and other conditions of the mind of a person may be plead generally.

Jones v. Bock

Prisoner (P) v. State (D)

549 U.S. 199 (2007)

NATURE OF CASE: Appeal to Supreme Court on issue of pleading requirements.

FACT SUMMARY: Lorenzo Jones (P) was a prisoner in Michigan. He sued the State (D) after he suffered injuries in custody when the staff refused to reassign him to work he could perform in light of his injuries.

⚖ RULE OF LAW

A plaintiff need not plead and demonstrate exhaustion of administrative remedies in the complaint.

FACTS: Lorenzo Jones (P) was a prisoner in Michigan. He sued the State (D) after he suffered injuries in custody when the staff refused to reassign him to work he could perform in light of his injuries.

ISSUE: Must a plaintiff plead and demonstrate exhaustion of administrative remedies in the complaint?

HOLDING AND DECISION: (Roberts, C.J.) No. A plaintiff need not plead and demonstrate exhaustion of administrative remedies in the complaint. The Federal Rules of Civil Procedure do not require that exhaustion be pleaded, and Rule 8(c) identifies a non-exhaustive list of affirmative defenses that must be pleaded in response, leaving room for exhaustion as an affirmative defense. In addition, the Prison Litigation Reform Act, which deals extensively with the subject of exhaustion, is silent on the issue whether exhaustion must be pleaded by the plaintiff or is an affirmative defense. This supports the fact that the usual practice should be followed, and the usual practice under the Federal Rules is to regard exhaustion as an affirmative defense. The reasons behind the decisions of some lower courts to impose a pleading requirement on plaintiffs in this context, which are to separate, when it comes to prisoner suits, those claims that have merit and those that have none and will merely clog the process, are understandable. But the way to establishing higher pleading requirements is to amend the rules, not on a case-by-case basis in courts.

▶ ANALYSIS

The outcome of this case is in keeping with the Roberts Court's general idea that policy considerations and courts should not expand the requirements of the Federal Rules of Civil Procedure. The general belief is that expansion of the Rules should be made through the Rules amendment process.

━━━

Quicknotes

AFFIRMATIVE DEFENSE A manner of defending oneself against a claim not by denying the truth of the charge, but by the introduction of some evidence challenging the plaintiff's right to bring the claim.

EXHAUSTION REMEDIES Requirement that a party exhaust all administrative remedies available before a court will intervene in the controversy.

━━━

Walker v. Norwest Corp.

Minor (P) v. Fiduciary (D)

108 F.3d 158 (8th Cir. 1996)

NATURE OF CASE: Appeal of an award of Rule 11 sanctions.

FACT SUMMARY: Jimmy Lee Walker, III (P), his guardian, Cynthia Walker (P), and their attorney, James Harrison Massey, appealed Fed. R. Civ. P. 11 sanctions imposed against Massey when Massey failed to amend or dismiss a clearly defective complaint he had filed.

🏛 RULE OF LAW
Fed. R. Civ. P. 11 sanctions may be appropriate for an attorney's filing of a clearly defective complaint and taking no steps to amend or dismiss it.

FACTS: Jimmy Walker (P), a minor, through his attorney, James Harrison Massey, filed a complaint in federal court against Norwest Corp. (D), in which the attorney failed to plead complete diversity of citizenship, and indeed, pleaded facts that tended to show there was not complete diversity. Upon receiving the complaint, Norwest (D) wrote to Massey informing him that the complaint showed on its face that there was no diversity jurisdiction. The letter asked Massey to dismiss the complaint and warned that if he did not, Norwest (D) would seek sanctions, including attorney's fees. Massey acknowledged Norwest's (D) correspondence but made no substantive response to the deficiency that Norwest's (D) counsel had pointed out. The federal district court granted Norwest's (D) motion to dismiss and for Fed. R. Civ. P. 11 sanctions against Walker (P) and Massey, and Walker (P) and Massey appealed.

ISSUE: May Fed. R. Civ. P. 11 sanctions be appropriate for an attorney's filing of a clearly defective complaint and taking no steps to amend or dismiss it?

HOLDING AND DECISION: (Gibson, J.) Yes. Fed. R. Civ. P. 11 sanctions may be appropriate for an attorney's filing of a clearly defective complaint and taking no steps to amend or dismiss it. Even though it was the Walkers' (P) burden to plead, and if necessary, prove diversity, they did not allege that all of the defendants were domiciled in a state other than South Dakota. Instead, they argued that finding out the defendants' (D) citizenship would be more trouble than they should be expected to take. However, this is a burden that plaintiffs desiring to invoke diversity jurisdiction have assumed since the days of Chief Justice Marshall. As to Massey's contention that the court should have inquired into his financial circumstances before imposing the monetary sanction, not only did Massey fail to argue this point to the district court, but there was no evidence in the record to support such an argu-

ment. Finally, Massey never did allege citizenship for many of the defendants and never identified which defendants should be dismissed to create diversity jurisdiction. Affirmed.

▶ ANALYSIS

In *Walker*, the U.S. Court of Appeals for the Eighth Circuit made clear that a district court is not obliged to do a party's research for them.

Quicknotes

DIVERSITY OF CITIZENSHIP Parties are citizens of different states, or one party is an alien; a factor, along with a statutorily set dollar value of the matter in controversy, that allows a federal district court to exercise its authority to hear a lawsuit based on diversity jurisdiction.

DIVERSITY JURISDICTION The authority of a federal court to hear and determine cases involving parties who are of different states and an amount in controversy greater than a statutorily set amount.

FED. R. CIV. P. 11 Sets forth: the requirement that every pleading or written paper be signed by at least one attorney of record; the representations made by the attorney to the court upon the signing of such document; and the sanctions for violation of the provision.

Christian v. Mattel, Inc.

Alleged infringed toymaker (P) v. Alleged infringing toymaker (D)

286 F.3d 1118 (9th Cir. 2003)

NATURE OF CASE: Appeal of an award of Fed. R. Civ. P. 11 sanctions.

FACT SUMMARY: When the court awarded Fed. R. Civ. P. 11 sanctions against Claudene Christian (P) and her attorney, Hicks, for a combination of frivolous pleading and improper discovery tactics, Christian (P) and Hicks argued that Rule 11 sanctions must be limited to papers signed in violation of the rule, not to other conduct.

RULE OF LAW
Fed. R. Civ. P. 11 sanctions are limited to papers signed in violation of the rule, not to other conduct.

FACTS: Claudene Christian (P), who created and marketed a cheerleader doll, filed a complaint alleging that the toymaker Mattel, Inc. (D) infringed the copyright on her doll. Mattel (D) proffered evidence that its copyright predated Christian's (P) doll. However, Christian (P), through her attorney Hicks, refused voluntarily to dismiss the suit. The federal district court granted Mattel's (D) motion for summary judgment and for Fed. R. Civ. P. 11 sanctions, finding that Christian's (P) attorney, Hicks, had filed a meritless claim and that Hicks had demonstrated that his conduct fell far below the proper standards of attorneys, including, among other things, unprofessional behavior during discovery proceedings and misrepresentations to the court during oral arguments. The court awarded Mattel (D) $501,565 in attorney's fees. Christian (P) and Hicks appealed.

ISSUE: Are Fed. R. Civ. P. 11 sanctions limited to papers signed in violation of the rule, not to other conduct?

HOLDING AND DECISION: (McKeown, J.) Yes. Fed. R. Civ. P. 11 sanctions are limited to papers signed in violation of the rule, not to other conduct. While the laundry list of Hicks's outlandish conduct is a long one and raises questions as to his respect for the judicial process, nonetheless Rule 11 sanctions are limited to papers signed. Conduct in depositions, discovery meetings of counsel, oral representations at hearings, and behavior in prior proceedings do not fall within the ambit of Rule 11. Here, the orders clearly demonstrate that the district court decided, at least in part, to sanction Hicks because he signed and filed a factually and legally meritless complaint, and also, strongly suggest that the court considered "extra-pleadings conduct" as a basis for the Rule 11 sanctions. Because it cannot from the record be determined for certain whether the district court granted

Mattel's (P) Rule 11 motion as a result of an impermissible intertwining of its conclusion about the complaint's frivolity and Hicks's extrinsic misconduct, the district court Rule 11 order is vacated, and the matter is remanded to delineate the factual and legal basis for its sanctions orders.

ANALYSIS

In *Christian*, the court emphasized that Fed. R. Civ. P. 11 does not authorize sanctions for "extra-pleadings conduct" such as, for example, discovery abuses or misstatements made to the court during an oral presentation.

Quicknotes

FED. R. CIV. P. 11 Sets forth: the requirement that every pleading or written paper be signed by at least one attorney of record; the representations made by the attorney to the court upon the signing of such document; and the sanctions for violation of the provision.

Zielinski v. Philadelphia Piers, Inc.

Injured forklift operator (P) v. Rival forklift company (D)

139 F. Supp. 408 (E.D. Pa. 1956)

NATURE OF CASE: Action in torts to recover damages for personal injuries.

FACT SUMMARY: Philadelphia Piers (D) was estopped to deny ownership of a forklift and the agency of the operator.

🏛 RULE OF LAW

In the federal courts, a defendant who knowingly makes inaccurate statements may be estopped from denying those inaccurate statements at the trial.

FACTS: Zielinski (P) was injured on February 9, 1953, while operating a forklift on Pier 96 for J.A. McCarthy. Zielinski (P) alleged in his complaint that Sandy Johnson was operating a forklift owned by Philadelphia Piers (D) and was their agent as well. Because of the negligent manner in which Sandy Johnson operated the forklift, Zielinski (P) was injured. A complaint was served on Philadelphia Piers (D). Actually, Sandy Johnson worked for Carload Contractors, Inc., who had leased the forklift from Philadelphia Piers, Inc. (D). Sandy Johnson had worked for Philadelphia Piers (D) for the previous 15 years and wasn't aware that he was now working for Carload Contractors, Inc. Sandy Johnson testified at a deposition taken August 18, 1953, that he had worked for Philadelphia Piers, Inc. (D). As soon as Carload Contractors, Inc. found out about the accident, they made a report to their insurance company. When Philadelphia Piers (D) received the complaint, they forwarded it on to their insurance company, which was the same insurance company of Carload Contractors, Inc., telling them of the mistake and asking them to take care of it. Philadelphia Piers (D) was at the deposition when Sandy Johnson testified that he worked for Philadelphia Piers (D), and by receiving the complaint and the letter they sent to their insurance company, it was clear that they knew of Zielinski's (P) mistake. Zielinski (P) didn't find out that he was suing the wrong party until the pretrial conference held on September 27, 1955. Zielinski (P) requested a ruling that for the purposes of this case the forklift operated by Sandy Johnson was owned by Philadelphia Piers (D), and that Sandy Johnson was its agent acting in the course of his employment. In other words, Philadelphia Piers (D) would be estopped to deny the facts they allowed Zielinski (P) to believe.

ISSUE: If a defendant makes an ineffective denial of part of the complaint and knowingly allows the plaintiff to continue to rely on the facts as stated in the complaint, may the defendant be estopped to deny the facts as they are contained in the complaint?

HOLDING AND DECISION: (Van Dusen, J.) Yes. Philadelphia Piers (D) made a general denial of the paragraph in the complaint that alleged that Sandy Johnson was an agent of Philadelphia Piers (D) and was driving their forklift. It was clear from interrogatories that they were aware of the accident and the facts involved because they made an investigation and forwarded their report to their insurance company. Philadelphia Piers (D) should have made a specific denial of parts of the complaint they believed and knew to be false and admitted the parts that were true. This would have warned Zielinski (P) that he was suing the wrong party. This case was being tried in the district court sitting in Pennsylvania and there were no federal court decisions on this point, so the Pennsylvania law was used. The Pennsylvania rule is that where an improper and ineffective answer has been filed, an allegation of agency in the complaint requires a statement to the jury that agency is admitted if the time allowed to amend an answer has already passed. Philadelphia Piers (D) was under no duty to advise Zielinski (P) of his error other than by appropriate pleadings, but neither did they have a right, knowing of the mistake, to foster it by its acts of omission. Therefore, Philadelphia Piers (D) will be estopped to deny Sandy Johnson's agency and their ownership of the forklift and the jury will be instructed as Zielinski (P) requested. Philadelphia Piers (D) will not be prejudiced by having to defend this action, because it will be its insurance company who will have to do it and they are the insurance company for the proper defendants. A pre-trial order may be modified at trial if justice so requires.

▶ ANALYSIS

Fed. R. Civ. P. 8(b) requires that denials fairly meet the substance of the averments denied. This requirement, together with the basic requirement of good faith in pleading contained in Fed. R. Civ. P. 11, probably would provide adequate grounds for the decision in this case. Rule 8(b) also requires that the party shall state in short and plain terms his defenses to each claim asserted against him. If Philadelphia Piers (D) had stated that their defense to the complaint was that they were not the employers or owners of the personnel or machinery involved, Zielinski (P) would have been able to bring this action against the proper party. Philadelphia Piers (D) seemed to lack the good faith the federal rules require because they waited until

Continued on next page.

the time of trial to raise their defense that Zielinski had sued the wrong party.

Quicknotes

COMPLAINT The initial pleading commencing litigation which sets forth a claim for relief.

FED. R. CIV. P. 8 Sets forth the general rules of pleading a claim for relief.

GENERAL DENIAL Type of pleading contradicting all the assertions of a former pleading.

Beeck v. Aquaslide 'N' Dive Corp.

Injured slide user (P) v. Slide manufacturer (D)

562 F.2d 537 (8th Cir. 1977)

NATURE OF CASE: Appeal from grant of leave to amend.

FACT SUMMARY: Beeck (P) was injured on a pool slide alleged to have been manufactured by Aquaslide 'N' Dive Corp. (Aquaslide) (D), and after Aquaslide (D) admitted manufacture in its answer, the district court granted it leave to amend to deny manufacture over Beeck's (P) objection.

> 🏛 **RULE OF LAW**
> The opponent of a motion for leave to amend must show he will be prejudiced by the grant of leave under Fed. R. Civ. P. 15(a)[2].

FACTS: Beeck (P) was injured while using the slide at a social gathering at Kimberly Village, Davenport, Iowa. Beeck (P) then brought this action in district court under diversity jurisdiction alleging that Aquaslide 'N' Dive Corp. (Aquaslide) (D) was liable under theories of negligence, strict liability, and breach of implied warranty. Aquaslide (D) answered the complaint, admitting that it manufactured the slide in question in reliance upon the opinions of insurance investigators. The district court then granted Aquaslide (D) leave to amend the answer to deny this fact and permitted a separate trial on the question of manufacture over the objection of Beeck (P). The jury found for Aquaslide (D) and the court entered summary judgment against Beeck (P). By the time of the amendment, the statute of limitations for Beeck's (P) cause of action had run, and Beeck (P) appealed.

ISSUE: Must an opponent of a motion for leave to amend show he will be prejudiced by the grant of leave under Fed. R. Civ. P. 15(a)[2]?

HOLDING AND DECISION: (Benson, J.) Yes. Fed. R. Civ. P. 15(a)[2] provides that "leave shall be freely given when justice so requires." The grant or denial of such leave to amend is within the sound discretion of the trial judge. The party opposing the motion for leave must show he will be prejudiced by the grant of leave under Fed. R. Civ. P. 15(a)[2]. In this case, Aquaslide (D) relied upon the conclusions of three separate insurance companies and their investigators and were thus not negligent in determining the facts in question, and it was not an abuse of discretion to give Aquaslide (D) a chance to correct a fact disputed. Beeck (P) alleged that he was prejudiced because his action was foreclosed by the running of the statute of limitations. This argument required the trial judge to assume that Aquaslide (D) would prevail on the manufacturing issue, and the judge properly refused to so

presume. Neither was the grant of separate trials improper. A substantial issue of material fact was raised that would exonerate Aquaslide (D) if resolved in its favor. There was thus no abuse of discretion. Affirmed.

▶ **ANALYSIS**

Because of the running of the statute of limitations, it would be unlikely, if not impossible, that Beeck (P) would be able to move against any other party. The court had to counterbalance this injustice against that of precluding Aquaslide (D) from proving that it did not manufacture the slide that caused the injury. Since the amendment and the separate trial gave Beeck (P) a chance to disprove Aquaslide's (D) argument, and since the Federal Rules of Civil Procedure technically permitted the amendment and severance, the balance was struck in Aquaslide's (D) favor.

▬▬

Quicknotes

AMENDMENT TO PLEADING The modification of a pleading either as a matter of course upon motion to the court or by consent of both parties; a party is entitled to change its pleading once as a matter of course before a responsive pleading has been served.

ISSUE OF MATERIAL FACT A fact that is disputed between two or more parties to litigation that is essential to proving an element of the cause of action or a defense asserted or would otherwise affect the outcome of the proceeding.

▬▬

Moore v. Baker

Patient (P) v. Physician (D)

989 F.2d 1129 (11th Cir. 1993)

NATURE OF CASE: Appeal of denial of motion to amend pleading in nonconsent action.

FACT SUMMARY: Moore (P) initially alleged that Dr. Baker (D) violated the informed-consent law, but then sought to include a claim for medical malpractice.

🏛 RULE OF LAW

A claim that does not arise out of the same conduct, transaction, or occurrence as the original claim does not relate back to the original pleading.

FACTS: Moore (P) consulted Dr. Baker (D) to correct a blockage of her carotid artery. Baker (D) recommended surgery and warned Moore (P) of the risks. The operation left Moore (P) permanently disabled. Moore's (P) initial complaint alleged only a violation of Georgia's informed-consent law. The trial court granted Baker's (D) motion for summary judgment. The statute of limitations ran the day after Moore (P) filed the original complaint. Moore (P) then sought to amend the complaint to include a claim for negligence, asserting that the new claim should relate back to the date of the original complaint. The trial court denied Moore's (P) motion, and Moore (P) appealed.

ISSUE: May a claim that does not arise out of the same conduct, transaction, or occurrence as the original claim relate back to the original pleading?

HOLDING AND DECISION: (Morgan, J.) No. A claim that does not arise out of the same conduct, transaction, or occurrence as the original claim may not relate back to the original pleading. In this case, the new claim arises out of alleged actions that are distinct in time and involve separate and distinct conduct. The failure-to-warn claim focused on actions prior to surgery, while the negligence claim focuses on actions during and post-surgery. Affirmed.

▶ ANALYSIS

Whether the conduct, transaction, or occurrence in the amended complaint relates back to the original complaint to avoid the bar of a statute of limitations is a subjective test open to argument and interpretation. The role of the appellate court is to decide whether the trial court abused its discretion in applying this test to the facts of the case.

◼▬◼

Quicknotes

AMENDMENT TO PLEADING The modification of a pleading either as a matter of course upon motion to the court or

by consent of both parties; a party is entitled to change its pleading once as a matter of course before a responsive pleading has been served.

RELATION BACK DOCTRINE Doctrine that holds that a party may not amend its pleading to set forth a new or different claim or defense unless it involves the subject matter of the original pleading; under Fed. R. Civ. P. 15(c), if a party amends its pleading as a matter of course before a responsive pleading is served, such amendment is said to relate back to the original pleading if it involves the subject matter of the original pleading.

◼▬◼

Bonerb v. Richard J. Caron Foundation

Injured basketball player (P) v. Foundation (D)

159 F.R.D. 16 (W.D.N.Y. 1994)

NATURE OF CASE: Motion to amend complaint in personal-injury action.

FACT SUMMARY: After Bonerb (P) filed suit for injuries received on a basketball court while he was being treated at the Richard J. Caron Foundation (Foundation) (D), he sought to amend his complaint to add a cause of action for "counseling malpractice."

🏛 RULE OF LAW
When allegations in an amended complaint and the original complaint derive from the same nucleus of operative facts, the amended complaint relates back to the date of the original complaint.

FACTS: Bonerb (P) slipped and fell while playing basketball at the Richard J. Caron Foundation (Foundation) (D) while participating in the Foundation's (D) mandatory exercise program. Bonerb's (P) original complaint alleged the Foundation's (D) basketball court was negligently maintained. Bonerb (P) sought to amend the complaint to include a new claim for counseling malpractice. Bonerb (P) sought to relate back the malpractice claim to the date of the original complaint since the statute of limitations had expired for asserting a malpractice claim.

ISSUE: May allegations in an amended complaint relate back to the date of the original complaint when the new claim derives from the same nucleus of operative facts as the original complaint?

HOLDING AND DECISION: (Heckmann, J.) Yes. Allegations in an amended complaint may relate back to the date of the original complaint when the new claim derives from the same nucleus of operative facts as the original complaint. The determining factor is whether the facts stated in the original complaint put the defendant on notice of the claim which plaintiff later seeks to add. Here, Bonerb (P) is using the same factual allegations in the amended complaint as in the original complaint. Bonerb (P) has merely changed the legal theory upon which the claim is based. Motion to amend is granted.

▌ ANALYSIS

Amendment to a pleading may occur in an answer as well as a complaint. Fed. R. Civ. P. 15(a) allows relation back for claims and defenses asserted in the original pleading or attempted to be set forth in the original pleading, which arose from the conduct, transaction, or occurrence of the original pleading.

Quicknotes

NUCLEUS OF OPERATIVE FACTS An underlying fact situation common to those pleadings asserting it.

RELATION BACK DOCTRINE Doctrine that holds that a party may not amend its pleading to set forth a new or different claim or defense unless it involves the subject matter of the original pleading; under Fed. R. Civ. P. 15(c), if a party amends its pleading as a matter of course before a responsive pleading is served, such amendment is said to relate back to the original pleading if it involves the subject matter of the original pleading.

Quick Reference Rules of Law

Zubulake v. UBS Warburg LLC

Former employee (P) v. Employer (D)

229 F.R.D. 422 (S.D.N.Y. 2004)

NATURE OF CASE: Action for sanctions for destruction of evidence.

FACT SUMMARY: Laura Zubulake (P) moved to sanction UBS Warburg LLC (D) for failure to produce relevant information and for late production of material.

🏛 RULE OF LAW
An attorney's duty to produce evidence is not discharged upon notification to the parties and witnesses that all possibly relevant evidence must be preserved for litigation.

FACTS: Laura Zubulake (P) moved to sanction UBS Warburg LLC (UBS) (D) for failure to produce relevant information and for late production of material. UBS (D) employees had deleted some e-mails and other electronic files that were relevant to Zubulake's (P) case against UBS (D). In addition, UBS's (D) lawyers failed to request certain information from one employee and to give the litigation hold instructions to another. They also did not communicate effectively about how the employees should maintain their computer files for litigation and about how to safeguard backup tapes that might have contained some of the deleted e-mails.

ISSUE: Is an attorney's duty to produce evidence discharged upon notification to the parties and witnesses that all possibly relevant evidence must be preserved for litigation?

HOLDING AND DECISION: (Scheindlin, J.) No. An attorney's duty to produce evidence is not discharged upon notification to the parties and witnesses that all possibly relevant evidence must be preserved for litigation. The attorney must issue a "litigation hold" at the outset of litigation and should periodically reissue it so that new employees are aware of it. The attorney should also communicate directly with key players in the litigation. And employees should be instructed by attorneys that they must produce electronic copies of their relevant active files, and that backup media must be identified and stored safely and separate from other, non-relevant backup material. But the attorney's role is still limited, and the ultimate responsibility for preserving evidence rests with the parties. [Here, UBS (D) acted willfully in destroying potentially relevant information, and sanctions were therefore warranted to put Zubulake (P) in the position she would have been in had UBS (D) faithfully discharged its discovery obligations. The jury was instructed to construe the missing e-mails in Zubulake's (P) favor, since most of the existing e-mails support her case.]

▶ ANALYSIS

The court's goal in imposing sanctions was to put the plaintiff in the position she would have been, had the destruction of evidence not occurred. But in this case, there was other evidence that supported the plaintiff's case, and therefore the court instructed the jury to weigh the destroyed evidence against the defendant. A different result would occur, however, if there were not additional evidence supporting the plaintiff's case, even if all of the destroyed evidence would have supported her case.

■■■

Quicknotes

EVIDENTIARY FACTS Those facts necessary for the determination of the ultimate facts.

RELEVANT EVIDENCE Evidence having any tendency to prove or disprove a disputed fact.

■■■

Favale v. Roman Catholic Diocese of Bridgeport

Former employee (P) v. Former employer (D)

233 F.R.D. 243 (D. Conn. 2005)

NATURE OF CASE: Motions to compel and for a protective order in action for, inter alia, sexual harassment, retaliation, negligent hiring, and negligent supervision.

FACT SUMMARY: Maryann Favale (P), a former employee of the Roman Catholic Diocese of Bridgeport (the Diocese) (D) who claimed that her former supervisor, Sister Stobierski, sexually harassed Favale (P), sought to compel Stobierski to testify as to Stobierski's treatment for anger management, psychological and psychiatric conditions, and sought to compel the Diocese (D) to produce any records it had of any such treatment. The Diocese (D) sought a protective order barring such discovery.

RULE OF LAW
Discovery of highly personal information will not be compelled where it is not relevant to conduct alleged to have caused the plaintiff's harms.

FACTS: Maryann Favale (P) was an administrative assistant at a school run by the Roman Catholic Diocese of Bridgeport (the Diocese) (D). At some point, Sister Stobierski became the school's principal. Favale (P) brought suit alleging that Stobierski had sexually harassed her. She sought damages for sexual harassment, retaliation, defamation, intentional and negligent infliction of emotional distress, negligent hiring, negligent supervision, and other causes of action. Favale (P) moved to compel Stobierski to testify to any prior treatment she may have received for her alleged anger management history and psychological or psychiatric conditions. Favale (P) also move to compel the Diocese (D) to produce any records it had of any such treatment. The Diocese (D), asserting that the discovery sought by Favale (P) was irrelevant and privileged, moved for a protective order barring the discovery. Favale (P) countered that the discovery was relevant to the claims of negligent hiring and negligent supervision.

ISSUE: Will discovery of highly personal information be compelled where it is not relevant to conduct alleged to have caused the plaintiff's harms?

HOLDING AND DECISION: (Squatrito, J.) No. Discovery of highly personal information will not be compelled where it is not relevant to conduct alleged to have caused the plaintiff's harms. To prove a claim for negligent hiring, a plaintiff must show that she suffered harm as a result of the defendant's negligence in hiring an employee who was unfit or incompetent to perform the work for which the employee was hired, and that her injuries resulted from the employee's unfit or incompetent performance. To prove a negligent supervision claim, the plaintiff must prove that defendant knew or reasonably should have known of the employee's propensity to engage in the type of tortious conduct that caused the plaintiff's injuries. Here, Favale's (P) alleged injuries resulted from Stobierski's alleged repeated acts of sexual harassment—not from anger management or other psychological or psychiatric conditions. Accordingly, Stobierski's testimony as to those conditions would be irrelevant to the defense or claim of either party. Even if the Diocese (D) had been aware of Stobierski's alleged anger management history or psychological or psychiatric conditions, this knowledge would have no bearing on Favale's (P) claims for negligent supervision and negligent hiring because the wrongful conduct of which the Diocese (D) would have had notice of was not the same type of wrongful conduct that caused Favale (P) harm. For the same reasons, if the Diocese (D) possessed records relating to Stobierski's alleged conditions, these records would not establish Stobierski's propensity for the type of behavior that caused Favale (P) harm because they would not demonstrate a propensity for sexual harassment. For these reasons, Favale's (P) motion to compel is denied, and the Diocese's (D) motion for a protective order barring the type of discovery sought by Favale (P) is granted, especially since the type of information Favale (P) is seeking is "profoundly personal."

ANALYSIS

This case illustrates the principle that there are boundaries to discovery. A court can limit discovery if it determines, among other things, the discovery is: (1) unreasonably cumulative or duplicative; (2) obtainable from another source that is more convenient, less burdensome, or less expensive; or (3) the burden or expense of the proposed discovery outweighs its likely benefit. In addition, a district court enjoys broad discretion when resolving discovery disputes. When exercising such discretion, the court should—as the court did here—determine the relevance of discovery requests, assess oppressiveness, and weigh these factors in deciding whether discovery should be compelled.

Quicknotes

DISCOVERY Pretrial procedure during which one party makes certain information available to the other.

Cerrato v. Nutribullet, LLC

Individual (P) v. Corporation (D)

2017 WL 3608266 (M.D. Fla. 2017)

NATURE OF CASE: Consideration of plaintiff's motion to compel production of the prior accident reports relating to the product that allegedly caused injuries to the plaintiff.

FACT SUMMARY: Phyllis Cerrato (P) was allegedly injured when a blender designed by Nutribullet (D) exploded while she was operating it.

🏛 RULE OF LAW
Courts will generally find discovery requests that do not include time limitations or do not accurately define the type of information requested to be overbroad and not proportional to the needs of the case.

FACTS: Phyllis Cerrato (P) was allegedly injured when a blender designed by Nutribullet (D) exploded while she was operating it. The alleged defect in the product was that it could not be turned off. The explosion caused hot liquids to burn Cerrato (P) and caused property damage to Cerrato's (P) kitchen. Cerrato (P) brought a products liability action against Nutribullet (D). During discovery, Cerrato (P) requested any and all documents relating to any injuries caused by the product at any time. She also requested any consumer complaints relating to the product. Nutribullet (D) objected to both requests on the grounds they were overbroad and unduly burdensome. Cerrato (P) filed a motion to compel the discovery.

ISSUE: Will courts find discovery requests that do not include time limitations or do not accurately define the type of information requested to be overbroad and not proportional to the needs of the case?

HOLDING AND DECISION: (Sneed, J.) Yes. Courts will generally find discovery requests that do not include time limitations or do not accurately define the type of information requested to be overbroad and not proportional to the needs of the case. In this case, Cerrato's (P) requests are not proportional. They include no time limitations, no limitation on the type of injuries caused in the past by the product or the nature of the defect in those prior cases. Accordingly, the court orders that Nutribullet (D) produce all accident reports and complaints that relate to incidents where the product could not be turned off. The time frame shall be five years prior to the date of the incident to the date of the filing of the complaint. Nutribullet (D) shall be allowed to redact the consumer names on those complaints, as that information is irrelevant to the claims at issue. Motion granted in part and denied in part.

▶ ANALYSIS

Trial court judges at both the federal and state levels have broad discretion to determine the scope of discovery in a case. They are closest to the matter and are familiar with the claims as well as the amount of discovery potentially available in the case. Appellate court judges do not typically overturn trial court judges' rulings on discovery matters, unless there is an abuse of discretion, which is a very difficult standard to prove.

Quicknotes

DISCOVERY Pretrial procedure during which one party makes certain information available to the other.

PRODUCTS LIABILITY The legal liability of manufacturers and sellers for damages and injuries suffered by buyers, users, or bystanders because of defects in goods purchased.

Wagoner v. Lewis Gale Medical Center, LLC

Individual (P) v. Corporation (D)

2016 WL 3893135 (W.D. Va. 2016)

NATURE OF CASE: Consideration of plaintiff's motion to compel production of e-mails from the defendant.

FACT SUMMARY: Lewis Gale Medical Center, LLC (D) terminated Wagoner (P), a security guard, after two months on the job.

🏛 RULE OF LAW
Relevant electronically stored information may not be discoverable if the party in possession can show the information is not reasonably accessible because of undue burden or cost.

FACTS: Lewis Gale Medical Center, LLC (Lewis Gale) (D) terminated Wagoner (P), a security guard, after two months on the job. Wagoner (P) filed suit alleging that Lewis Gale (D) wrongfully terminated him in violation of the Americans with Disabilities Act, based upon his dyslexia. During discovery, Wagoner (P) requested four months of documents and e-mails from two other custodians at the hospital. The request sought documents using specific search terms such as "Wagoner," "dyslexia," "reading," and "copying," among others. Lewis Gale (D) objected on the grounds it would cost them almost $45,000 to search its computer systems and then review any documents with those search terms. It alleged there were over 30,000 e-mails that would be responsive to the request. Wagoner (P) filed a motion to compel.

ISSUE: May relevant electronically stored information not be discoverable if the party in possession can show the information is not reasonably accessible because of undue burden or cost?

HOLDING AND DECISION: (Ballou, J.) Yes. Relevant electronically stored information may not be discoverable if the party in possession can show the information is not reasonably accessible because of undue burden or cost. Fed. R. Civ. P. 26(b)(2)(B). Courts also can order cost sharing in particular cases. In this matter, Lewis Gale (D) has not shown that the information Wagoner (P) is seeking is not reasonably accessible. Whether production of documents is unduly burdensome or expensive depends on whether the data is physically accessible. Lewis Gale (D) has not shown the information has to be restored or reconstructed in any manner. The issue here is that Lewis Gale (D) employs a computer system that does not preserve any e-mails beyond three days. This makes it costly for Lewis Gale (D) to search and find e-mails when faced with legal claims. That Lewis Gale (D) chose a system that makes it expensive for them to find the documents should

not be held against Wagoner (P). Accordingly, Lewis Gale (D) must produce the records requested. For the same reason, cost shifting is not appropriate and the principle that each party bears the costs of producing its own discovery shall apply. Motion to compel granted.

▶ ANALYSIS

In this matter, the discovery request was limited in time to four months and sought e-mails with a limited set of search parameters. Once the court finds that a request is relevant and proportional, it will be difficult for the other party to claim that cost alone prohibits the production of the documents.

■▤■

Quicknotes

DISCOVERY Pretrial procedure during which one party makes certain information available to the other.

WRONGFUL TERMINATION Unlawful termination of an individual's employment.

■▤■

Rengifo v. Erevos Enterprises, Inc.

Former employee (P) v. Former employer (D)

2007 WL 894376 (S.D.N.Y. Mar. 20, 2007)

NATURE OF CASE: Motion for protective order in action to recover unpaid overtime wages.

FACT SUMMARY: Willy Rengifo (P), who brought an action against his former employer, Erevos Enterprises, Inc. (Erevos) (D), to recover unpaid overtime wages, sought a protective order barring discovery related to his immigration status, social security number, and authorization to work in the United States.

🏛 RULE OF LAW
In an action to enforce employment rights, a protective order barring discovery related to the plaintiff's immigration status, social security number, and authorization to work in the United States will be granted where, at most, such discovery is related to collateral issues.

FACTS: Willy Rengifo (P), a former employee of Erevos Enterprises, Inc. (Erevos) (D), brought suit against Erevos (D) to recover unpaid overtime wages under federal and state law. Erevos (D) sought discovery related to Rengifo's (P) immigration status, authorization to work in the United States, and social security number, contending that these were relevant to his right to recover unpaid wages, as well as to his credibility. Rengifo (P) sought a protective order, asserting that the discovery sought by Erevos (D) was irrelevant to his right to overtime pay, and that the intimidating effect of requiring disclosure of immigration status was sufficient to establish "good cause" for the protective order since the question of immigration status only went to a collateral issue. Erevos (D) also argued that because Rengifo (P) had failed to produce a complete set of pay stubs that reflected all of the compensation he had received, and because he had not produced any records regarding the number of hours he had worked on a weekly basis, discovery of documents containing his tax identification number or social security number, such as tax returns, was necessary and relevant to obtain this information.

ISSUE: In an action to enforce employment rights, will a protective order barring discovery related to the plaintiff's immigration status, social security number, and authorization to work in the United States be granted where, at most, such discovery is related to collateral issues?

HOLDING AND DECISION: (Ellis, J.) Yes. In an action to enforce employment rights, a protective order barring discovery related to the plaintiff's immigration status, social security number, and authorization to work in the United States will be granted where, at most, such

discovery is related to collateral issues. As to discovery regarding Rengifo's (P) immigration status, courts have recognized the in terrorem effect of inquiring into a party's immigration status and authorization to work in the U.S. when such inquiry is irrelevant to any material claim, because it presents a danger of intimidation that would inhibit plaintiffs in pursuing their rights. Here, Rengifo's (P) immigration status and authority to work is a collateral issue, so that a protective order is necessary to prevent him from being intimidated to the point where he would rather withdraw from the suit than face potential deportation or criminal charges. Additionally, Rengifo (P) seeks to prevent disclosure of his social security number or tax identification number. These identifying data are irrelevant to Rengifo's (P) claims for unpaid overtime wages, and, in any event, Erevos (D) possesses relevant data on hours and compensation, and there is no reason to assume that its records are less reliable than any records maintained by Rengifo (P). Erevos (D) also argues that by applying for a job and providing his social security number, Rengifo (P) represented that he was a legal resident, and that Erevos (D) is entitled to test the truthfulness of that information. Erevos (D) further argues that if Rengifo (P) filed tax returns, this information would be relevant to his overtime claim, but if he failed to file tax returns, this fact would affect the veracity of statements he would potentially make at trial. Although credibility is always an issue, it seems that Erevos's (D) attempt to discover tax identification numbers on the basis of testing credibility is a back-door attempt to learn of immigration status. The opportunity to test the credibility of a party based on representations made when seeking employment does not outweigh the chilling effect that disclosure of immigration status has on employees seeking to enforce their rights. If an employee is undocumented, allowing an employer to inquire into immigration status in employment cases would allow the employer to implicitly raise threats of deportation or criminal prosecution when a worker reports illegal practices. Even limiting disclosure of immigrant status to the case at bar through a confidentiality agreement would not eliminate the danger of intimidation and of destroying the cause of action. In sum, giving Erevos (D) opportunity to test the credibility of Rengifo does not outweigh the public interest in allowing employees to enforce their rights. For these reasons, Rengifo's (P) application for a protective order is granted.

Continued on next page.

► *ANALYSIS*

According to Rule 26(b)(1) of the Federal Rules of Civil Procedure, a party "may obtain discovery regarding any matter, not privileged, which is relevant to the subject matter involved in the pending action." However, Rule 26 (c) authorizes courts, for good cause, to "make any order which justice requires to protect a party or person from annoyance, embarrassment, oppression, or undue burden or expense, including . . . that certain matters not be inquired into, or that the scope of the disclosure or discovery be limited to certain matters . . ." The burden is upon the party seeking non-disclosure or a protective order to show good cause. Thus, in this case, Rengifo (P) carried the burden of showing there was good cause for the protective order he was requesting by showing that the damage and prejudice that would result to him if discovery into his immigration status were permitted far outweighed its probative value.

Quicknotes

DISCOVERY Pretrial procedure during which one party makes certain information available to the other.

PROTECTIVE ORDER Court order protecting a party against potential abusive treatment through use of the legal process.

Hickman v. Taylor

Representative of deceased (P) v. Tug owner (D)

329 U.S. 495 (1947)

NATURE OF CASE: Action for damages for wrongful death.

FACT SUMMARY: Five crew members drowned when a tug sank. In anticipation of litigation, the attorney for Taylor (D), the tug owner, interviewed the survivors. Hickman (P), as representative of one of the deceased, brought this action and tried by means of discovery to obtain copies of the statements Taylor's (D) attorney obtained from the survivors.

RULE OF LAW
Material obtained by counsel in preparation for litigation is the work product of the lawyer, and while such material is not protected by the attorney-client privilege, it is not discoverable on mere demand without a showing of necessity or justification.

FACTS: Five of nine crew members drowned when a tug sank. A public hearing was held at which the four survivors were examined. Their testimony was recorded and was made available to all interested parties. A short time later, the attorney for Taylor (D), the tug owner, interviewed the survivors, in preparation for possible litigation. He also interviewed other persons believed to have information on the accident. Ultimately, claims were brought by representatives of all five of the deceased. Four were settled. Hickman (P), the fifth claimant, brought this action. He filed interrogatories asking for any statements taken from crew members as well as any oral or written statements, records, reports, or other memoranda made concerning any matter relative to the towing operation, the tug's sinking, the salvaging and repair of the tug, and the death of the deceased. Taylor (D) refused to summarize or set forth the material on the grounds that it was protected by the attorney-client privilege.

ISSUE: Does a party seeking to discover material obtained by an adverse party's counsel in preparation for possible litigation have a burden to show a justification for such production?

HOLDING AND DECISION: (Murphy, J.) Yes. The deposition-discovery rules are to be accorded a broad and liberal treatment, since mutual knowledge of all the relevant facts gathered by both parties is essential to proper litigation. But discovery does have ultimate and necessary boundaries. Limitations arise upon a showing of bad faith or harassment or when the inquiry seeks material that is irrelevant or privileged. In this case, the material sought by Hickman (P) is not protected by the attorney-client privilege. However, such material as that sought here does constitute the work product of the lawyer. The general policy against invading the privacy of an attorney in performing his various duties is so well recognized and so essential to the orderly working of our legal system that the party seeking work-product material has a burden to show reasons to justify such production. Interviews, statements, memoranda, correspondence, briefs, mental impressions, etc., obtained in the course of preparation for possible or anticipated litigation fall within the work product. Such material is not free from discovery in all cases. Where relevant and nonprivileged facts remain hidden in an attorney's file and where production of those facts is essential to the preparation of one's case, discovery may be had. But there must be a showing of necessity and justification. In this case, Hickman (P) seeks discovery of oral and written statements of witnesses whose identity is well known and whose availability to Hickman (P) appears unimpaired. Here no attempt was made to show why it was necessary that Taylor's (D) attorney produce the material. No reasons were given to justify this invasion of the attorney's privacy. Hickman's (P) counsel admitted he wanted the statements only to help him prepare for trial. That is insufficient to warrant an exception to the policy of protecting the privacy of an attorney's professional activities.

CONCURRENCE: (Jackson, J.) A common law trial is and always should be an adversary proceeding. Discovery was hardly intended to enable a learned profession to perform its functions either without wits or on wits borrowed from the adversary. I can conceive of no practice more demoralizing to the bar than to require a lawyer to write out and deliver to the adversary an account of what witnesses have told him.

▶ ANALYSIS

The *Hickman* decision left open a number of questions as to the scope of the work product doctrine and the showing needed to discover work product material. In 1970, Fed. R. Civ. P. 26(b)(3) was added to deal with the discovery of work product. It provides that documents and tangible things that were prepared in anticipation of litigation or for trial are discoverable only upon a showing that the party seeking such materials has substantial need of them and that he is unable without undue hardship to obtain the substantial equivalent of the materials by other means. The rule states mental impressions, conclusions,

Continued on next page.

opinions, or legal theories of an attorney or other representative of a party are to be protected against disclosure.

Quicknotes

ATTORNEY-CLIENT PRIVILEGE A doctrine precluding the admission into evidence of confidential communications between an attorney and his client made in the course of obtaining professional assistance.

ATTORNEY WORK-PRODUCT DOCTRINE A doctrine excluding from discovery work performed by an attorney in preparation for litigation.

DEPOSITION A pretrial discovery procedure whereby oral or written questions are asked by one party of a witness of the opposing party under oath in preparation for litigation.

DISCOVERY Pretrial procedure during which one party makes certain information available to the other.

Thompson v. The Haskell Co.

Sexually harassed employee (P) v. Employer (D)

65 F. Empl. Prac. Cas. (BNA) 1088 (M.D. Fla. 1994)

NATURE OF CASE: Motion for protective order in sexual-harassment suit.

FACT SUMMARY: Thompson (P) sought to protect her psychologist's report from discovery.

🏛 RULE OF LAW
Under exceptional circumstances, if it is impractical for the party seeking discovery to obtain facts or opinions on the same subject by other means, a party may, by interrogatories or by deposition, discover information by an expert who has been retained or specially employed by another party in anticipation of litigation and who is not to be called as a witness.

FACTS: Thompson (P) sued The Haskell Co. (D) and Zona (D), a supervisor of The Haskell Co. (D), alleging sexual harassment and that her employment with The Haskell Co. (D) was terminated when she refused to acquiesce to Zona's (D) advances. Thompson's (P) former counsel employed Dr. Lucas, a psychologist, to perform a diagnostic review and personality profile ten days after Thompson (P) was terminated. Thompson (P) sought an order to protect the psychological records possessed by Dr. Lucas.

ISSUE: May a party, under exceptional circumstances, obtain discovery of information by an opposing party's expert who has been retained or employed by a party in anticipation of litigation and who is not to be called as a witness?

HOLDING AND DECISION: (Snyder, J.) Yes. Under exceptional circumstances, a party may obtain discovery of information by an opposing party's expert who has been retained or employed by a party in anticipation of litigation and who is not to be called as a witness. Here, Dr. Lucas's report was made ten days after Thompson (P) was terminated and is the only evidence available which is probative of Thompson's (P) emotional state at that time. Motion denied.

▶ ANALYSIS

Thompson (P) did not file her complaint until several months after she was terminated. Thus, opposing counsel had no opportunity to obtain psychological information from Thompson (P) shortly after her termination that would be probative of her emotional state during that time. This factor provided the exceptional circumstance in the present case.

■=■

Quicknotes

DEPOSITION A pretrial discovery procedure whereby oral or written questions are asked by one party of a witness of the opposing party under oath in preparation for litigation.

DISCOVERY Pretrial procedure during which one party makes certain information available to the other.

EXPERT WITNESS A witness providing testimony at trial who is specially qualified regarding the particular subject matter involved.

INTERROGATORY A method of pretrial discovery in which written questions are provided by one party to another who must respond in writing under oath.

■=■

Chiquita International Ltd. v. M/V Bolero Reefer

Shipper (P) v. Cargo carrier (D)

1994 U.S. Dist. LEXIS 5820 (S.D.N.Y. 1994)

NATURE OF CASE: Motion to compel discovery.

FACT SUMMARY: International Reefer Ltd. (D), a carrier, sought to compel discovery of a marine surveyor who had evaluated its loading cranes and side ports.

RULE OF LAW
A nontestifying expert is immune from discovery unless exceptional circumstances apply.

FACTS: Shipper Chiquita International Ltd. (Chiquita) (P) sued International Reefer Services, S.A. (D), a cargo carrier, for cargo loss and damage. Chiquita (P) alleged that loading cranes and side ports on International Reefer's (D) carrier failed to function properly, which prevented the carrier from shipping the full load of Chiquita (P) bananas to Germany and unloading them before spoilage in accord with their contract. International Reefer (D) requested an order compelling discovery from Winer, a marine surveyor Chiquita (P) had employed to inspect the carrier upon arrival in Germany. International Reefer (D) asserted that Winer was a fact witness rather than an expert and that even if Winer were a nontestifying expert, exceptional circumstances existed to compel discovery. Chiquita (P) objected.

ISSUE: May a nontestifying expert be subject to discovery?

HOLDING AND DECISION: (Francis, J.) No. A nontestifying expert may not be subject to discovery unless exceptional circumstances apply. A fact witness is a witness whose information was obtained in the normal course of business; however, a nontestifying expert is a person hired to make an evaluation in connection with expected litigation. Winer was hired by Chiquita (P) to make an observation in anticipation of litigation; thus, he is a nontestifying expert. Because International Reefer (D) could have employed its own expert to examine its carrier, and Chiquita (P) did not prevent another expert from being retained, no exceptional circumstances apply here. Application for Winer's deposition is denied.

▶ ANALYSIS

It is often not clear whether a person is a fact witness or nontestifying expert; thus, this is a favorite topic for law school examinations. Another favorite topic is determining if exceptional circumstances apply that would warrant compelling discovery from a nontestifying expert.

Quicknotes

DEPOSITION A pretrial discovery procedure whereby oral or written questions are asked by one party of a witness of the opposing party under oath in preparation for litigation.

DISCOVERY Pretrial procedure during which one party makes certain information available to the other.

EXPERT WITNESS A witness providing testimony at trial who is specially qualified regarding the particular subject matter involved.

Mueller v. Swift

Individual (P) v. Individuals (D)

2017 WL 3058027 (D. Colo. 2017)

NATURE OF CASE: Consideration of defendants' motion for sanctions against the plaintiff due to plaintiff's alleged spoliation of evidence.

FACT SUMMARY: David Mueller (P), a radio disc jockey, brought claims against Taylor Swift (D) and his employer for tortious interference with his employment contract after the employer terminated him because of allegations Swift (D) made relating to inappropriate touching by Mueller (P) during a photo opportunity.

🏛 RULE OF LAW
A court may order sanctions or an adverse inference where a party has a duty to preserve evidence because it knew litigation was imminent and the other party was prejudiced by the destruction or loss of the evidence at issue.

FACTS: Prior to one of her concerts, Taylor Swift (D) attended a backstage photo opportunity with David Mueller (P). Swift (D) later alleged to Mueller's (P) employer, radio station KYGO (D), that Mueller (P) inappropriately touched her buttocks under her dress during the shoot. The following day, Mueller (P) met with his superiors, Eddie Haskell (D) and Robert Call (D), to discuss the allegations. Unbeknownst to them, Mueller (P) recorded the entire two-hour conversation. KYGO (D) terminated Mueller (P) on the grounds that Mueller (P) had changed his version of events that he did not touch Swift (D) as alleged to a new version that it was only incidental. Mueller (P) brought suit against the defendants for tortious interference with his employment contract. Regarding the recording, Mueller (P) edited down the recording and sent only clips of it to his attorney. Mueller (P) then allegedly spilled coffee on the laptop that contained the full recording and it could not be preserved. During discovery, the defendants filed this motion for sanctions based on Mueller's (P) spoliation of evidence by not preserving a copy of the entire recording.

ISSUE: May a court order sanctions or an adverse inference where a party has a duty to preserve evidence because it knew litigation was imminent and the other party was prejudiced by the destruction or loss of the evidence at issue?

HOLDING AND DECISION: (Martínez, J.) Yes. A court may order sanctions or an adverse inference where a party has a duty to preserve evidence because it knew litigation was imminent and the other party was prejudiced by the destruction or loss of the evidence at issue. Two factors are paramount in this scenario: (1) the degree of culpability of the party that did not preserve the evidence; and (2) the actual degree of prejudice to the other parties. Mueller (P) does not dispute he had a duty to preserve the entire recording. He clearly knew or should have known that litigation was imminent. It is very likely Mueller (P) was aware litigation was possible and that is the reason he created the recording. The recording is also relevant to Mueller's (P) claims that Haskell (D) and Call (D) improperly interfered with his employment relationship with KYGO (D). The recording likely contained evidence that would tend to prove or disprove that claim. The recording could also potentially prove whether Mueller (P) did indeed change his story while speaking with Haskell (D) and Call (D). The spoliation of evidence also prejudiced the defendants. If the recording had been preserved, it would have saved time and expense during discovery and allowed for better preparation for trial. Regarding culpability, there is not enough evidence for the court to find that Mueller (P) acted in bad faith, warranting the issuance of an adverse inference instruction at trial. Nor will the court characterize the loss as mere negligence. The court cannot find that Mueller (P) acted in bad faith because the record does not establish that he acted with intent to deprive the other parties of evidence. However, Mueller (P) did alter the recording to preserve evidence that was helpful to his claims. Accordingly, there will [be] no instruction of an adverse inference at trial. To be fair, the defendants will be able to cross examine Muller (P) during trial about his (P) spoliation of the recording. This will allow the jury to make its own assessment of the degree of Mueller's (P) culpability and the prejudice to the defendants. If the jury believes Mueller (P) acted in bad faith, it will draw its own adverse inferences. Mueller's (P) credibility is central to his claims and the credibility of witnesses at trial falls within the province of the jury, not the court. The motion for spoliation of evidence is granted, but the defendants' request for an adverse inference instruction is denied.

▶ ANALYSIS

The adverse inference instruction typically states to a jury it must find that the entirety of a lost or destroyed piece of evidence would have been unfavorable to the party guilty of the spoliation. In extreme cases, courts may even dismiss a plaintiff's entire case if it finds the plaintiff acted in bad faith and the defendants were so prejudiced by the loss of evidence that they are unable to defend the claims.

■-■□■

Continued on next page.

Quicknotes

ADVERSE INFERENCE A harmful conclusion made by the fact-finder from a party's not producing evidence that the party has within its control.

BAD FAITH Conduct that is intentionally misleading or deceptive.

SANCTIONS A penalty imposed in order to ensure compliance with a statute or regulation.

SPOLIATION OF EVIDENCE When a party has a duty to preserve evidence because it knew litigation was imminent and the other party was prejudiced by the destruction or loss of the evidence at issue.

TORTIOUS INTERFERENCE WITH CONTRACTUAL RELATIONSHIP An intentional tort whereby a defendant intentionally elicits the breach of a valid contract resulting in damages.

Security National Bank of Sioux City v. Abbott Laboratories

[Parties not identified.]

299 F.R.D. 595 (N.D. Iowa 2014) *rev'd sub nom. Security Natl. Bank of Sioux City v. Day*, 800 F.3d 936 (8th Cir. 2015)

NATURE OF CASE: Attorney sanctions for discovery abuses in action for products liability.

FACT SUMMARY: As attorney sanctions for an unwarranted number of "obstructionist" objections and interruptions, as well as coaching, that an attorney made during depositions, the judge ordered the attorney to write and create a video that could serve as a guide to other attorneys for avoiding the obstructionist conduct the attorney had engaged in.

🏛 RULE OF LAW
Where a judge has determined that counsel has engaged in discovery abuse, the judge may specially tailor a sanction designed to deter the specific abuses the attorney has engaged in.

FACTS: A district judge who was reviewing depositions in a products liability case determined that one of the attorneys in the case (whom the judge called "Counsel") had engaged in obstructionist conduct by making hundreds of unnecessary and meritless objections and interruptions, as well as coaching. The judge determined that sanctions were appropriate. The judge, while believing that substantial monetary sanctions would be appropriate, felt that these would not serve as well as a specially tailored sanction to deter the attorney, and other attorneys, from engaging in the type of obstructionist conduct the attorney had exhibited. Accordingly, the judge ordered the attorney to write and create a video that could serve as a guide to other attorneys for avoiding the obstructionist conduct the attorney had engaged in. [The judge's holding and decision elaborates the judge's rationale and details the specifics of the sanction.]

ISSUE: Where a judge has determined that counsel has engaged in discovery abuse, may the judge specially tailor a sanction designed to deter the specific abuses the attorney has engaged in?

HOLDING AND DECISION: (Bennett, J.) Yes. Where a judge has determined that counsel has engaged in discovery abuse, the judge may specially tailor a sanction designed to deter the specific abuses the attorney has engaged in. Based on Counsel's deposition conduct, the court would be well within its discretion to impose substantial monetary sanctions on Counsel. However, the court is less interested in negatively affecting Counsel's pocketbook than in positively affecting Counsel's obstructive deposition practices. The court also is interested in deterring others who might be inclined to comport themselves similarly to Counsel. Deterrence is especially important given

that so many litigators are trained to make obstructionist objections. In light of this goal, the following sanction is imposed: Counsel must write and produce a training video in which Counsel, or another partner in Counsel's firm, appears and explains the holding and rationale of this opinion, and provides specific steps lawyers must take to comply with its rationale in future depositions in any federal and state court. The lawyer in the video must state that the video is being produced and distributed pursuant to a federal court's sanction order regarding a partner in the firm, but the lawyer need not state the name of the partner, the case the sanctions arose under, or the court issuing this order. Upon completing the video, Counsel must file it with this court, under seal, for the court's review and approval. If and when the court approves the video Counsel must (1) notify certain lawyers at Counsel's firm about the video via e-mail and (2) provide those lawyers with access to the video. The lawyers who must receive this notice and access include each lawyer at Counsel's firm—including branch offices worldwide—who engages in federal or state litigation or who work in any practice group in which at least two of the lawyers have filed an appearance in any state or federal case in the United States. After providing these lawyers with notice of and access to the video, Counsel must file in this court, under seal, (1) an affidavit certifying that Counsel complied with this order and received no assistance (other than technical help or help from the lawyer appearing in the video) in creating the video's content and (2) a copy of the e-mail notifying the appropriate lawyers in Counsel's firm about the video. Failure to comply with this order within 90 days may result in additional sanctions.

▌ ANALYSIS

The Federal Rules of Civil Procedure specifically acknowledge that one function of discovery sanctions should be deterrence. The advisory committee notes (1983 amendments) to Fed. R. Civ. P. 26, state that "Sanctions to deter discovery abuse would be more effective if they were diligently applied not merely to penalize those whose conduct may be deemed to warrant such a sanction, but to deter those who might be tempted to such conduct in the absence of such a deterrent." On appeal, notwithstanding that court of appeals found that the district judge's goal of deterring other attorneys was proper, that the judge had the discretion to raise the matter sua sponte, and that the specially-crafted sanction was not inappropriate, the court

Continued on next page.

of appeals reversed, on the grounds that the judge's sanction—which came almost two years after the depositions at issue—had not been imposed within a time frame that had a nexus to the behavior sought to be deterred, and because the attorney being sanctioned had not been provided with notice of the specially-tailored sanction in a manner that would have enabled the attorney to respond. See *Sec. Natl. Bank of Sioux City v. Abbott Labs.,* 800 F.3d 936 (8th Cir. 2015).

■═■

Quicknotes

OBSTRUCTION   To interfere with, hinder, or delay.

SUA SPONTE   An action taken by the court by its own motion and without the suggestion of one of the parties.

■═■

Resolution Without Trial

Quick Reference Rules of Law

Peralta v. Heights Medical Center

Employer/guarantor (P) v. Hospital (D)

485 U.S. 80 (1988)

NATURE OF CASE: Review of summary judgment dismissing bill of review.

FACT SUMMARY: A trial court refused to set aside a default entered after improper service when Peralta (P) could not show a meritorious defense to the action.

RULE OF LAW

A meritorious defense is not required to set aside a default entered after improper service.

FACTS: Heights Medical Center, Inc. (Heights Medical) (D) sued Peralta (P) on a guarantee to pay medical expenses on an employee of Peralta (P). Peralta (P) was improperly served. Heights Medical (D) nonetheless entered a default on Peralta's (P) failure to respond and a judgment lien was placed on certain real estate belonging to Peralta (P). The property was sold at a marshal's sale at a large discount. Peralta (P), upon discovering the sale, filed an action to void the sale and have the default set aside, as the service was invalid. The trial court granted summary judgment, dismissing the action, holding that Peralta (P) had to show meritorious defense to the underlying action, which he could not do. The Texas Court of Appeals affirmed. The United States Supreme Court accepted review.

ISSUE: Is a meritorious defense required to set aside a default entered after improper service?

HOLDING AND DECISION: (White, J.) No. A meritorious defense is not required to set aside a default entered after improper service. It is basic to due process before a judgment can be entered against a person, he must be given legally sufficient notice of the action and be given an opportunity to defend. It is no defense to a due process claim that the defendant would have lost on the merits. There are avenues that can be employed by a litigant in a losing posture, such as settling or impleading other parties. For the defendant to do this, he must have notice of the suit. Here, Peralta (P) was not given such notice, and due process therefore demands that the default be set aside. Reversed.

ANALYSIS

Various avenues exist to challenge a default. The most direct manner is to move for relief in the same action in which the default is entered. However, most states place time limitations on this, as did Texas in this instance. This

forced Peralta (P) to file a bill of review, a collateral proceeding.

■◆■

Quicknotes

DEFAULT JUDGMENT A judgment entered against a defendant due to his failure to appear in a court or defend himself against the allegations of the opposing party.

SERVICE OF PROCESS The communication of reasonable notice of a court proceeding to a defendant in order to provide him with an opportunity to be heard.

■◆■

Kalinauskas v. Wong

Former employee (P) v. Employer (D)

151 F.R.D. 363 (D. Nev. 1993)

NATURE OF CASE: Motion for protective order.

FACT SUMMARY: Caesars Palace Hotel & Casino (D) sought to enforce a confidential settlement agreement with a former employee.

🏛 RULE OF LAW
A protective order or confidentiality agreement can be modified to place private litigants in a position they would otherwise reach only after repetition of another's discovery if modification would not tangibly prejudice substantial rights of the party opposing modification.

FACTS: Kalinauskas (P) sued Desert Palace, Inc. (D), doing business as Caesars (D), for sexual discrimination. She sought to depose Thomas, a former Caesars (D) employee, who had sued Caesars (D) for sexual harassment the previous year. Thomas had settled her claim with Caesars (D) and agreed to a confidential settlement agreement that stated in part that Thomas "shall not discuss any aspect of plaintiff's employment at Caesars other than to state the dates of her employment and her job title." Caesars (D) sought a protective order to enforce the confidential settlement agreement and to bar Thomas's deposition. Kalinauskas (P) opposed the order.

ISSUE: May a protective order or confidentiality agreement be modified to place private litigants in a position they would otherwise reach only after repetition of another's discovery if modification would not tangibly prejudice substantial rights of the party opposing modification?

HOLDING AND DECISION: (Johnston, J.) Yes. A protective order or confidentiality agreement can be modified to place private litigants in a position they would otherwise reach only after repetition of another's discovery if modification would not tangibly prejudice substantial rights of the party opposing modification. Here, Kalinauskas's (P) claim duplicates Thomas's claim both factually and legally. Thus, to force Kalinauskas (P) to duplicate all of Thomas's work would be wasteful. The protective order is granted to the extent that during the deposition of Thomas no information regarding the settlement itself may be disclosed and is denied as to all other aspects. Protective order granted in part and denied in part.

▶ ANALYSIS

The party seeking to enforce a protective order against a party seeking discovery information has the burden of showing that allowing modification of the order would substantially prejudice that party's rights. As the case above indicates, this burden could be met by showing that an applicable privilege applies to the information sought to be disclosed or that the party would suffer potential injury or prejudice if the information were to be disclosed.

Quicknotes

DISCOVERY Pretrial procedure during which one party makes certain information available to the other.

PROTECTIVE ORDER Court order protecting a party against potential abusive treatment through use of the legal process.

Ferguson v. Countrywide Credit Industries, Inc.

Employee (P) v. Employer (D)

298 F.3d 778 (9th Cir. 2002)

NATURE OF CASE: Appeal of denial of motion to compel arbitration.

FACT SUMMARY: Misty Ferguson (P) sued Countrywide Credit Industries Inc. (Countrywide) (D) and her supervisor for sexual harassment, retaliation, and hostile work environment, and Countrywide (D) moved to compel the matter to arbitration. The district court denied Countrywide's (D) motion.

🏛 RULE OF LAW

An arbitration agreement is unconscionable, and therefore unenforceable, where it is a prerequisite to employment, job applicants are not permitted to modify the terms of the agreement, and the terms are one sided, favoring the employer.

FACTS: Misty Ferguson (P) sued Countrywide Credit Industries Inc. (Countrywide) (D) and her supervisor for sexual harassment, retaliation, and hostile work environment. Countrywide (D) moved to compel the matter to arbitration pursuant to an employment contract, which required Ferguson (P) to arbitrate her claims. The district court refused to compel arbitration, holding that the arbitration agreement was unenforceable under the doctrine of unconscionability.

ISSUE: Is an arbitration agreement unconscionable, and therefore unenforceable, where it is a prerequisite to employment, job applicants are not permitted to modify the terms of the agreement, and the terms are one-sided, favoring the employer?

HOLDING AND DECISION: (Pregerson, J.) Yes. An arbitration agreement is unconscionable, and therefore unenforceable, where it is a prerequisite to employment, job applicants are not permitted to modify the terms of the agreement, and the terms are one sided, favoring the employer. A contract is unenforceable under the doctrine of unconscionability where there is both procedural and substantive unconscionability. Procedural unconscionability exists here, because the bargaining power of each party is unequal: Ferguson (P) had to sign the agreement, and accept all of its terms, or not get the job applied for. Substantive unconscionability also exists here, because the terms of the agreement are one sided: The agreement compels arbitration of Ferguson's (P) claims but exempts from arbitration the claims of Countrywide (D). In addition, Countrywide's (D) agreement requires Ferguson (P) to pay filing fees for arbitration, which could exceed the costs of litigation. Finally, the agreement includes limitations on the number of subjects Ferguson (P) could raise

during discovery. While the discovery provision in the arbitration agreement is not so one sided it alone could be called unconscionable, in the context of an arbitration agreement that overall favors Countrywide (D), it too is unconscionable. Affirmed.

▶ ANALYSIS

The outcome of this case, decided in California, stands in direct contrast to *Carter v. Countrywide Credit Industries, Inc.*, 362 F.3d 294 (5th Cir. 2004), also set forth in your casebook. *Carter* was decided in Texas, which is generally much more lenient on arbitration agreements.

Quicknotes

SUBSTANTIVE UNCONSCIONABILITY Rule of law whereby a court may excuse performance of a contract, or of a particular contract term, if it determines that such terms are unduly oppressive or unfair to one party to the contract and violate the subordinate party's reasonable expectations.

Epic Systems v. Lewis

Corporations (D) v. Individuals (P)

584 U.S. __ (2018)

NATURE OF CASE: Appeal from appellate court's decision in favor of the plaintiffs.

FACT SUMMARY: Three employees at different companies brought similar wage claims against their employers in federal court. The federal courts dismissed the suits on the grounds the employees had signed a valid agreement to arbitrate all claims.

🏛 RULE OF LAW

Via the Federal Arbitration Act, Congress has instructed federal courts to enforce valid arbitration agreements and the parties' chosen arbitration procedures.

FACTS: Three employees at different companies brought similar wage claims against their employers in federal court. The federal courts dismissed the suits on the grounds the employees had signed a valid agreement to arbitrate all claims. In this decision, the United States Supreme Court focused on the facts of *Ernst and Young LLP v. Morris*, one of three cases consolidated for this appeal. Upon his hire, Morris (P) and Ernst and Young (D) signed an agreement to arbitrate any disputes that arose from the employment relationship. Morris (P) filed a claim in federal court, alleging that Ernst and Young (D) violated the Fair Labor Standards Act by not paying salaried employees for overtime. The district court dismissed the case on the grounds Morris (P) had agreed to arbitration as the sole avenue to address any legal claims. The U.S. Circuit Court of Appeals for the Ninth Circuit disagreed and found that the Federal Arbitration Act allowed suits like Morris's to proceed in federal court. Ernst and Young (D) appealed.

ISSUE: Via the Federal Arbitration Act, has Congress instructed federal courts to enforce valid arbitration agreements and the parties' chosen arbitration procedures?

HOLDING AND DECISION: (Gorsuch, J.) Yes. Via the Federal Arbitration Act, Congress has instructed federal courts to enforce valid arbitration agreements and the parties' chosen arbitration procedures. The validity of arbitration agreements has been settled law for quite some time. Here, the parties in each of the three consolidated cases executed valid agreements to arbitrate. The agreements specified the arbitration procedures and also required that the employee could not file or join any class action proceedings for claims arising from the employment relationship. Morris (P) argues the Federal Arbitration Act's Savings Clause allows his case to proceed in federal court. He argues courts can refuse to enforce such agree-ments or clauses just as they can for any type of contract. Contracts created where fraud, duress, or unconscionability is present are often struck down as a matter of law. Here, there is no evidence in the record the employees signed the arbitration agreements because of fraud or duress. Accordingly, the Ninth Circuit was incorrect when it held that Morris's (P) claims could move forward in federal court. Reversed.

DISSENT: (Ginsburg, J.) The National Labor Relations Act allows for class action suits to enforce workplace rights. Employers are prohibited from interfering with or restraining employees' rights that are granted to them in the Act, including the right to join in concerted litigation activities. While the employees may not be able to bring a suit in federal court, it is clear the Labor Relations Act prohibits employers from requiring employees to give up their rights to join in a class action suit.

▶ ANALYSIS

While there is some tension between the Federal Arbitration Act and the National Labor Relations Act, courts typically review arbitration agreements just like they do other contracts or agreements. If the parties voluntarily enter the agreement without undue fraud or duress and the agreement includes valid consideration given by each side, a court will uphold the parties' decision to arbitrate claims.

Quicknotes

ARBITRATION AGREEMENT A mutual understanding entered by parties wishing to submit to the decision-making authority of a neutral third party, selected by the parties and charged with rendering a decision.

NATIONAL LABOR RELATIONS ACT Guarantees employees the right to engage in collective bargaining and regulates labor unions.

Celotex Corp. v. Catrett

Asbestos product manufacturer (D) v. Wife of decedent (P)

477 U.S. 317 (1986)

NATURE OF CASE: Appeal from reversal of summary judgment denying damages for asbestos exposure.

FACT SUMMARY: In Catrett's (P) action against Celotex Corp. (D) for the death of her husband as a result of his exposure to asbestos manufactured by Celotex (D), Celotex (D) moved for summary judgment, contending that Catrett (P) had failed to identify, in answering interrogatories specifically requesting such information, any witnesses who could testify about the decedent's exposure to Celotex's (D) asbestos.

RULE OF LAW

The plain language of Fed. R. Civ. P. 56(c) mandates the entry of summary judgment, after adequate time for discovery, against a party who fails to make a showing sufficient to establish the existence of an element essential to that party's case.

FACTS: Catrett (P) sued Celotex Corp. (D), alleging that the death of her husband resulted from his exposure to products containing asbestos manufactured by Celotex (D). At trial, Celotex (D) moved for summary judgment, contending that Catrett (P) had failed to identify, in answering interrogatories specifically requesting such information, any witnesses who could testify about the decedent's exposure to Celotex's (D) asbestos products. The district court granted Celotex's (D) motion because there was no showing that the decedent was exposed to Celotex's (D) product within the statutory period. Catrett (P) appealed.

ISSUE: Does the plain language of Fed. R. Civ. P. 56(c) mandate the entry of summary judgment, after adequate time for discovery, against a party who fails to make a showing sufficient to establish the existence of an element essential to that party's case?

HOLDING AND DECISION: (Rehnquist, J.) Yes. The plain language of Fed. R. Civ. P. 56(c) mandates the entry of summary judgment, after adequate time for discovery, against a party who fails to make a showing sufficient to establish the existence of an element essential to that party's case. In such a situation, there can be "no genuine issue as to any material fact," since a complete failure of proof concerning an essential element of the nonmoving party's case necessarily renders all other facts immaterial. Here, Catrett (P) failed to identify any witnesses who could testify about her husband's exposure to Celotex's (D) asbestos products. There was also no showing that the decedent was exposed to Celotex's (D) product

within the statutory period. Catrett's (P) failure to show sufficient evidence to establish essential elements of her case makes summary judgment proper. Reversed and remanded.

CONCURRENCE: (White, J.) If respondent Catrett (P) had named a witness to support her claim, summary judgment could not have been granted without Celotex (D) somehow showing that the named witness's testimony raised no genuine issue of material fact.

ANALYSIS

Celotex is an important case in two ways. First, it integrates the burden of proof borne by the parties at trial with the corresponding burdens on a summary judgment motion. Second, it hints at a larger, more significant role for summary judgment in deciding cases.

■■■

Quicknotes

MATERIAL FACT A fact without the existence of which a contract would not have been entered.

SUMMARY JUDGMENT Judgment rendered by a court in response to a motion by one of the parties, claiming that the lack of a question of material fact in respect to an issue warrants disposition of the issue without consideration by the jury.

■■■

Tolan v. Cotton

Police shooting victim (P) v. Police officer (D)

134 S. Ct. 1861 (2014)

NATURE OF CASE: Appeal from affirmance of summary judgment for defendant in action brought under 42 U.S.C. § 1983.

FACT SUMMARY: Robert Tolan (P), who claimed that police officer Jeffrey Cotton (D) shot him using excessive force, contended that the U.S. Court of Appeals for the Fifth Circuit improperly failed to credit evidence he presented that contradicted Cotton's (D) evidence, so that the court erroneously weighed the evidence and resolved disputed factual issues in favor of Cotton (D).

🏛 **RULE OF LAW**

In ruling on a motion for summary judgment, a court must credit the evidence of the nonmovant and draw all justifiable inferences in the nonmovant's favor, so that if it fails to do so, it erroneously weighs the evidence and resolves disputed issues in favor of the moving party.

FACTS: Police officer John Edwards incorrectly entered the license plate number of a car, which led to the car being identified as stolen, when in fact it was not. Edwards ordered the two men who had just exited the car—Robert Tolan (P) and his cousin Cooper—to the ground on the porch of Tolan's (P) house. Tolan's (P) parents, hearing the commotion, exited the house, and, like Tolan (P) before them, assured Edwards that the car was not stolen, and that this was where Tolan (P) lived and that they owned the house. In the meantime, officer Jeffrey Cotton (D) appeared on the scene, with his gun drawn. He ordered Tolan's (P) mother to stand against the garage door. The parties disputed what happened next. The Tolans claimed that Cotton (D) slammed Ms. Tolan against the garage door with extreme force. Cotton (D) claimed that when he escorted Ms. Tolan to the garage, she flipped her arms up and told him to get his hands off her. Tolan (P) claimed that upon seeing his mother being pushed, he rose to his knees. The officers claimed he rose to his feet. Both parties agreed that Tolan (P) then exclaimed, from roughly 15 to 20 feet away, "[G]et your fucking hands off my mom." The parties also agreed that Cotton (D) then drew his pistol and fired three shots at Tolan (P). Tolan (P) and his mother testified that these shots came with no verbal warning. One of the bullets entered Tolan's (P) chest, collapsing his right lung and piercing his liver. Tolan (P) filed suit against Cotton (D) under 42 U.S.C. § 1983 claiming that Cotton (D) had used excessive force in contravention of Tolan's (P) Fourth Amendment rights. Cotton (D) moved for summary judgment, which the district court granted, determining that Cotton's (D) use of force was not

unreasonable. The U.S. Court of Appeals for the Fifth Circuit affirmed. It held that even if Cotton's (D) conduct did violate the Fourth Amendment, Cotton (D) was entitled to qualified immunity because he did not violate a clearly established right. In reaching this conclusion, the Fifth Circuit relied on the following facts: the front porch had been dimly lit; Tolan's (P) mother had refused orders to remain quiet and calm; and Tolan's (P) words had amounted to a verbal threat. Most critically, the court also relied on the purported fact that Tolan (P) was moving to intervene in Cotton's (D) handling of his mother, and that Cotton (D) therefore could reasonably have feared for his life. The United States Supreme Court granted certiorari.

ISSUE: In ruling on a motion for summary judgment, must a court credit the evidence of the nonmovant and draw all justifiable inferences in the nonmovant's favor, so that if it fails to do so, it erroneously weighs the evidence and resolves disputed issues in favor of the moving party?

HOLDING AND DECISION: (Per curiam) Yes. In ruling on a motion for summary judgment, a court must credit the evidence of the nonmovant and draw all justifiable inferences in the nonmovant's favor, so that if it fails to do so, it erroneously weighs the evidence and resolves disputed issues in favor of the moving party. In holding that Cotton's (D) actions did not violate clearly established law, the Fifth Circuit failed to view the evidence at summary judgment in the light most favorable to Tolan (P) with respect to the central facts of this case. By failing to credit evidence that contradicted some of its key factual conclusions, the court improperly weighed the evidence and resolved disputed issues in favor of the moving party. The Fifth Circuit ignored evidence that contradicted Cotton's (D) testimony that the porch was dimly lit. The court also ignored evidence that Tolan's (P) mother was not agitated or aggravated when she spoke to Cotton (D)—which contradicted the evidence presented by Cotton (D). The court also concluded that Tolan (P) was "shouting," and "verbally threatening" the officer, but the court ignored directly contradictory evidence from which a jury could conclude that Tolan (P) was not being threatening but instead was pleading with Cotton (D) to cease assaulting his mother. Finally, the court concluded that Tolan (P) was moving towards Cotton (D) at the time of the shooting, but it failed to credit evidence that Tolan (P) was on his knees and not going anywhere. Considered together,

Continued on next page.

these facts lead to the inescapable conclusion that the court below credited the movant's evidence and failed properly to acknowledge key evidence offered by the nonmovant. The disputed factual issues should have been resolved by a jury, instead of on summary judgment. Vacated and remanded.

▶ ANALYSIS

This case illustrates the rule that courts may not resolve genuine disputes of fact in favor of the party seeking summary judgment. This rule is simply an application of the more general rule that a judge's function at summary judgment is not to weigh the evidence and determine the truth of the matter but to determine whether there is a genuine issue for trial. Summary judgment is appropriate only if the movant shows that there is no genuine issue as to any material fact and the movant is entitled to judgment as a matter of law. In making that determination, a court must view the evidence in the light most favorable to the opposing party.

Quicknotes

QUALIFIED IMMUNITY An affirmative defense relieving officials from civil liability for the performance of activities within their discretion so long as such conduct is not in violation of an individual's rights pursuant to law as determined by a reasonable person standard.

SUMMARY JUDGMENT Judgment rendered by a court in response to a motion made by one of the parties, claiming that the lack of a question of material fact in respect to an issue warrants disposition of the issue without consideration by the jury.

Bias v. Advantage International, Inc.

Estate of basketball player (P) v. Business affairs representative (D)

905 F.2d 1558 (D.C. Cir. 1990)

NATURE OF CASE: Appeal of the granting of a motion for summary judgment.

FACT SUMMARY: Basketball star Leonard Bias (P) died from a cocaine overdose. When his estate sued Bias's business manager, Advantage International, Inc. (D) for failure to procure insurance for Bias (P) as it had promised to do, Advantage International (D) argued that no insurer would have insured a cocaine user.

🏛 RULE OF LAW
Once a moving party has made a prima facie showing to support a motion for summary judgment, the motion will be granted unless the nonmoving party establishes specific facts showing a genuine issue for trial.

FACTS: The estate of basketball star Leonard Bias (P) brought suit against Advantage International, Inc. (Advantage) (D) which was Bias's (P) management company, for failing to secure life insurance for Bias (P) as it had promised to do. Bias (P) died from a cocaine overdose without the one million dollar life insurance policy that Advantage (D) had represented it had obtained. Advantage (D) moved for a summary judgment on the grounds that Bias's estate (P) did not suffer any damage from the failure of Advantage (D) to try to obtain life insurance for Bias (P) because even if they had attempted to obtain such a policy, they would not have been able to do so because of Bias's (P) known cocaine use. The district court agreed and granted the motion. Bias's estate (P) appealed.

ISSUE: Once a moving party has made a prima facie showing to support a motion for summary judgment, will the motion be granted unless the nonmoving party establishes specific facts showing a genuine issue for trial?

HOLDING AND DECISION: (Sentelle, J.) Yes. Once a moving party has made a prima facie showing to support a motion for summary judgment, the motion will be granted unless the nonmoving party establishes specific facts showing a genuine issue for trial. Here, Advantage (D) offered testimony of witnesses that clearly tended to show that Bias (P) was a cocaine user who would therefore have been uninsurable. Bias's estate (P) could have deposed these witnesses, or otherwise attempted to impeach their testimony, but failed to do so or even to try. Advantage (D) offered evidence that every insurance company inquires about prior drug use at some point in the application process. Bias's (P) evidence that some insurance companies existed in 1986 that did not inquire about prior drug use at certain particular stages in the application process does not

undermine Advantage's (D) claim that at some point every insurance company did inquire about drug use, particularly where a jumbo policy was involved. Bias's estate (P) failed to name a single particular company or provide other evidence that a single company existed that would have issued a jumbo policy in 1986 without inquiring about an applicant's drug use. Because Bias's estate (P) failed to do more than show that there was "some metaphysical doubt as to the material facts," the district court properly concluded there was no genuine issue of material fact as to the insurability of a drug user. Affirmed.

▌ ANALYSIS

In *Bias*, the court noted that, rather than presenting any evidence or questioning any witnesses, to try to establish a case on non-cocaine use, Bias's estate (P) relied instead "on bare arguments and allegations" or on evidence that did not actually create a genuine issue for trial.

Quicknotes

MATERIAL FACT A fact without the existence of which a contract would not have been entered.

PRIMA FACIE An action in which the plaintiff introduces sufficient evidence to submit an issue to the judge or jury for determination.

SUMMARY JUDGMENT Judgment rendered by a court in response to a motion by one of the parties, claiming that the lack of a question of material fact in respect to an issue warrants disposition of the issue without consideration by the jury.

The Trier and the Trial

Quick Reference Rules of Law

Caperton v. A.T. Massey Coal Co.

Business associate (P) v. Coal company (D)

556 U.S. 868 (2009)

NATURE OF CASE: Grant of writ of certiorari.

FACT SUMMARY: A judge in a state court who was elected to the bench after receiving $3 million from a donor refused to recuse himself when the court heard a case in which a verdict had been entered against that donor for $50 million. The plaintiff in the case objected that he did not receive a fair trial.

🏛 RULE OF LAW

It is unconstitutional for a state court judge to hear a case involving the financial interests of a major backer of the judge's election campaign.

FACTS: Hugh Caperton (P) brought suit against A.T. Massey Coal Co. (Massey) (D) for unlawfully cancelling a contract that bankrupted Caperton (P). A West Virginia jury returned a verdict that found Massey (D) and its affiliates liable for fraudulent misrepresentation, concealment, and tortious interference with existing contractual relations. The jury awarded Caperton (P) the sum of $50 million in compensatory and punitive damages. After the verdict but before the appeal, West Virginia held its 2004 judicial elections, and Don Blankenship, Massey's (D) chairman, chief executive officer, and president, supported Brent Benjamin in the election. He contributed the $1,000 statutory maximum to Benjamin's campaign committee, donated almost $2.5 million to a political organization that supported Benjamin, and just over $500,000 on independent expenditures to support Benjamin. Blankenship's $3 million in contributions were more than the total amount spent by all other Benjamin supporters and three times the amount spent by Benjamin's own committee. Benjamin won the election. Caperton (P) moved to disqualify now-Justice Benjamin under the Due Process Clause and the West Virginia Code of Judicial Conduct, based on the conflict caused by Blankenship's campaign involvement. Justice Benjamin denied the motion. Massey (D) then filed its petition for appeal to challenge the jury verdict. The court of appeals granted review and reversed the $50 million verdict against Massey (D). Justice Benjamin joined the majority opinion. Caperton (P) sought rehearing, and the parties moved for disqualification of three of the five justices who decided the appeal. Justice Benjamin again denied Caperton's (P) recusal motion. The court granted rehearing. Caperton (P) moved a third time for disqualification. Justice Benjamin again refused. A divided court again reversed the jury verdict.

ISSUE: Is it unconstitutional for a state court judge to hear a case involving the financial interests of a major backer of the judge's election campaign?

HOLDING AND DECISION: (Kennedy, J.) Yes. It is unconstitutional for a state court judge to hear a case involving the financial interests of a major backer of the judge's election campaign. The Due Process Clause requires a fair and impartial trial. The leading case on the subject is *Tumey v. Ohio*, 273 U.S. 510 (1927), where it was concluded that the Due Process Clause incorporated the common law rule that a judge must recuse himself when he has "a direct, personal, substantial, pecuniary interest" in a case. Under this rule, personal bias or prejudice "alone" would not be sufficient basis for imposing a constitutional requirement under the Due Process Clause. Over time, the Court has identified additional instances that, as an objective matter, require recusal. These are cases in which the probability of actual bias on the part of the judge is too high to be constitutionally tolerable. For example, where a judge has a financial interest in the outcome of a case, although the interest was less than what would have been considered personal or direct at common law, recusal is required. Similarly, in the criminal contempt context, where a judge had no pecuniary interest in the case but was challenged because of a conflict arising from his participation in an earlier proceeding, recusal was required. The problem in this case arises in the context of judicial elections, a framework not presented in the precedents. Not every campaign contribution by a litigant or attorney creates a probability of bias that requires a judge's recusal, but this is an exceptional case. Here, there is a serious risk of actual bias because a person with a personal stake in the case had a significant and disproportionate influence in placing the judge on the case by raising funds or directing the judge's election campaign when the case was pending or imminent. The inquiry centers on the contribution's relative size in comparison to the total amount of money contributed to the campaign, the total amount spent in the election, and the apparent effect such contribution had on the outcome of the election. Proving what ultimately drives the electorate to choose a particular candidate is a difficult endeavor, but Blankenship's campaign efforts had a significant and disproportionate influence in placing Justice Benjamin on the case. Blankenship contributed some $3 million to unseat the incumbent and replace him with Benjamin. His contributions eclipsed the total amount spent by all other Benjamin supporters and exceeded by 300 percent the amount spent by Benjamin's campaign committee. In the end the people of West Virginia elected him, and they may have done so based on many reasons

Continued on next page.

other than Blankenship's efforts, but whether Blankenship's campaign contributions were a necessary and sufficient cause of Benjamin's victory is not the proper inquiry. The risk that Blankenship's influence engendered actual bias is sufficiently substantial that it "must be forbidden if the guarantee of due process is to be adequately implemented." The temporal relationship between the campaign contributions, the justice's election, and the pendency of the case is also critical. It was reasonably foreseeable, when the campaign contributions were made, that the pending case would be before the newly elected justice. The $50 million adverse jury verdict had been entered before the election, and the Supreme Court of Appeals was the next step once the state trial court dealt with post-trial motions. So it became at once apparent that, absent recusal, Justice Benjamin would review a judgment that cost his biggest donor's company $50 million. Although there is no allegation of a quid pro quo agreement, the fact remains that Blankenship's extraordinary contributions were made at a time when he had a vested stake in the outcome. Just as no man is allowed to be a judge in his own cause, similar fears of bias may arise when—without the consent of the other parties—a man chooses the judge in his own cause. And applying this principle to the judicial election process, there was here a serious, objective risk of actual bias that required Justice Benjamin's recusal. Justice Benjamin did undertake an extensive search for actual bias. But that is just one step in the judicial process. Objective standards may also require recusal whether or not actual bias exists or can be proved. Blankenship's significant and disproportionate influence—coupled with the temporal relationship between the election and the pending case—"offer a possible temptation to the average . . . judge to . . . lead him not to hold the balance nice, clear and true." On these extreme facts the probability of actual bias rises to an unconstitutional level. Reversed and remanded.

DISSENT: (Roberts, C.J.) The majority imprudently expanded the standard for which a judge need recuse himself by merely showing a "probability of bias." The "probability of bias" standard formulated by the majority was excessively vague and discretionary. It fails to provide clear, workable guidance for future cases. At the most basic level, it is unclear whether the new probability of bias standard is somehow limited to financial support in judicial elections or applies to judicial recusal questions more generally. Forty questions are unanswered by the majority opinion [the casebook excerpt does not list all 40], but these are only a few uncertainties that quickly come to mind.

DISSENT: (Scalia, J.) The majority performed its duties poorly as a clarifying body by making an area of the law vastly more uncertain. That area of law can be raised in all litigated cases in (at least) those 39 states that elect their judges. This course was urged upon us on grounds that it would preserve the public's confidence in the judicial system, but the decision will have the opposite effect. What above all else is eroding public confidence in the judicial system is the perception that litigation is just a game, that the party with the most resourceful lawyer can play it to win, and that our legal proceedings are self-perpetuating but incapable of delivering real-world justice. The majority opinion will reinforce that perception.

ANALYSIS

This case is important for the fact that through it, the Supreme Court set a new standard for judges to recuse themselves from cases, ruling a state supreme court justice who benefited from $3 million in campaign contributions from a coal executive should have stayed out of a lawsuit involving the executive's company. In light of the fact that many states—39 by last count—currently elect judges to courts, the case will have wide-reaching consequences.

Quicknotes

DUE PROCESS CLAUSE Clauses found in the Fifth and Fourteenth Amendments to the United States Constitution, providing, that no person shall be deprived of "life, liberty, or property, without due process of law."

QUID PRO QUO What for what; in the contract context used synonymously with consideration to refer to the mutual promises between two parties rendering a contract enforceable.

RECUSAL Procedure whereby a judge is disqualified from hearing a case either on his own behalf, or on the objection of a party, due to some bias or interest on the part of the judge in the subject matter of the suit.

Monfore v. Phillips

Spouse of deceased patient (P) v. Physician (D)

778 F.3d 849 (10th Cir. 2015)

NATURE OF CASE: Appeal from denial of motion to amend a final pretrial order in action for negligence.

FACT SUMMARY: Phillips (D), a physician accused of negligence, contended that his motion to amend a final pretrial order days before jury selection was to commence—so he could completely change his litigation strategy after 20 months of discovery and motions practice—should have been granted, and that the denial of such motion was reversible error.

RULE OF LAW

It is not reversible error for a district court to deny a motion to amend a final pretrial order days before jury selection is to start, and 20 months after motions practice and discovery, so that the movant may introduce new jury instructions, exhibits, and witnesses aimed at advancing an entirely new defense.

FACTS: Tests showed Shatwell had throat cancer, but through a series of blunders, he never received the news, and, as a result he died. His widowed wife (P) brought suit against the hospital and physicians, asserting claims of negligence. For 20 months, through motions practice and discovery, the defendants denied any responsibility. Then, two weeks prior to trial, some of the defendants settled. Phillips (D), one of the physicians, was not among the settling defendants. Instead, just days before jury selection was to start, Phillips (D) moved to amend the final pretrial order so he could completely change his defense strategy by blaming some of the defendants who had settled. His motion sought permission to introduce new jury instructions, exhibits, and witnesses aimed at advancing his new defense. However, the district court denied the motion, and at the trial's end, the jury found him liable for damages of a little over $1 million. Phillips (D) appealed, contending that the district court's refusal to amend the final pretrial order and allow his new defense amounted to reversible error. The U.S. Court of Appeals for the Tenth Circuit granted review.

ISSUE: Is it reversible error for a district court to deny a motion to amend a final pretrial order days before jury selection is to start, and 20 months after motions practice and discovery, so that the movant may introduce new jury instructions, exhibits, and witnesses aimed at advancing an entirely new defense?

HOLDING AND DECISION: (Gorsuch, J.) No. It is not reversible error for a district court to deny a motion to amend a final pretrial order days before jury selection is to start, and 20 months after motions practice

and discovery, so that the movant may introduce new jury instructions, exhibits, and witnesses aimed at advancing an entirely new defense. Final pretrial orders are intended to formulate a trial plan and to focus the parties on trial. Given the Federal Rules' liberal approach to discovery and pretrial practices, such orders are intended to separate the wheat from the chaff, as it were, and have the parties disclose something approximating their real trial intentions to opposing counsel and the court. Toward those ends, the parties are often asked—as they were in this case—to specify the witnesses and exhibits, supply the proposed jury instructions, and identify the claims and defenses they actually intend to introduce at trial. Under Fed. R. Civ. P. 16(e), a final pretrial order focused on formulating a plan for an impending trial may be amended "only to prevent manifest injustice." This standard is as high as it is to ensure everyone involved has sufficient incentive to fulfill the order's dual purposes of encouraging self-editing and providing reasonably fair disclosure to the court and opposing parties alike of their real trial intentions. Despite his protestations that he was surprised by his co-defendants' change of heart, Phillips (D) could not have been surprised that they did so. What happened was hardly unforeseeable, given that virtually all cases settle in part or in whole, many on the eve of trial, especially in multi-party litigation, where an incentive exists to break ranks, settle relatively cheaply, and leave others on the hook before the jury. Multiparty litigation presents a variety of collective action problems and other strategic pitfalls, and those Phillips (D) encountered here are well known, not the stuff of surprise. The prejudice to the other side also cannot be ignored. Phillips (D) essentially sought to force the plaintiff to prepare for an entirely different trial on a few days' notice. The defendants adduced hardly any evidence or experts relating to contributory negligence. Thus, the plaintiff and her lawyers had some reasonable expectations about what trial would look like and the sort of evidence they would—and would not—need. They knew they'd need to prove negligence by the defendants who chose to go to trial but they wouldn't have to worry about finger pointing between defendants. Under such circumstances, a district court does not abuse its discretion in holding a party to a long-scheduled trial and to the strategy he articulated though pleading and discovery and in the face of such obvious risks, especially when indulging an eleventh-hour strategic shift would mean either imposing prejudice on the other side or inviting more delay. Affirmed.

Continued on next page.

ANALYSIS

There are four primary factors that typically are considered in determining whether a district court has abused its discretion in denying a motion to amend the pretrial order: (1) prejudice or surprise to opposing party; (2) ability of the opposing party to cure the prejudice; (3) potential disruption of trial; and (4) any bad faith of moving party. Here, the court of appeals, without considering these separate factors, concluded that the district court properly exercised its discretion in refusing to permit Phillips (D) to amend the pretrial order. Judge Moritz, concurring in the opinion, argues that consideration of the relevant factors would have demonstrated that the district court could just as easily have exercised its discretion to permit Phillips (D) to amend the pretrial order, and that, contrary to the majority opinion, denying Phillips's (D) motion may not have been the only reasonable course of action.

Quicknotes

DISCRETION The authority conferred upon a public official to act reasonably in accordance with his own judgment under certain circumstances.

REVERSIBLE ERROR A substantial error that might reasonably have prejudiced the party complaining.

Pennsylvania Railroad v. Chamberlain

Railroad company (D) v. Estate of brakeman (P)

288 U.S. 333 (1933)

NATURE OF CASE: Appeal of an action for negligent homicide.

FACT SUMMARY: When deceased was killed while routing railroad cars, Chamberlain (P) sued Pennsylvania Railroad (D) for negligently bringing about a collision. Three eyewitnesses testified there was no such collision and one witness gave testimony that would have given equal inferential support for both collision and no collision.

🏛 RULE OF LAW
Where evidence is so insubstantial that if a verdict is rendered for one of the parties, the other would be entitled to a new trial, it is up to the judge to direct a verdict according to the court's view of all the evidence.

FACTS: Chamberlain (P) sued Pennsylvania Railroad (D) to recover for the death of a brakeman who was killed while routing train cars in a railroad yard. The complaint alleged that certain railroad cars were negligently brought into collision with the cars the deceased was riding on, causing him to fall off and be run over. There was corroborated testimony by three eyewitnesses that there was no such collision. Bainbridge, a witness for Chamberlain (P), testified that a loud crash occurred before the accident. He also stated that he stood about 900 feet away from the body of the deceased, was not paying particular attention, and loud crashes were not an unusual event. The trial court entered a directed verdict for Pennsylvania Railroad (D). Reversed on appeal. Certiorari granted.

ISSUE: Should a judge refrain from ordering a directed verdict where the evidence, taken in toto, would require a new trial to be ordered for one party should the other manage to prevail with the jury?

HOLDING AND DECISION: (Sutherland, J.) No. Where there is a true conflict of testimony, evidence must be left to the jury. Here, there was no such conflict. There was an inference drawn from Bainbridge's testimony that there had been a collision, but the testimony gave equal support to an inference that there was no collision. Argument that a collision took place is mere speculation in light of the witness's limited observations. Bainbridge's testimony was so insubstantial that it did not justify submission to the jury, as there was no evidence that a jury could have properly proceeded to a verdict for the party offering it as proof. Judgment of appellate court reversed. District court judgment affirmed.

▶ ANALYSIS

This case points up the distinctly minority rule for determining the propriety of a motion for directed verdict. In most jurisdictions, the trial court may look only to the evidence presented by the party against whom a directed verdict is sought to determine whether as a matter of law the evidence is insufficient to support such party's case. In *Chamberlain*, and a minority of jurisdictions, however, the trial court may look to all the evidence presented by both sides to determine whether "reasonable minds could differ" as to the ultimate disposition of the case. Note, of course, that this "minority view" is the majority view for determining the right to a new trial, a fact that gives rise to substantial criticism of the rule as too liberal (since the effect of a new trial is somewhat less drastic than that of a directed verdict).

▄▄▄

Quicknotes

DIRECTED VERDICT A verdict ordered by the court in a jury trial.

▄▄▄

Unitherm Food Systems, Inc. v. Swift-Eckrich, Inc.

Corporation (P) v. Corporation (D)

546 U.S. 394 (2006)

NATURE OF CASE: Appeal from intermediate court's decision to overturn a jury verdict in favor of the plaintiff.

FACT SUMMARY: ConAgra (D), owned by Swift-Eckrich, Inc. (D), attempted to enforce a patent for a product and method to brown precooked meats. Unitherm Food Systems, Inc. (P) invented a similar process six years earlier than ConAgra (D).

🏛 RULE OF LAW
In the absence of a Fed. R. Civ. P. 50(b) post-verdict motion to set aside an adverse jury verdict on the grounds the evidence was legally insufficient, an appellate court may not set aside a jury verdict that a district court has allowed to stand.

FACTS: ConAgra (D), owned by Swift-Eckrich, Inc. (D), attempted to enforce a patent for a product and method to brown precooked meats. Unitherm Food Systems, Inc. (Unitherm) (P) invented a similar process six years earlier than ConAgra (D). Unitherm (P) brought a lawsuit against ConAgra (D) on the grounds its patent was invalid and that ConAgra (D) violated the Sherman Act by attempting to enforce a patent that was obtained by committing a fraud on the Patent and Trademark Office. After the close of evidence at trial, ConAgra (D) filed a Rule 50(a) motion requesting that the court find the evidence presented was legally insufficient to support an adverse jury verdict against it. The district court denied the motion and the jury returned a verdict for Unitherm (P). ConAgra (D) did not file a Fed. R. Civ. P. 50(b) motion after the verdict to request that the court set aside the jury verdict based upon the insufficiency of the evidence. The Federal Circuit Court of Appeals reversed, finding that: (1) it had the authority to vacate the jury's verdict even though ConAgra (D) failed to file a Rule 50(b) motion; and (2) the evidence was insufficient to support a verdict in favor of Unitherm (P) on the Sherman Act claim.

ISSUE: In the absence of a Fed. R. Civ. P. 50(b) post-verdict motion to set aside an adverse jury verdict on the grounds the evidence was legally insufficient, may an appellate court set aside a jury verdict that a district court has allowed to stand?

HOLDING AND DECISION: (Thomas, J.) No. In the absence of a Fed. R. Civ. P. 50(b) post-verdict motion to set aside an adverse jury verdict on the grounds the evidence was legally insufficient, an appellate court may not set aside a jury verdict that a district court has allowed to stand. A post-verdict motion is required because it allows the judge who heard the case and listened to the witnesses to make the first determination whether a jury verdict may be set aside. This holding applies to both Fed. R. Civ. P. 50(b) motions and motions for a new trial. A Rule 50(a) motion is at the discretion of the trial court. A denial of that motion, prior to the jury's consideration of the case, cannot serve as the basis of an appeal because the court is not required to grant the motion, even if it feels the evidence is insufficient. The accepted practice in civil litigation is, except in limited circumstances, to allow cases to proceed to a jury verdict and then rule upon the sufficiency of the evidence after the verdict. The only error in this matter was counsel's failure to file the post-verdict motion. Federal Circuit's decision is reversed and the jury's verdict is reinstated. Reversed.

DISSENT: (Stevens, J.) 28 U.S.C. 2106 allows the Supreme Court or any appellate court to affirm, modify, or vacate a judgment of a lower court. Nothing in the text of Rule 50(b) limits the grant of this authority to the appellate courts. A party's failure to file a Rule 50(b) motion precludes only the district court from issuing a directed verdict.

▶ ANALYSIS

It is a primary rule of litigation to ensure that all appellate avenues are preserved during the course of trial. Well before trial, competent counsel will have prepared all motions in limine, a motion for a directed verdict at the close of all evidence, and a motion for a directed verdict or a new trial after a jury's verdict is issued.

■═■

Quicknotes

DIRECTED VERDICT A verdict ordered by the court in a jury trial.

MOTION IN LIMINE Motion by one party brought prior to trial to exclude the potential introduction of prejudicial evidence.

■═■

Lind v. Schenley Industries

Sales negotiator (P) v. Employer company (D)

278 F.2d 79 (3d Cir. 1960)

NATURE OF CASE: Appeal from granting of judgment notwithstanding the verdict and, in the alternative, a new trial.

FACT SUMMARY: Although a jury awarded Lind (P) damages in his breach of contract suit against his employer, Schenley Industries, Inc. (D), the trial judge set aside the award as being against the weight of the evidence.

🏛 RULE OF LAW
Where nothing indicates that the jury was not properly presented with correct evidence, the judge may not nullify the jury verdict by granting a new trial so long as the evidence admits of the conclusion made by the jury.

FACTS: Lind (P) sued his employer Schenley Industries, Inc. (Schenley) (D), alleging that Schenley (D) had breached its oral promise to give him an increase in pay and a share of commissions. Lind (P) and his secretary testified to such promises. Schenley's (D) agents denied making the promises. The jury found that a contract was created and awarded damages to Lind (P). The trial judge granted Schenley's (D) motion for judgment notwithstanding the verdict and, alternatively, for a new trial. Lind (P) appealed.

ISSUE: Where nothing indicates that the jury was not properly presented with correct evidence, may the judge nullify the jury verdict by granting a new trial if the evidence admits of the conclusion made by the jury?

HOLDING AND DECISION: (Biggs, J.) No. The jury found the testimony of the plaintiff and his secretary credible. The judge disagreed. The evidence given as to what Lind (P) had received as a result of his negotiations demonstrates that the jury's finding was not against the weight of the evidence, however. Furthermore, there was evidence enough to sustain the finding that the contract was not too indefinite to be sustainable. Where nothing indicates that the jury was not properly presented with the correct evidence, the judge may not nullify the jury verdict by granting a new trial if the evidence admits of the conclusion made by the jury. Reversed and remanded.

DISSENT: (Hastie, J.) A judge may not substitute his own verdict for that of the jury. But he may avoid what in his professionally trained and experienced judgment is an unjust verdict by vacating it and causing the matter to be tried again. Here, there was a sharp conflict of testimony as to the offers and promises. It was not an abuse of discretion to grant the new trial.

▶ ANALYSIS

A reversal of an order granting a new trial requires an abuse of discretion by the granting judge. Showing an abuse of discretion is not an easy proposition, but it is possible. Where the new trial is granted despite a logically defensible jury verdict based on properly admitted correct evidence, such an abuse is shown.

Quicknotes

ABUSE OF DISCRETION A determination by an appellate court that a lower court's decision was based on an error of law.

DIRECTED VERDICT A verdict ordered by the court in a jury trial.

Peterson v. Wilson

Employee (P) v. Employer (D)

141 F.3d 573 (5th Cir. 1998)

NATURE OF CASE: Appeal from judgment in a retrial of wrongful-termination action.

FACT SUMMARY: The trial court ordered a new trial on its own motion after meeting with a jury after their verdict.

🏛 RULE OF LAW
The admission of juror testimony to impeach a jury verdict is prohibited.

FACTS: Peterson (P) filed suit in district court after he was fired as grant director at Texas Southern University (D). After a trial, a jury awarded Peterson (P) $187,000. The defendants moved for a new trial. Four months later, the district court granted the new trial, but its order revealed that it did so because comments made by the jurors after the verdict indicated that they had disregarded the court's instructions. The case was re-tried and Peterson's (P) claims were rejected by the second jury. Peterson (P) appealed the grant of a new trial.

ISSUE: Is the admission of juror testimony to impeach a jury verdict prohibited?

HOLDING AND DECISION: (Wiener, J.) Yes. The admission of juror testimony to impeach a jury verdict is prohibited. A jury's verdict can be disregarded if it is against the great weight of the evidence. However, in the present case, the district court clearly granted the new trial due to its meeting with jurors following the verdict and the comments made at that time. This post-verdict, ex parte meeting was impermissible. Rule 606(b) of the Fed. R. Evid. provides jurors may not testify as to statements made in deliberations or concerning the mental process of decision making. The only exception is for extraneous and outside influences on the jury. This reflects a conscious decision to disallow juror testimony as to their fidelity to the court's instructions. Given this rule, the court's granting of a new trial in the present case was clearly erroneous. The only reason given for granting the new trial was the comments made by the jurors after the verdict. Therefore, the judgment in the second trial must be vacated and the results of the first trial reinstated. Grant of a new trial reversed, second trial judgment vacated, first trial reinstated, and case remanded.

▶ ANALYSIS

The court also awarded Peterson (P) his costs and attorney's fees incurred in both trials and on appeal. The decision also found that the original verdict was not against the weight of the evidence, even if the district court had used this legal reason for granting the new trial. The exception to the rule in this case is a situation where the jurors are influenced by evidence that is brought illegally into the jury room.

Quicknotes

EX PARTE A proceeding commenced by one party.

WRONGFUL TERMINATION Unlawful termination of an individual's employment.

Quick Reference Rules of Law

Aetna Casualty & Surety Co. v. Cunningham

Insurer (P) v. Contractor (D)

224 F.2d 478 (5th Cir. 1955)

NATURE OF CASE: Appeal of breach of trial court judgment.

FACT SUMMARY: [After the insured, a contractor, failed to finish a building project, Aetna Casualty & Surety Co. (P), the insurer, financed the remainder of the project, and then tried to recover from the contractor.]

🏛 **RULE OF LAW**

A plaintiff who is denied relief to which it claims to be entitled raises contentions of error on appeal.

FACTS: [Cunningham (D), a building contractor, failed to complete a project. Aetna Casualty & Surety Co. (Aetna) (P), the insurer, financed the remainder of the project. Aetna (P) then tried to recover from the contractor based on two theories for recovery: that the terms of the insurance contract permitted such recovery and that the contractor/insured had committed fraud in applying for the policy, and that Aetna's (P) loss was traceable to that fraud. The district court found for Aetna (P) on the contract claim but ruled that the contractor had not committed fraud. Both Aetna (P) and the contractor (D) appealed.]

ISSUE: May a plaintiff who is denied relief to which it claims to be entitled raise contentions of error on appeal?

HOLDING AND DECISION: [Judge not identified in casebook excerpt.] Yes. A plaintiff who is denied relief to which it claims to be entitled raises contentions of error on appeal. To rule on the effect of bankruptcy on a judgment on either claim would be premature, as would a ruling on whether the finding that Cunningham's (D) representations were not fraudulent would be res judicata as to the operation of a discharge in bankruptcy. But since Aetna (P) was denied judgment of the quality to which it laid claim, it is a party aggrieved on appeal. When, as a practical matter, the denial of any one claim results in the plaintiff not getting the relief to which it claims to be entitled, whether in the amount or in the quality of the judgment, it has a right to be heard on appeal.

▶ **ANALYSIS**

This decision is a straightforward illustration of the well-known rule that the plaintiff may appeal on any relevant ground when denied the relief sought, regardless of whether it has to do with the amount or in the nature of the judgment.

Quicknotes

RES JUDICATA The rule of law a final judgment by a court precludes subsequent litigation between the parties regarding the same cause of action.

Liberty Mutual Insurance Co. v. Wetzel

Insurer (D) v. Employer insured (P)

424 U.S. 737 (1976)

NATURE OF CASE: Appeal from finding of liability for violation of Title VII of the Civil Rights Act of 1964.

FACT SUMMARY: Wetzel (P) alleged that Liberty Mutual Insurance Company's (D) employee insurance benefits and maternity leave regulations discriminated against women in violation of Title VII of the Civil Rights Act of 1964.

 RULE OF LAW
An interlocutory appeal under Fed. R. Civ. P. 54(b) is limited expressly to multiple-claims actions.

FACTS: Wetzel (P) filed a complaint that asserted that Liberty Mutual Insurance Company's (Liberty Mutual) (D) employee insurance benefits and maternity leave regulations discriminated against women in violation of Title VII of the Civil Rights Act of 1964. Wetzel's (P) complaint sought several forms of relief, including monetary damages, attorney's fees, and injunctive relief. On January 9, 1974, after finding no issues of material fact in dispute, the district court granted partial summary judgment for Wetzel (P) on the issue of liability only. On February 20, 1974, the district court issued an order of final judgment as to Liberty Mutual's (D) liability but granted none of the relief requested in Wetzel's (P) complaint. The U.S. Court of Appeals for the Third Circuit held that it had jurisdiction over Liberty Mutual's (D) appeal under 28 U.S.C. § 1291 and affirmed the judgment of the district court.

ISSUE: Is an interlocutory appeal under Fed. R. Civ. P. 54(b) limited expressly to multiple-claims actions?

HOLDING AND DECISION: (Rehnquist, J.) Yes. Fed. R. Civ. P. 54(b) is limited expressly to multiple-claims actions in which one or more, but less than all, of the multiple claims have been finally decided and are found otherwise to be ready for appeal. Here, Wetzel's (P) complaint set forth a single claim, which advanced a single legal theory that was applied to only one set of facts. Even if the district court's order was a declaratory judgment on the issue of liability, it still left unresolved Wetzel's (P) requests for an injunction, for compensatory and exemplary damages, and for attorney's fees. Although it might be argued that the order of the district court, insofar as it failed to include the injunctive relief requested, was an interlocutory order refusing an injunction within the meaning of 28 U.S.C. § 1292(a)(1), even if this would have allowed the obtaining of a review in the court of appeals, there was no denial of any injunction sought. Nor was the order appealable under § 1292(b). There can

be no assurance that had the requirements of § 1292(b) been complied with, the court of appeals would have exercised its discretion to entertain the interlocutory appeal. The district court's order is therefore not appealable pursuant to 28 U.S.C. § 1291. Vacated and remanded.

▶ ANALYSIS

The basic rationale for the policy in federal courts of requiring final judgments is one based upon a cost-benefit analysis. If the trial judge turns out to have been correct, the cost of allowing an interlocutory appeal is the cost of an unnecessary extra appeal. Conversely, if the trial judge turns out to have been wrong in his or her judgment, the cost of not allowing an interlocutory appeal is the sum expended for an unnecessary or an unnecessarily long trial. However, because trial judges are affirmed far more often than they are reversed, the federal policy seems to be logical.

Quicknotes

INTERLOCUTORY APPEAL The appeal of an issue that does not resolve the disposition of the case but is essential to a determination of the parties' legal rights.

Lauro Lines, s.r.l. v. Chasser

Ship company (D) v. Passenger (P)

490 U.S. 495 (1989)

NATURE OF CASE: Interlocutory appeal of a denial of a motion to dismiss action for damages for personal injuries.

FACT SUMMARY: After the district court denied Lauro Line's (Lauro's) (D) motion for dismissal based on a forum-selection clause that purportedly limited Chasser (P) to suing in Naples, Italy, Lauro (D) sought to overturn the denial on interlocutory appeal.

> ## 🏛 RULE OF LAW
> Under the collateral-order doctrine, a prejudgment order may be appealed only when it conclusively determines the disputed question, resolves an important issue completely separable from the merits of the action, and is effectively unreviewable on appeal from a final judgment.

FACTS: Chasser (P) and the other plaintiffs were passengers aboard Lauro Line's (Lauro's) (D) ship, the Achille Lauro, when it was hijacked in the Mediterranean Sea by terrorists. Lauro (D) moved to dismiss Chasser's (P) personal-injury suit on the grounds that a forum-selection clause printed on the passenger tickets limited any passenger to suing in Naples, Italy. The district court denied the motion, holding that the ticket did not give passengers reasonable notice that they were giving up the right to sue in the United States. The U.S. Court of Appeals for the Second Circuit dismissed Lauro's (D) appeal, finding that the district court's order was interlocutory and not appealable. Lauro (D) appealed to the United States Supreme Court.

ISSUE: Is a prejudgment order subject to interlocutory appeal when it can be effectively reviewed on appeal from a final judgment?

HOLDING AND DECISION: (Brennan, J.) No. Under the collateral-order doctrine, a prejudgment order may be appealed only when it conclusively determines the disputed question, resolves an important issue completely separable from the merits of the action, and is effectively unreviewable on appeal from a final judgment. An order is "effectively" unreviewable on final judgment when the order involves an asserted right, the practical value of which would be destroyed if it were not vindicated before trial. Thus, interlocutory appeal is allowed when the defendant asserts a right that is not an ultimate right upon which the suit is brought. Here, Lauro (D) only asserted a right not to be sued in a particular forum. This right was not lost. Lauro (D) could assert the forum-selection clause in appealing any unfavorable final judgment. If an appeals

court agreed with Lauro's (D) position, it could vacate trial judgment and limit the refiling of the case in Naples. Affirmed.

CONCURRENCE: (Scalia, J.) Implicit in the Court's ruling is that Lauro's (D) right of forum selection is not important enough to require vindication on interlocutory appeal.

▶ ANALYSIS

Where a criminal defendant asserts a right not to be tried, an order denying that right is reviewable on interlocutory appeal. In civil cases, a partial list of orders reviewable on interlocutory appeal includes denial of a motion to dismiss based on a claim of absolute or qualified official immunity, an order denying a party leave to proceed in forma pauperis, an order requiring class action defendants to bear the cost of notifying members of the plaintiff class, and an order vacating attachment of a vessel.

■=■

Quicknotes

COLLATERAL ORDER Doctrine pursuant to which an appeal from an interlocutory order may be brought in order to hear and determine claims which are collateral to the merits of the case and which could not be granted adequate review on appeal.

IN FORMA PAUPERIS Permission to proceed with litigation without incurring fees or costs.

INTERLOCUTORY APPEAL The appeal of an issue that does not resolve the disposition of the case but is essential to a determination of the parties' legal rights.

JUDGMENT ON THE MERITS A determination of the rights of the parties to litigation based on the presentation evidence, barring the party from initiating the same suit again.

■=■

Anderson v. Bessemer City

Sex discrimination claimant (P) v. Municipality (D)

470 U.S. 564 (1985)

NATURE OF CASE: Appeal of finding of discriminatory intent in action brought under Title VII of the Civil Rights Act of 1964.

FACT SUMMARY: In Anderson's (P) action against Bessemer City (D) for discrimination in an action brought under Title VII of the Civil Rights Act of 1964, Anderson (P), a woman applying for a job as a Recreation Director for Bessemer City (D), alleged that she had been denied the position because of her sex, and that the district court's finding of discriminatory intent in Anderson's (P) action was a factual finding that could be overturned on appeal only if it was clearly erroneous.

🏛 RULE OF LAW
Under Fed. R. Civ. P. 52(a), a finding is clearly erroneous only when, although there is evidence to support it, the reviewing court, on the entire evidence, is left with the definite and firm conviction that a mistake has been made.

FACTS: In Anderson's (P) action against Bessemer City (D) for discrimination in an action brought under Title VII of the Civil Rights Act of 1964, Anderson (P), a woman, alleged that she had been denied a position as Recreation Director in a city athletic program because of her sex. After a two-day trial, the court issued a memorandum of decision setting forth its finding that Anderson (P) had been denied the position because of her sex and that male members of the Bessemer City (D) hiring commission for the position had been biased against Anderson (P) because she was a woman. The City (D) appealed and the U.S. Court of Appeals for the Fourth Circuit reversed, holding that the lower court's findings were clearly erroneous. Anderson (P) appealed.

ISSUE: Under Fed. R. Civ. P. 52(a), is a finding clearly erroneous only when, although there is evidence to support it, the reviewing court, on the entire evidence, is left with the definite and firm conviction that a mistake has been made?

HOLDING AND DECISION: (White, J.) Yes. Under Fed. R. Civ. P. 52(a), a finding is clearly erroneous only when, although there is evidence to support it, the reviewing court, on the entire evidence, is left with the definite and firm conviction that a mistake has been made. Application of the foregoing principles to the facts of this case lays bare the errors committed. The Fourth Circuit improperly conducted what amounted to a de novo weighing of the evidence in the record. The district court's findings were based on essentially undisputed evidence and

from the evidence, the court determined that Anderson's (P) more varied educational and employment background and her extensive experience in variety of civil activities left her better qualified to implement such a rounded program than the other job applicants. Our determination that the findings of the district court regarding Anderson's (P) qualifications, the conduct of her interview, and the bias of the male committee members were not clearly erroneous leads this Court to conclude that the court's finding that Anderson (P) was discriminated against on account of her sex was also not clearly erroneous. Reversed.

▶ ANALYSIS

Anderson v. Bessemer City grows out of a practice that has its roots in the distinction between law and equity. Because cases in equity were considered only on a written record and the appellate court was able to read the record as the trial court, the rule evolved in equity that the appellate court reviewed equity decisions de novo. That standard came to dominate appellate review not just of decisions in equity, but of all decisions by a judge sitting without a jury.

Quicknotes

DE NOVO The review of a lower court decision by an appellate court, which is hearing the case as if it had not been previously heard and as if no judgment had been rendered.

FED. R. CIV. P. 52(a)(6) Requires that findings of fact not be set aside unless clearly erroneous.

Van Zee v. Hanson

Individual (P) v. Individual (D)

630 F.3d 1126 (8th Cir. 2011)

NATURE OF CASE: Appeal from district court's dismissal of the complaint.

FACT SUMMARY: The United States Army cancelled Van Zee's (P) enlistment when it learned from Hanson (D), a court clerk, that Van Zee (P) had a juvenile court record.

🏛 RULE OF LAW
Consideration of matters or evidence outside of the pleadings at the motion to dismiss stage is harmless if the reviewing court gives the nonmoving party notice and the opportunity to respond.

FACTS: While Van Zee (P) was applying for enlistment into the United States Army, he completed a release form for his court records, allowing Hanson (D), the Clerk of Courts for the Sixth Judicial District of South Dakota, to release his records to the Army recruiter. When Hanson (D) did so, the Army rescinded Van Zee's (P) enlistment. Van Zee (P) brought suit against Hanson (D) in federal court for allegedly violating his right to privacy under the Fourteenth Amendment. Hanson (D) filed a motion to dismiss. In a written order, the district court required Van Zee (P) to produce the release form that granted Hanson (D) the legal ability to produce the court records. The district court then granted Hanson's (D) motion to dismiss. Van Zee (P) appealed.

ISSUE: Is consideration of matters or evidence outside of the pleadings at the motion to dismiss stage harmless if the reviewing court gives the nonmoving party notice and the opportunity to respond?

HOLDING AND DECISION: (Benton, J.) Yes. Consideration of matters or evidence outside of the pleadings at the motion to dismiss stage is harmless if the reviewing court gives the nonmoving party notice and the opportunity to respond. First, to violate the right to privacy, the information disclosed must be a shocking degradation, an egregious humiliation, or a breach of a pledge of confidentiality. Here, the district court correctly found that Van Zee (P) lacked an expectation of privacy when he had specifically signed a valid form allowing for the release of the court records. Van Zee (P) argues on appeal that the district court's reliance on the release form converted Hanson's (D) motion to dismiss into a motion for summary judgment, without giving Van Zee (P) an opportunity to respond. Typically, if a court reviews matters beyond the plaintiff's complaint, it should convert the motion to dismiss to a summary judgment motion and provide each party with an opportunity to adequately brief the issues. However, constructive notice that a court intends to consider evidence beyond the complaint satisfies this standard. Van Zee (P) had constructive notice that the district court was going to rely upon the release form when the court issued a written order requesting the submission of the form to the court in August 2009. The court dismissed the case in February 2010. Van Zee (P) had adequate notice and the opportunity to respond to the motion and the court's consideration of the release form. Affirmed.

▶ ANALYSIS

Because the appellate court was convinced that Van Zee (P) was going to be unable to prove his claim, it was able to find that the district court's consideration of matters outside of the pleadings was harmless error. Typically, trial courts at the state and federal level will be more explicit in converting motions to dismiss to motions for summary judgment. This will better insulate the trial court's handling of the case at the appellate stage.

Quicknotes

HARMLESS ERROR An error taking place during trial that does not require the reviewing court to overturn or modify the trial court's judgment in that it did not affect the appellant's substantial rights or the disposition of the action.

MOTION TO DISMISS Motion to terminate an action based on the adequacy of the pleadings, improper service or venue, etc.

Respect for Judgments

Quick Reference Rules of Law

Frier v. City of Vandalia

Owner of towed car (P) v. Municipality (D)

770 F.2d 699 (7th Cir. 1985)

NATURE OF CASE: Appeal of dismissal of action for deprivation of property without due process under color of law.

FACT SUMMARY: After Charles Frier (P) lost his state court suit against the City of Vandalia (D) for replevin of his car, he then sued Vandalia (D) in federal court under 42 U.S.C. § 1983 for depriving him of his car without due process under color of law.

🏛 RULE OF LAW
Claim preclusion bars a second suit where the first suit arose out of the same transaction.

FACTS: City of Vandalia (D) police had a garage tow Charles Frier's (P) car because it was parked in traffic. Frier (P) did not receive a citation or a hearing either before the car was towed or after he refused to pay to retrieve it. Frier (P) sued Vandalia (D) and the garage in state court for replevin of his car. After a trial, the court decided that Vandalia (D) had the right to tow Frier's (P) car because it was obstructing traffic. Therefore, the court did not issue the writ of replevin. Frier (P) then filed a 42 U.S.C. § 1983 suit in federal court, seeking equitable relief and compensatory and punitive damages from Vandalia (D) for depriving him of his car without due process under color of law. The district court dismissed Frier's (P) suit for failure to state a claim, and Frier (P) appealed, arguing that he was not precluded from filing a federal suit under a different legal theory than the one on which he based his state court action.

ISSUE: Does claim preclusion bar a second suit where the first suit arose out of the same transaction?

HOLDING AND DECISION: (Easterbrook, J.) Yes. Claim preclusion bars a second suit where the first suit arose out of the same transaction. Claim preclusion, also called res judicata, is designed to impel parties to consolidate all closely related matters in the same suit. First, this prevents oppression of defendants through multiple cases. Second, when the facts and issues of all theories of liability are closely related, there is no good reason to incur the cost of litigation more than once. Frier (P) could have sued in his state court action for both replevin, to get his car back, and under § 1983, for damages. Both theories alleged the same conduct: that Vandalia (D) towed and detained his cars without lawful process, i.e., without a determination of a parking violation. Thus, claim preclusion bars Frier's (P) federal suit. The district court, though it properly dismissed the case, should not have reached the merits. Affirmed.

CONCURRENCE: (Swygert, J.) Frier's (P) suit should properly have been dismissed on summary judgment, but not for claim preclusion. Illinois law, applicable in this case, follows the narrower, traditional rule of claim preclusion, not the broader Restatement rule applied by the majority. Under the traditional rule, one suit bars a second where the evidence necessary to sustain a second verdict would have sustained the first, i.e., where the causes of action are based on a common core of operative facts. To prevail on his replevin claim, Frier (P) would have had to prove a superior right to possession of the car, which turned on whether he had parked illegally. However, under § 1983, the legality of Frier's (P) parking was irrelevant. The issues as to § 1983 were whether Frier (P) had notice that he would be towed for parking where he did, and whether he had a fair hearing on the detaining of his car. The fact that Frier (P) could have brought the two causes of action in the same suit is irrelevant under the traditional rule of claim preclusion.

▶ ANALYSIS

Judge Easterbrook and Judge Swygert agree that under the "same transaction" rule Frier's (P) second suit was barred by claim preclusion or res judicata. However, Judge Swygert applied the narrower, traditional, "core of operative facts" rule to reach the opposite result on the claim preclusion issue. The federal courts and most states follow the "same transaction" rule, which is codified in the Restatement (Second) of Judgments § 24 (1982).

Quicknotes

42 U.S.C. § 1983 The Civil Rights Act; usually invoked when a party commences suit based on the alleged state's violation of the party's civil rights.

CLAIM The demand for a right to payment or equitable relief; the fact or facts giving rise to such demand.

RES JUDICATA The rule of law a final judgment by a court precludes subsequent litigation between the parties regarding the same cause of action.

Semtek Intl. Inc. v. Lockheed Martin Corp.

Injured party (P) v. Alleged wrongdoer (D)

531 U.S. 497 (2001)

NATURE OF CASE: Appeal from affirmance of dismissal of state action on res judicata grounds, giving effect to dismissal by federal court sitting in diversity jurisdiction.

FACT SUMMARY: When Semtek International, Inc.'s (Semtek's) (P) breach of contract and tort claims against Lockheed Martin Corp. (D) were barred by California's two-year statute of limitations, Semtek (P) filed the same claims in state court in Maryland, which had a three-year statute of limitations.

🏛 **RULE OF LAW**
As a matter of federal common law, a state rule of claim preclusion applies to dismissals ordered by either state or federal courts, except where state law is incompatible with federal interests.

FACTS: Semtek International, Inc. (Semtek) (P) sued Lockheed Martin Corp. (Lockheed) (D) for breach of contract and tort claims. After removal to federal court in California, the action was dismissed because it was barred by California's two-year statute of limitations. Semtek (P) filed the same claims in state court in Maryland, which had a three-year statute of limitations. The Maryland court dismissed the case on res judicata grounds. In affirming, the Maryland Court of Special Appeals held that, regardless of whether California state law would have accorded claim preclusive effect to a statute-of-limitations dismissal by one of its own courts, the California federal court's dismissal barred the Maryland complaint because the res judicata effect of federal diversity judgments is prescribed by federal law, under which the earlier dismissal was on the merits and claim preclusive.

ISSUE: As a matter of federal common law, does a state rule of claim preclusion apply to dismissals ordered by either state or federal courts, except where state law is incompatible with federal interests?

HOLDING AND DECISION: (Scalia, J.) Yes. As a matter of federal common law, a state rule of claim preclusion applies to dismissals ordered by either state or federal courts, except where state law is incompatible with federal interests. Semtek (P) asserts that *Dupasseur v. Rochereau*, 21 Wall. 130 (1875), which held that the res judicata effect of a federal diversity judgment "is such as would belong to judgments of the State courts rendered under similar circumstances," governs here. That case is not dispositive, however, because it was decided under the Conformity Act of 1872, which required federal courts to apply the procedural law of the forum state in nonequity

cases. However, claim-preclusive effect is not, as Lockheed (D) asserts, required by Fed. R. Civ. P. § 41(b), which provides that, unless the court "otherwise specifies," an involuntary dismissal, other than a dismissal for lack of jurisdiction, improper venue, or failure to join a party under Rule 19, "operates as an adjudication upon the merits." Although the original connotation of a judgment "on the merits" was one that passes directly on the substance of a claim (which would be claim-preclusive), the meaning of the term has changed, and does not necessarily designate a judgment effecting claim preclusion. There are a number of reasons that support this conclusion. First, it would be peculiar to announce a federally prescribed rule on claim preclusion in a default rule for determining a dismissal's import, or to find a rule governing the effect to be accorded federal judgments by other courts ensconced in rules governing the internal procedures of the rendering court itself. Moreover, if the rule were interpreted as Lockheed (D) suggests, it would in many cases violate the federalism principle of *Erie R. Co. v. Tompkins*, 304 U.S. 64 (1938), by engendering substantial variations in outcomes between state and federal litigation that would likely influence forum choice. Finally, the Court itself has never relied upon Rule 41(b) when recognizing the claim-preclusive effect of federal judgments in federal-question cases. Rule 41(a) makes clear "an adjudication upon the merits" in Rule 41(b) is the opposite of a dismissal without prejudice, which means that it prevents refiling of the claim in the same court. That is undoubtedly a necessary condition, but not a sufficient one, for claim-preclusive effect in other courts. Given that neither Semtek's (P) approach, nor Lockheed's (D) approach is satisfactory, what does govern the claim-preclusive effect of the California federal diversity judgment in Maryland state court? The answer is that federal common law governs the claim-preclusive effect of a dismissal by a federal court sitting in diversity, and that it is up to this Court to determine the appropriate federal rule. Since in diversity cases state, rather than federal, substantive law is at issue, there is no need for a uniform federal rule; and nationwide uniformity is better served by having the same claim-preclusive rule (the state rule) apply whether the dismissal has been ordered by a state or a federal court. Any other rule would produce the sort of forum shopping and inequitable administration of the laws that *Erie* seeks to avoid. While the federal reference to state law will not be workable in situations in which the state law

Continued on next page.

is incompatible with federal interests, no such conflict exists here. Reversed and remanded.

▶ *ANALYSIS*

An example of where federal reference to state law will not work is where state law has not given claim-preclusive effect to dismissals for willful violation of discovery orders. In such a case, the federal courts' interest in the integrity of their own processes might justify a federal rule of claim preclusion that does not reflect state law. Of course, that kind of exceptional case was not before the court.

■=■=■

Quicknotes

CLAIM PRECLUSION A procedural rule or order prohibiting the support or opposition to certain claims or defenses.

***ERIE* DOCTRINE** Federal courts must apply state substantive law and federal procedural law.

RES JUDICATA The rule of law that a final judgment by a court precludes subsequent litigation between the parties regarding the same cause of action.

■=■=■

Taylor v. Sturgell

FOIA requester (P) v. Federal official (D)

553 U.S. 880 (2008)

NATURE OF CASE: Appeal from affirmance of summary judgment for defendant in action under the Freedom of Information Act (FOIA).

FACT SUMMARY: Taylor (P) contended that his Freedom of Information Act suit seeking records from the Federal Aviation Administration (D) should not have been dismissed on grounds of claim preclusion—on the theory of "virtual representation"—merely because his friend and close associate, Herrick, had filed a similar suit seeking the same records.

🏛 RULE OF LAW
A claim may not be precluded under a doctrine of "virtual representation" where a second claimant brings a suit identical to a first claimant and, although the claimants know each other, there is no legal relationship between them and there is no evidence that the second claimant controlled, financed, participated in, or even had notice of the earlier suit.

FACTS: Herrick, an antique aircraft enthusiast sought to restore a vintage airplane manufactured by the Fairchild Engine and Airplane Corporation (FEAC). He filed a Freedom of Information Act (FOIA) request asking the Federal Aviation Administration (FAA) (D) for copies of technical documents related to the airplane. The FAA (D) denied his request based on FOIA's exemption for trade secrets. Herrick took an administrative appeal, but when Fairchild Corporation (Fairchild) (D), FEAC's successor, objected to the documents' release, the FAA (D) adhered to its original decision. Herrick then filed a FOIA lawsuit to secure the documents, which was dismissed on summary judgment by the district court and later affirmed by the court of appeals. Less than a month after that suit was resolved, Taylor (P), Herrick's friend and an antique aircraft enthusiast himself, made a FOIA request for the same documents Herrick had unsuccessfully sued to obtain. When the FAA (D) failed to respond, Taylor (P) filed suit in federal district court. Holding the suit barred by claim preclusion, the district court granted summary judgment to the FAA (D) and to Fairchild (D), as intervener in Taylor's (P) action. The court acknowledged that Taylor (P) was not a party to Herrick's suit, but held that a nonparty may be bound by a judgment if she was "virtually represented" by a party. The court of appeals affirmed, announcing a five-factor test for "virtual representation." The first two factors of that test—"identity of interests" and "adequate representation" are necessary but not sufficient for virtual representation. In addition, at least one of three other factors must be established: "a close relationship between

the present party and his putative representative," "substantial participation by the present party in the first case," or "tactical maneuvering on the part of the present party to avoid preclusion by the prior judgment." The court of appeals acknowledged the absence of any indication that Taylor (P) participated in, or even had notice of, Herrick's suit. It nonetheless found the "identity of interests," "adequate representation," and "close relationship" factors satisfied because the two men sought release of the same documents, were "close associates," had discussed working together to restore Herrick's plane, had used the same lawyer to pursue their suits, and Herrick had given Taylor (P) documents Herrick had obtained from the FAA (D) during discovery in his suit. Because these conditions sufficed to establish virtual representation, the court left open the question whether Taylor (P) had engaged in tactical maneuvering to avoid preclusion. The United States Supreme Court granted certiorari.

ISSUE: May a claim be precluded under a doctrine of "virtual representation" where a second claimant brings a suit identical to a first claimant and, although the claimants know each other, there is no legal relationship between them and there is no evidence that the second claimant controlled, financed, participated in, or even had notice of the earlier suit?

HOLDING AND DECISION: (Ginsburg, J.) No. A claim may not be precluded under a doctrine of "virtual representation" where a second claimant brings a suit identical to a first claimant and, although the claimants know each other, there is no legal relationship between them and there is no evidence that the second claimant controlled, financed, participated in, or even had notice of the earlier suit. The preclusive effect of a federal-court judgment is determined by federal common law, subject to due process limitations. Extending the preclusive effect of a judgment to a nonparty runs up against the "deep-rooted historic tradition that everyone should have his own day in court." Indicating the strength of that tradition, this Court has often repeated the general rule that "one is not bound by a judgment in personam in a litigation in which he is not designated a party or to which he has not been made a party by service of process." The rule against nonparty preclusion is subject to exceptions, currently grouped into six categories. First, "[a] person who agrees to be bound by the determination of issues in an action between others is bound in accordance with the [agree-

Continued on next page.

ment's] terms," Restatement (Second) of Judgments § 40. Second, nonparty preclusion may be based on a pre-existing substantive legal relationship between the person to be bound and a party to the judgment, e.g., assignee and assignor. Third, "in certain limited circumstances," a nonparty may be bound by a judgment because she was "adequately represented by someone with the same interests who [wa]s a party" to the suit. Fourth, a nonparty is bound by a judgment if he "assume[d] control" over the litigation in which that judgment was rendered. Fifth, a party bound by a judgment may not avoid its preclusive force by relitigating through a proxy. Preclusion is thus in order when a person who did not participate in litigation later brings suit as the designated representative or agent of a person who was a party to the prior adjudication. Sixth, a special statutory scheme otherwise consistent with due process, e.g., bankruptcy proceedings, may "expressly fore-clos[e] successive litigation by nonlitigants." Reaching beyond these six categories, the court of appeals recognized a broad "virtual representation" exception to the rule against nonparty preclusion. None of the arguments advanced by that court, the FAA (D), or Fairchild (D) justify such an expansive doctrine. The court of appeals purported to ground its doctrine in this Court's statements that, in some circumstances, a person may be bound by a judgment if she was adequately represented by a party to the proceeding yielding that judgment. But the court of appeals' definition of "adequate representation" strayed from the meaning this Court has attributed to that term. In one case, *Richards v. Jefferson County*, 517 U.S. 793 (1996), the Alabama Supreme Court had held a tax challenge barred by a judgment upholding the same tax in a suit by different taxpayers. This Court reversed, holding that nonparty preclusion was inconsistent with due process where there was no showing (1) that the court in the first suit "took care to protect the interests" of absent parties, or (2) that the parties to the first litigation "understood their suit to be on behalf of absent [parties]." In holding that representation can be "adequate" for purposes of nonparty preclusion even where these two factors are absent, the court of appeals misapplied *Richards*. Fairchild (D) and the FAA (D) ask the Court to abandon altogether the attempt to delineate discrete grounds and clear rules for nonparty preclusion. Instead, they contend, only an equitable and heavily fact-driven inquiry can account for all the situations in which nonparty preclusion is appropriate. This argument is rejected. First, the balancing test they propose is at odds with the constrained approach advanced by this Court's decisions, which have endeavored to delineate discrete, limited exceptions to the fundamental rule that a litigant is not bound by a judgment to which she was not a party. Second, a party's representation of a nonparty is "adequate" for preclusion purposes only if, at a minimum: (1) the interests of the nonparty and her representative are aligned, and (2) either the party understood herself to be acting in a representative capacity or the original court took care to protect the nonparty's interests. Adequate

representation may also require (3) notice of the original suit to the persons alleged to have been represented. In the class-action context, these limitations are implemented by Fed. R. Civ. P. 23's procedural safeguards. But an expansive virtual representation doctrine would recognize a common-law kind of class action that would lack these protections. Third, a diffuse balancing approach to nonparty preclusion would likely complicate the task of district courts faced in the first instance with preclusion questions. Finally, the FAA (D) maintains that nonparty preclusion should apply more broadly in "public-law" litigation than in "private-law" controversies. First, the FAA (D) points to *Richards's* acknowledgment that when a taxpayer challenges "an alleged misuse of public funds" or "other public action," the suit "has only an indirect impact on [the plaintiff's] interests," and "the States have wide latitude to establish procedures [limiting] the number of judicial proceedings that may be entertained." In contrast to the public-law litigation contemplated in *Richards*, however, a successful FOIA action results in a grant of relief to the individual plaintiff, not a decree benefiting the public at large. Furthermore, *Richards* said only that, for the type of public-law claims there envisioned, states were free to adopt procedures limiting repetitive litigation. While it appears equally evident that Congress can adopt such procedures, it hardly follows that this Court should proscribe or confine successive FOIA suits by different requesters. Second, the FAA (D) argues that, because the number of plaintiffs in public-law cases is potentially limitless, it is theoretically possible for several persons to coordinate a series of vexatious repetitive lawsuits. But this risk does not justify departing from the usual nonparty preclusion rules. Stare decisis will allow courts to dispose of repetitive suits in the same circuit, and even when stare decisis is not dispositive, the human inclination not to waste money should discourage suits based on claims or issues already decided. The remaining question is whether the result reached by the courts below can be justified based on one of the six established grounds for nonparty preclusion. With one exception, those grounds plainly have no application here. The FAA (D) and Fairchild (D) argue that Taylor's (P) suit is a collusive attempt to relitigate Herrick's claim. That argument justifies a remand to allow the courts below the opportunity to determine whether the fifth ground for nonparty preclusion—preclusion because a nonparty to earlier litigation has brought suit as an agent of a party bound by the prior adjudication—applies to Taylor's (P) suit. However, courts should be cautious about finding preclusion on the basis of agency. A mere whiff of "tactical maneuvering" will not suffice; instead, principles of agency law indicate that preclusion is appropriate only if the putative agent's conduct of the suit is subject to the control of the party who is bound by the

Continued on next page.

prior adjudication. Finally, the Court rejects Fairchild's (D) suggestion that Taylor (P) must bear the burden of proving he is not acting as Herrick's agent. Claim preclusion is an affirmative defense for the defendant to plead and prove. Vacated and remanded.

▶ ANALYSIS

This case presented an issue of first impression in the sense that the Supreme Court had never before addressed the doctrine of "virtual representation" adopted (in varying forms) by several circuits and relied upon by the district court and court of appeals below. For example, the Eighth Circuit had developed a seven-factor test for virtual representation, which was adopted by the district court in this case. The Eighth Circuit test requires an "identity of interests" between the person to be bound and a party to the judgment. Six additional factors counsel in favor of virtual representation under the Eighth Circuit's test, but are not prerequisites: (1) a "close relationship" between the present party and a party to the judgment alleged to be preclusive; (2) "participation in the prior litigation" by the present party; (3) the present party's "apparent acquiescence" to the preclusive effect of the judgment; (4) "deliberat[e] maneuver[ing]" to avoid the effect of the judgment; (5) adequate representation of the present party by a party to the prior adjudication; and (6) a suit raising a "public law" rather than a "private law" issue. These factors, the court of appeals (D.C. Circuit) in this case observed, "constitute a fluid test with imprecise boundaries" and call for "a broad, case-by-case inquiry." The D.C. Circuit adopted a five-factor test. The Supreme Court resolved these different approaches by rejecting the doctrine of virtual representation altogether, instead relying on well-established principles of due process and claim preclusion.

Quicknotes

CLAIM PRECLUSION A procedural rule or order prohibiting the support or opposition to certain claims or defenses.

DUE PROCESS The constitutional mandate requiring the courts to protect and enforce individuals' rights and liberties consistent with prevailing principles of fairness and justice and prohibiting the federal and state governments from such activities that deprive its citizens of life, liberty, or property interest.

INTERVENOR A party, not an initial party to the action, who is admitted to the action in order to assert an interest in the subject matter of a lawsuit.

PARTY Person designated as either the defendant or plaintiff in a lawsuit.

Gargallo v. Merrill Lynch, Pierce, Fenner & Smith

Client (P) v. Broker (D)

918 F.2d 658 (6th Cir. 1990)

NATURE OF CASE: Appeal from dismissal of action for securities violations.

FACT SUMMARY: Gargallo's (P) federal court action was dismissed because in a previous state court case, his counterclaim involving the same issues was rejected.

RULE OF LAW
A judgment rendered by a court lacking subject matter jurisdiction does not have claim preclusive effect in subsequent proceedings.

FACTS: Gargallo (P) had a brokerage account with Merrill Lynch, Pierce, Fenner & Smith (Merrill Lynch) (D). When the investments went poorly, Gargallo (P) ended up owing Merrill Lynch (D) $17,000. The broker (D) brought suit in Ohio state court for collection of the debt, and Gargallo (P) filed a counterclaim alleging that the losses were caused by violation of federal securities law. The Ohio court dismissed the counterclaim with prejudice for Gargallo's (P) failure to comply with discovery requests and orders. Gargallo (P) then filed a complaint in U.S. District Court. The court dismissed the action on res judicata grounds, finding that the claims were the same as those dismissed by the Ohio court. Gargallo (P) appealed.

ISSUE: Does a judgment rendered by a court lacking subject matter jurisdiction have claim preclusive effect in subsequent proceedings?

HOLDING AND DECISION: (Ryan, J.) No. A judgment rendered by a court lacking subject matter jurisdiction does not have claim preclusive effect in subsequent proceedings. The doctrine of res judicata provides that a final judgment by a court is conclusive of the rights, questions and facts at issue with respect to the parties in all other actions. In the present case, it is clear Gargallo's (P) federal court complaint alleges the same violations that were alleged in the state court counterclaim. Ordinarily, federal courts are required to give state court judgments the same preclusive effect such judgment would have in a state court. Ohio subscribes to the position that res judicata does not apply where the original court did not have subject matter jurisdiction over the issue. In the present case, Ohio did not have jurisdiction over Gargallo's (P) allegations of securities violations by Merrill Lynch (D). Thus, the dismissal should not have been given preclusive effect in federal district court. Reversed and remanded.

ANALYSIS

The decision did not directly address the issue that Gargallo's (P) state court counterclaim was not really decided on the merits. It was dismissed because of failure to abide by discovery requirements. However, it would still have been subject to res judicata if the state court had had subject matter jurisdiction.

Quicknotes

JUDGMENT ON THE MERITS A determination of the rights of the parties to litigation based on the presentation evidence, barring the party from initiating the same suit again.

RES JUDICATA The rule of law a final judgment by a court precludes subsequent litigation between the parties regarding the same cause of action.

SUBJECT MATTER JURISDICTION A court's ability to adjudicate a specific category of cases based on the subject matter of the dispute.

Illinois Central Gulf Railroad v. Parks

Railroad company (D) v. Injured car occupants (P)

Ind. Ct. App., 181 Ind. App. 141, 390 N.E.2d 1078 (1979)

NATURE OF CASE: Interlocutory appeal from denial of motion for summary judgment.

FACT SUMMARY: Parks (P) was injured when his car collided with an Illinois Central Gulf Railroad (D) train.

🏛 RULE OF LAW
The doctrine of estoppel by verdict allows a judgment in a prior action to operate as a complete bar to those facts or issues actually litigated and determined in the prior action.

FACTS: Parks (P) and his wife were injured when their car collided with an Illinois Central Gulf Railroad (Illinois Central) (D) train. Parks's (P) wife recovered $30,000 on her claim for damages for personal injuries, but judgment was rendered for Illinois Central (D) on Parks's (P) own claim for damages for loss of services and loss of consortium. Parks (P) then sued Illinois Central (D) to recover damages for his own injuries. On Illinois Central's (D) motion for summary judgment, the trial court held that Parks's (P) claim was not barred by res judicata, and that the prior action did not collaterally estop Parks (P) on the issue of contributory negligence.

ISSUE: Does the doctrine of estoppel by verdict allow a judgment in a prior action to operate as complete bar to those facts or issues actually litigated and determined in the prior action?

HOLDING AND DECISION: (Lybrook, J.) Yes. The doctrine of estoppel by verdict allows the judgment in a prior action to operate as an estoppel as to those facts or questions actually litigated and determined in the prior action. Where a prior judgment may have been based upon either or any of two or more distinct facts, a party desiring to plead the judgment as an estoppel by verdict must show the actual basis for the prior judgment. Here, the basis for the prior judgment against Parks (P) could have been predicated on a finding by the jury that either Parks (P) had sustained no damages, or that his own negligence was a proximate cause of his damages. Illinois Central (D) failed to show that the judgment against Parks (P) in the prior action was based upon a finding that Parks (P) was contributorily negligent in the accident. Affirmed.

▶ ANALYSIS

The doctrine of collateral estoppel is reflective of the policy that the needs of judicial finality and efficiency outweigh the possible gains of fairness or accuracy that would result from the continued litigation of an issue that had been decided in prior judicial proceedings. There is a strong policy favoring consistency of judicial rulings in both state and federal courts.

Quicknotes

COLLATERAL ESTOPPEL A doctrine whereby issues litigated and determined in a prior proceeding are binding upon all subsequent litigation between the parties regarding that issue.

Parklane Hosiery Co. v. Shore

Hosiery company (D) v. Shareholder (P)

439 U.S. 322 (1979)

NATURE OF CASE: Review of denial of relitigation of issue determined in a separate case.

FACT SUMMARY: Shore (P) sought rescission of a merger on the grounds that Parklane Hosiery Co. (Parklane) (D), a party to the merger, had issued a false and misleading proxy statement, and in a separate action filed by the Securities Exchange Commission, the district court found the proxy statement to be false, so Shore (P) moved for partial summary judgment in this action on that issue, alleging that Parklane (D) was collaterally estopped from relitigating the issue.

RULE OF LAW

A trial judge has broad discretion to permit the offensive use of collateral estoppel to establish an element of a plaintiff's case where it is not unfair to the defendant.

FACTS: Shore (P) brought a shareholder's class action against Parklane Hosiery Co. (Parklane) (D) alleging that Parklane (D) had issued a materially false and misleading proxy statement in violation of §§ 14(a), 10(b), and 20(a) of the Securities Exchange Act. Shore (P) sought rescission of merger to which Parklane (D) was a party because of the proxy statement, which related to the merger. Before trial, however, the Securities Exchange Commission (SEC) filed suit on the same basis seeking injunctive relief. The court in that suit found the statement false and misleading and entered a declaratory judgment to that effect. Shore (P) then moved for partial summary judgment on the issue of falsity, alleging that Parklane (D) was collaterally estopped from relitigating the issue. The district court denied the motion, but the court of appeals reversed. The United States Supreme Court granted certiorari.

ISSUE: Has a trial judge broad discretion to permit the offensive use of collateral estoppel to establish an element of a plaintiff's case where it is not unfair to the defendant?

HOLDING AND DECISION: (Stewart, J.) Yes. A trial judge has broad discretion to permit the offensive use of collateral estoppel to establish an element of a plaintiff's case where it is not unfair to the defendant. The defensive use of collateral estoppel to prevent relitigation of issues previously litigated and lost by a plaintiff against another defendant has been upheld by this Court. But the present case involves the offensive use of collateral estoppel to prevent relitigation of issues by a defendant against whom a different plaintiff has obtained a ruling. It is argued that such offensive use will not promote judicial economy because plaintiffs can await a ruling in another matter without intervening, and then be relieved of making proofs if the issue is resolved to their satisfaction, but not be foreclosed from raising it again if it is not. SEC injunction suit, so that this argument is inapplicable. Another argument is that a defendant may have little incentive to defend in an action for small or nominal damages and should not be subjected to unforeseeable future suits against which he will not be adequately able to defend. But here, Parklane (D) had a strong incentive for offensive use of collateral estoppel to establish an element of a plaintiff's case where it is not unfair to the defendant. Under these circumstances, it is not unfair to use collateral estoppel against Parklane (D), who had a full and fair opportunity to litigate its claims. Preclusion did not violate the Seventh Amendment.

ANALYSIS

In a separate part of the opinion, the Court found that the offensive use of collateral estoppel in this case would violate Parklane's (D) right to a jury trial in the legal action as opposed to the SEC's equitable suit. This Seventh Amendment right did not, however, affect the propriety of use of collateral estoppel offensively where not unfair to the defendant if the jury trial right was not at issue.

Quicknotes

JOINDER OF PARTIES The joining of parties in one lawsuit.

OFFENSIVE COLLATERAL ESTOPPEL A doctrine that may be invoked by a plaintiff whereby a defendant is prohibited from relitigating issues litigated and determined in a prior proceeding against another plaintiff.

V.L v. E.L.

Individual (P) v. Individual (D)

136 S. Ct. 1017 (2016)

NATURE OF CASE: Appeal from Alabama Supreme Court's ruling in favor of the defendant.

FACT SUMMARY: V.L. (P) formally adopted E.L.'s (D) biological children in Georgia. After the couple later separated while living in Alabama, V.L. (P) sought to enforce her parental rights as granted to her by the earlier adoption proceedings in Georgia.

🏛 RULE OF LAW
The Full Faith and Credit Clause of the United States Constitution requires that each state recognize and give effect to valid judgments issued by the courts of all other states.

FACTS: V.L. (P) formally adopted E.L.'s (D) biological children in Georgia. After the couple later separated while living in Alabama, V.L. (P) sought to enforce her parental rights as granted to her by the earlier adoption proceedings in Georgia. V.L. (P) specifically sought the Alabama court to recognize her valid adoption from Georgia and to grant her some level of custody or visitation rights. The trial court agreed, but the Alabama Supreme Court reversed on the grounds that the Georgia court did not have proper jurisdiction to allow V.L. (P) to adopt the children. V.L. (P) appealed to the United States Supreme Court.

ISSUE: Does the Full Faith and Credit Clause of the United States Constitution require that each state recognize and give effect to valid judgments issued by the courts of all other states?

HOLDING AND DECISION: (Per curiam). Yes. The Full Faith and Credit Clause of the United States Constitution requires that each state recognize and give effect to valid judgments issued by the courts of all other states. The clause transformed the states of the early union from sovereign entities, each free to ignore the rulings of the others, into part of single nation. Any final judgment issued by a state court with subject matter and personal jurisdiction over the case shall be recognized as valid throughout the country. One state may not disregard the rulings of another state even if it disagrees with the ruling or the reasoning supporting the decision. Essentially, the Full Faith and Credit Clause prohibits one state court from inquiring into the merits of a valid final decision by another state court. The only caveat is that a court need not afford full faith and credit to another court's decision if that court did not have jurisdiction over the case. Here, Georgia clearly had subject matter jurisdiction over V.L.'s (P) adoption of E.L.'s (D) biological children. The Alabama Supreme Court relied upon a Georgia statue that stated

that a third party—here, V.L. (P)—could only adopt E.L.'s (D) children if E.L. (D) gave up her parental rights at the time. However, that statute is not a jurisdictional one. Georgia's interpretation of its own adoption scheme is not open to inquiry as it is clear the Georgia court had subject matter jurisdiction over the adoption. Reversed.

▶ ANALYSIS

This case is a straightforward example of the application of the Full Faith and Credit Clause. As with this case, the Clause is most often tested in the arena of family law, where individuals marry, separate, move among the states, and seek to enforce prior court orders issued by other states.

Quicknotes

FULL FAITH AND CREDIT CLAUSE As provided in the U.S. Constitution, Article IV, any state judicial proceedings shall have such faith and credit given them in every court in the United States as they would in their own state.

PER CURIAM Denotes a decision that represents the opinion of the entire court.

United States v. Beggerly

Federal government (D) v. Alleged property owner (P)

524 U.S. 38 (1998)

NATURE OF CASE: Appeal from dismissal of action to set aside settlement in prior quiet title litigation.

FACT SUMMARY: Beggerly (P) sought to set aside an earlier judgment based on a settlement.

🏛 RULE OF LAW
Independent actions pursuant to Fed. R. Civ. P. 60(b) are reserved for cases of injustice sufficiently gross to demand departure from adherence to the doctrine of res judicata.

FACTS: In 1979, the United States (D) brought a quiet title action in Mississippi against Beggerly (P) over certain real property. The issue was whether the land in question had been deeded prior to the date of the Louisiana Purchase in 1803. If not, the United States (D) would own it and not have to purchase it from Beggerly (P). During discovery, Beggerly (P) sought proof of title. A search by government officials of public records revealed nothing that proved a land grant prior to 1803. On the eve of trial, the case was settled for a modest sum and judgment entered based on the agreement. However, Beggerly (P) continued to search for information and in 1991, a specialist claimed to have found a grant in 1781. Beggerly (P) then filed a complaint seeking to set aside the settlement and award damages. The district court dismissed the case on jurisdictional grounds but the court of appeals reversed, deciding that it qualified as an independent action under Fed. R. Civ. P. 60(b).

ISSUE: Are independent actions pursuant to Fed. R. Civ. P. 60(b) reserved for cases of injustice sufficiently gross to demand departure from adherence to the doctrine of res judicata?

HOLDING AND DECISION: (Rehnquist, C.J.) Yes. Independent actions pursuant to Fed. R. Civ. P. 60(b) are reserved for cases of injustice sufficiently gross to demand departure from adherence to the doctrine of res judicata. Prior to the adoption of the Federal Rules of Civil Procedure, the availability of relief from a judgment turned on whether the court was still in the same term in which the challenged judgment was entered. The 1946 amendment to Fed. R. Civ. P. 60 made clear that all old forms of relief from a judgment were abolished except for the independent action. However, an independent action is only available to prevent a grave miscarriage of justice. In the present case, it is obvious that Beggerly's (P) allegations do not come close to meeting this standard. Beggerly (P) only alleges that the Government (D) failed to thoroughly search its record. It would surely result in no grave injustice to allow the settlement and judgment in the prior litigation to stand. Therefore, the court of appeals is reversed, and the case remanded.

▶ ANALYSIS

The decision noted that the alleged failure to furnish relevant information could possibly fit under Fed. R. Civ. P. 60(b)(3). This subsection provides for a one-year limit on motions. Given that the time limit had long expired, the court declined to fully rule on this possibility.

Quicknotes

ACTION TO QUIET TITLE Equitable action to resolve conflicting claims to an interest in real property.

RES JUDICATA The rule of law that a final judgment by a court precludes subsequent litigation between the parties regarding the same cause of action.

Quick Reference Rules of Law

Cordero v. Voltaire, LLC

Individuals (P) v. Corporation (D)

2013 WL 6415667 (W.D. Tex. 2013)

NATURE OF CASE: United States magistrate judge's report and recommendation to district court regarding plaintiffs' motion to dismiss defendant's counterclaims.

FACT SUMMARY: Cordero (P) and several other employees of Voltaire, LLC (D), a construction company, filed wage and hour claims against Voltaire (D) on the grounds the company failed to pay them for overtime. Voltaire (D) filed counterclaims for fraud and theft against the plaintiffs.

> ## 🏛 RULE OF LAW
> Federal courts may have supplemental jurisdiction pursuant to 28 U.S.C. 1367 over state law claims if those claims are so related to the federal claim as to form part of the same case or controversy under Article III of the United States Constitution.

FACTS: Cordero (P) and several other employees of Voltaire, LLC (D), a construction company, filed wage and hour claims against Voltaire (D) on the grounds the company failed to pay them for overtime in violation of the Fair Labor Standards Act (FLSA). Voltaire (D) filed counterclaims for fraud against Cordero (P) and the other plaintiffs on the grounds they falsified their timesheets. In addition, Voltaire (D) alleges the plaintiffs stole equipment and other construction materials from Voltaire. Cordero (P) and the plaintiffs filed a motion to dismiss all of Voltaire's (D) counterclaims on the grounds the federal court did not have supplemental jurisdiction over Voltaire's (D) state law claims. The case was referred to a United States magistrate judge to consider the plaintiffs' motion to dismiss.

ISSUE: May federal courts have supplemental jurisdiction pursuant to 28 U.S.C. 1367 over state law claims if those claims are so related to the federal claim as to form part of the same case or controversy under Article III of the United States Constitution?

HOLDING AND DECISION: (Austin, M.J.). Yes. Federal courts may have supplemental jurisdiction pursuant to 28 U.S.C. 1367 over state law claims if those claims are so related to the federal claim as to form part of the same case or controversy under Article III of the United States Constitution. Before 1990, whether a state law claim could be heard by a federal court depended mainly upon whether the claim was compulsory or permissive. Compulsory state law counterclaims were those that arose from the same transaction or occurrence as the plaintiff's federal claim. Under Fed. R. Civ. P. 13(a), the defendant must bring the claim or waive it. A permissive state law counterclaim, arising independently from the facts supporting the plaintiff's claim, must have an independent ground for federal subject matter jurisdiction. Congress essentially did away with the distinction of compulsory versus permissive counterclaims with the enactment of 28 U.S.C 1367 in 1990. Now, permissive counterclaims need not have an independent basis for jurisdiction, but they must be so related to the federal claim as to form the same case under Article III. Here, Voltaire's (D) counterclaim for fraud against Cordero (P) for falsifying timesheets arises from the same facts supporting Cordero's (P) FLSA claim. Both claims will rely upon similar evidence: number of hours worked, Cordero's (P) timesheets, and the amounts he was actually paid. Conversely, Voltaire's (D) claims against the plaintiffs that they stole equipment and materials from the company arise from a different set of facts. An entirely different body of evidence will be required to prove those particular claims. Those claims do not satisfy the standard of supplemental jurisdiction. Accordingly, it is recommended that the district court deny Cordero's (P) motion to dismiss Voltaire's (D) counterclaim for fraud but grant Cordero's (P) motion to dismiss Voltaire's (D) counterclaim for theft.

▶ ANALYSIS

The *Cordero v. Voltaire, LLC* decision also notes the accepted guidance that federal courts should be hesitant to allow employers to clutter up a plaintiff's wage and hour claim with counterclaims that are independent of the plaintiff's claims. The main function of federal courts when faced with a Fair Labor Standards Act claim is to determine whether a company paid its employees the proper wages.

■▬■

Quicknotes

COMPULSORY COUNTERCLAIM An independent cause of action brought by a defendant to a lawsuit that arises out of the same transaction or occurrence that is the subject matter of the plaintiff's claim.

FAIR LABOR STANDARDS ACT (FLSA) Enacted in 1938, the statute establishes a minimum wage applicable to all employees of covered employers and provides for mandatory overtime payment for covered employees who work more than 40 hours a week. Executive, administra-

Continued on next page.

tive and professional employees paid on a salary basis are exempt from the statute.

PERMISSIVE COUNTERCLAIM An independent cause of action brought by a defendant to a lawsuit in order to oppose or deduct from the plaintiff's claim that does not arise out of the transaction or occurrence that is the subject matter of the plaintiff's claim.

Mosley v. General Motors Corp.

Class-action plaintiffs (P) v. Car company (D)

497 F.2d 1330 (8th Cir. 1974)

NATURE OF CASE: Appeal from order requiring severance of joint action.

FACT SUMMARY: Mosley (P) and nine other plaintiffs brought this class action against General Motors Corp. (D) for various acts of race and sex discrimination, and the district court ordered the ten plaintiffs to bring ten separate actions due to the wide variety of the claims and the unmanageability of the joint proceeding.

🏛 RULE OF LAW

Permissive joinder of parties is to be broadly granted under Fed. R. Civ. P. 20 where each party seeks relief arising out of the same transaction or series of transactions and a common question of fact or law will arise in the action.

FACTS: Mosley (P) and nine other plaintiffs brought this class action against General Motors Corp. (GM) (D) alleging various different acts that in some cases they contended constituted racial discrimination and in others sex discrimination. They filed complaints individually with the Equal Employment Opportunity Commission (EEOC), and the EEOC notified each of their right to bring a civil action in federal court. At that point the plaintiffs joined in bringing the class action. The district court ordered that each plaintiff bring a separate action, separately filed, due to the differing types of claims alleged and the unmanageability of the joint proceeding. The judge found that there was no right to relief arising out of the same transaction or series of transactions or a common question of fact or law as required by Fed. R. Civ. P. 20. Mosley (P) appealed.

ISSUE: Is permissive joinder to be broadly granted under Fed. R. Civ. P. 20 where each party seeks relief arising out of the same transaction or series of transactions and a common question of fact or law will arise in the action?

HOLDING AND DECISION: (Ross, J.) Yes. The purpose of Fed. R. Civ. P. 20 is to promote trial convenience and expedite the final determination of disputes. The rules permit the trial judge, however, to order separate trials within his discretion if such an order will prevent delay or prejudice. Reversal of such an order depends upon an abuse of that discretion. In this case, a series of "logically related" events occurred, which has been held to constitute a single series of transactions as required. Furthermore, the rights asserted depend on a common question of law. The district court abused its discretion, therefore, in ordering the separate trials. Permissive joinder

is to be broadly granted under Fed. R. Civ. P. 20 where each party seeks relief arising out of the same transaction or series of transactions and a common question of fact or law will arise in the action. Reversed and remanded.

⯈ ANALYSIS

It is not often easy to determine a single series of transactions when distinct events have taken place. However, a series of employment or advancement decisions together appearing like a policy of discrimination is the kind of matter that Fed. R. Civ. P. 20 seeks to have determined in one action. It is when the rights of the parties suffer at the expense of judicial economy that Fed. R. Civ. P. 20(b) can be involved to require separate trials, rather than when the judge finds the case "unmanageable."

Quicknotes

FED. R. CIV. P. 20 Provides that parties requesting relief for injuries arising from the same transaction or common question of law or fact be permitted to consolidate their actions into a single action.

PERMISSIVE JOINDER The joining of parties or claims in a single suit if the claims against the parties arise from the same transaction or occurrence or involve common issues of law or fact; such joinder is not mandatory.

Price v. CTB, Inc.

Chicken farmer (P) v. Construction contractor (D)

168 F. Supp. 2d 1299 (M.D. Ala. 2001)

NATURE OF CASE: Motion to dismiss an impleaded party.

FACT SUMMARY: When Price (P) sued Latco (D) for faulty construction of a chicken house, Latco (D), in turn, impleaded ITW (D), the manufacturer of the nails, on theories of statutory and common-law indemnity.

🏛 **RULE OF LAW**
A defendant may assert a claim against anyone not a party to the original action if that third party's liability is in some way dependent upon the outcome of the original action.

FACTS: Price (P), a chicken farmer, hired Latco (D) to build a chicken house. Alleging defective construction, Price (P) sued CTB (D), which equips poultry houses, and Latco (D) who was the original defendant in the underlying suit concerning the quality of construction workmanship. Latco (D), in turn, moved to implead ITW (D), alleging that ITW (D), a nail manufacturer, defectively designed the nails used in the construction. The specific causes of action against ITW (D) included (1) breach of warranty, (2) Alabama's extended manufacturer's liability doctrine, and (3) common-law indemnity. ITW (D) moved that it be dismissed from the suit on the grounds that it had been improperly impleaded under Fed. R. Civ. P. Rule 14.

ISSUE: May a defendant assert a claim against anyone not a party to the original action if that third party's liability is in some way dependent upon the outcome of the original action?

HOLDING AND DECISION: (De Ment, J.) Yes. A defendant may assert a claim against anyone not a party to the original action if that third party's liability is in some way dependent upon the outcome of the original action. Under the doctrine of implied contractual indemnity, Alabama courts recognize that a manufacturer of a product has impliedly agreed to indemnify the seller when (1) the seller is without fault, (2) the manufacturer is responsible, and (3) the seller has been required to pay a monetary judgment. Here, under Latco's (D) theory, should it be found liable for its construction of the chicken houses, it can demonstrate that the true fault lies with the nail guns and the nails manufactured by ITW (D). Accordingly, Alabama law provides Latco (D) a cause of action under common-law indemnity against ITW (D). Although the doctrine permits recovery only when the party to be indemnified is without fault, whether such a factual scenario will be proven at trial is irrelevant for present purposes. The only issue presently is whether there is a legal basis to implead ITW (D), not whether ITW (D) is, in fact, liable to Latco (D). Since Fed. R. Civ. P. 14 permits Latco (D) to implead any party who "may be liable," it follows that the court must permit development of the factual-record so the extent of that liability may be determined. Furthermore, it is well established that a properly impleaded claim may serve as an anchor for separate and independent claims under Rule 18(a). In short, Latco (D) has properly impleaded ITW (D) under Rule 14(a). ITW's (D) motion to dismiss is denied.

▶ **ANALYSIS**

In *Price*, the court noted that there is a limitation on the general rule of permitting a defendant to assert a claim against anyone not a party to the original action if that third party's liability is in some way dependent upon the outcome of the original action. Even though it may arise out of the same general set of facts as the main claim, a third-party claim will not be permitted when it is based upon a separate and independent claim. Rather, the third-party liability must in some way be derivative of the original claim; a third party may be impleaded only when the original defendant is trying to pass all or part of the liability onto that third party.

Quicknotes

FED. R. CIV. P. 14 Permits the impleader of a party who is or may be liable in order to determine the rights of all parties in one proceeding.

IMPLEADER Procedure by which a third party, who may be liable for all or part of liability, is joined to an action so that all issues may be resolved in a single suit.

INDEMNITY The duty of a party to compensate another for damages sustained.

Temple v. Synthes Corp.

Medical implant user (P) v. Implant manufacturer (D)

498 U.S. 5, *reh'g. denied*, 498 U.S. 1092 (1990)

NATURE OF CASE: Appeal of dismissal with prejudice of action for damages for products liability, medical malpractice, and negligence.

FACT SUMMARY: Temple's (P) federal suit against Synthes Corp. (D), the manufacturer of a plate implanted in Temple's (P) back, was dismissed when Temple (P) failed to join the doctor and the hospital responsible for installing the plate.

 RULE OF LAW
Joint tortfeasors are not necessary parties under Fed. R. Civ. P. 19.

FACTS: A plate and screw device implanted in Temple's (P) back malfunctioned. Temple (P) filed a federal court products liability action against Synthes Corp. (D), the manufacturer of the device. Temple (P) also filed a state-court medical-malpractice and negligence action against the doctor who implanted the device and the hospital where the operation was performed. Synthes (D) filed a motion to dismiss the federal lawsuit under Fed. R. Civ. P. 19 for Temple's (P) failure to join necessary parties. The district court agreed that the doctor and the hospital were necessary parties and gave Temple (P) 20 days to join them. When Temple (P) did not, the court dismissed the suit with prejudice. The court of appeals affirmed, finding that Rule 19 allowed the district court to order joinder in the interest of complete, consistent, and efficient settlement of controversies. It further found that overlapping, separate lawsuits would have prejudiced Synthes (D) because Synthes (D) might claim the device was not defective but that the doctor and the hospital were negligent, and the doctor and the hospital might claim the opposite. Temple (P) appealed, arguing that joint tortfeasors are not necessary parties under Fed. R. Civ. P. 19.

ISSUE: Are joint tortfeasors necessary parties under Fed. R. Civ. P. 19?

HOLDING AND DECISION: (Per curiam) No. Joint tortfeasors are not necessary parties under Fed. R. Civ. P. 19. It has long been the rule that joint tortfeasors need not be named as defendants in a single lawsuit. Fed. R. Civ. P. 19 does not change that principle. The Advisory Committee Notes to Fed. R. Civ. P. 19(a) state that a tortfeasor with the usual joint and several liability is merely a permissive party. There is a public interest in avoiding multiple lawsuits. However, since the requirements of Fed. R. Civ. P. 19(a) have not been met, the district court had no authority to order dismissal. Reversed and remanded.

▶ **ANALYSIS**

The function of compulsory joinder codified in Fed. R. Civ. P. 19 is to bring all affected parties into the same lawsuit. Joinder is often required where the suit involves jointly held rights or liabilities, where more than one party claims the same property, or where granting relief necessarily would affect the rights of parties not in the lawsuit. Though there is a strong interest in "complete, consistent, and efficient settlement of controversies," compulsory joinder is limited. There is a strong tradition of allowing the parties themselves to determine who shall be a party, what claims shall be litigated, and what litigation strategies shall be followed.

Quicknotes

COMPULSORY JOINDER The joining of parties to a lawsuit that is mandatory if complete relief cannot be afforded to the parties in his absence or his absence will result in injustice.

FED. R. CIV. P. 19 Sets forth the rules governing joinder.

JOINDER The joining of claims or parties in one lawsuit.

JOINT TORTFEASORS Two or more parties that either act in concert, or whose individual acts combine to cause a single injury, rendering them jointly and severally liable for damages incurred.

NECESSARY PARTIES Parties whose joining in a lawsuit is essential to the disposition of the action.

Helzberg's Diamond Shops v. Valley West Des Moines Shopping Center

Jewelry stores (P) v. Shopping center (D)

564 F.2d 816 (8th Cir. 1977)

NATURE OF CASE: Appeal from denial of motion to dismiss for failure to join an indispensable party.

FACT SUMMARY: Helzberg's Diamond Shops (Helzberg's) (P) brought this suit to enjoin Valley West Des Moines Shopping Center (Valley West) (D), Helzberg's (P) commercial landlord, from breaching their lease agreement by leasing more than two full-line jewelry stores in the mall where Helzberg's (P) leasehold was located, and Valley West (D) unsuccessfully moved to dismiss on the ground that Helzberg's (P) failed to join the full-line jewelry store tenant, Lord's.

🏛 RULE OF LAW
A tenant under a lease that violates a clause in another tenant's lease from a common landlord is not an indispensable party under Fed. R. Civ. P. 19 to a suit by such other tenant against that landlord.

FACTS: Helzberg's Diamond Shops (Helzberg's) (P), a full-line jewelry store, leased space in Valley West Des Moines Shopping Center (Valley West) (D) shopping center to operate its store. The lease agreement provided that no more than two such stores would be allowed to rent space other than Helzberg's (P) in the mall. Valley West (D), however, leased space to a third such store, Lord's. Helzberg's (P) brought this action to enjoin such a lease, and Valley West (D) moved to dismiss on the ground that Lord's was not joined and was an indispensable party. Helzberg's (P) brought suit in district court in Missouri and could not obtain personal jurisdiction over Lord's, which had no Missouri contacts. The district court denied Valley West's (D) motion, and Valley West (D) appealed.

ISSUE: Is a tenant under a lease that violates a clause in another tenant's lease from a common landlord an indispensable party under Fed. R. Civ. P. 19 to a suit brought by such other tenant against that landlord?

HOLDING AND DECISION: (Alsop, J.) No. A tenant under a lease that violates a clause in another tenant's lease is not an indispensable party under Fed. R. Civ. P. 19 to a suit brought by such other tenant against their common landlord. Fed. R. Civ. P. 19 defines an indispensable party as one in whose absence complete relief cannot be accorded, or claims an interest related to the subject of the action and whose absence will impair or impede his ability to protect that interest or force him to risk multiple or inconsistent obligations. Valley West (D) contends that Lord's and Valley West's (D) rights under their contract cannot be adjudicated in Lord's absence. However, the determination that may result in this action is that Valley West (D) may be forced to terminate that contract, in which case Lord's will still be empowered to assert its rights under the contract for that eventuality. The claim that Valley West (D) may be subjected then to inconsistent obligations following another contract action also fails. Valley West's (D) inconsistent obligations will result from their voluntary execution of two lease agreements with inconsistent obligations required under them. The litigation here can proceed without Lord's, which is not an indispensable party under these circumstances. Affirmed.

▶ ANALYSIS
In federal practice, the court will balance the prejudice to an absent party against the desirability of ruling on a meritorious claim. The judge can shape the relief granted under his equitable powers so as to avoid any such prejudice so long as he renders an effective judgment.

Quicknotes

COMPULSORY JOINDER The joining of parties to a lawsuit that is mandatory if complete relief cannot be afforded to the parties in his absence or his absence will result in injustice.

FED. R. CIV. P. 19 Sets forth the rules governing joinder.

INDISPENSABLE PARTY Parties whose joining in a lawsuit is essential for the adequate disposition of the action and without whom the action cannot proceed.

Natural Resources Defense Council v. United States Nuclear Regulatory Commission

Federal regulatory agency (D) v. Federal commission (P)

578 F.2d 1341 (10th Cir. 1978)

NATURE OF CASE: Appeal of denial of motion to intervene.

FACT SUMMARY: The American Mining Congress and Kerr-McGee Nuclear Corporation appealed the denial of their motion to intervene in an action brought by the Natural Resources Defense Council (P) against the Nuclear Regulatory Commission (D) seeking a declaration that state-granted nuclear power operation licenses are subject to the requirement of filing an environmental impact statement and seeking an injunction of the grant of one such license by the New Mexico Environmental Improvement Agency.

RULE OF LAW
A party may intervene in an action under Fed. R. Civ. P. 24(a)(2) if the party has an interest upon which the disposition of that action will have a significant legal effect.

FACTS: The Nuclear Regulatory Commission (NRC) (D) is permitted by federal law to give the several states the power to grant licenses to operate nuclear power facilities. The NRC (D) is empowered to grant such licenses subject to a requirement that such "major federal action" be preceded by the preparation of an environmental impact statement. The NRC (D) entered into an agreement with the New Mexico Environmental Improvement Agency (NMEIA) permitting it to issue a license, which it did, to United Nuclear without preparing an environmental impact statement. The Natural Resources Defense Council (NRDC) (P) brought this action seeking a declaration that state-granted licenses are the product of "major federal action" and subject to the statement requirement and seeking an injunction against the issuance of the license. United Nuclear intervened without objection. Kerr-McGee Nuclear Corporation (KM), a potential recipient of an NMEIA license, and the American Mining Congress (AMC), a public interest group, sought to intervene, but their motions were denied. Both appealed.

ISSUE: May a party intervene in an action under Fed. R. Civ. P. 24(a)(2) if the party has an interest upon which the disposition of that action will have a significant legal effect?

HOLDING AND DECISION: (Doyle, J.) Yes. Fed. R. Civ. P. 24(a) gives a party the right to intervene when the party has a sufficiently protectable interest related to the property or transaction that is the subject of the action and the disposition will "as a practical matter, im-

pair or impede his ability to protect that interest." The argument that the effect upon the movant's right must be a res judicata effect is unpersuasive. The effect must "as a practical matter" impair or impede the ability to protect the right. A party may thus intervene in an action under Fed. R. Civ. P. 24(a)(2) if the party has an interest upon which the disposition of that action will have a significant legal effect. It need not be a strictly legal effect. KM and AMC each have rights, not protected by other parties to the litigation, which will be thus affected, and they must be allowed to intervene. Reversed and remanded.

▶ ANALYSIS

Fed. R. Civ. P. 24(a) covers the intervention of right, while Fed. R. Civ. P. 24(b) sets forth criteria for permissive intervention. Intervention is permissive if there is a common question of law or fact or if a statute gives a conditional right to intervene. In either case, an intervenor has the same status in the litigation as an original party, but he cannot raise any new issues. Ancillary jurisdiction attaches over the intervenor.

Quicknotes

FED. R. CIV. P. 24 Governs permissive intervention and intervention as a matter of right.

INTERVENTION The method by which a party, not an initial party to the action, is admitted to the action in order to assert an interest in the subject matter of a lawsuit.

Martin v. Wilks

Firefighters (P) v. Court (D)

490 U.S. 755 (1989)

NATURE OF CASE: Review of reversal of dismissal of reverse-discrimination action.

FACT SUMMARY: Several white firefighters challenged affirmative action plans mandated by a consent decree that was entered in an action of which they had knowledge but had not intervened.

🏛 RULE OF LAW

A party may not be bound by a judgment rendered in an action in which he was not a party, even if he had knowledge of the action.

FACTS: As part of a discrimination action, a consent decree was rendered between the City of Birmingham, Alabama, and a class of black firefighters. As part of the decree, the City instituted an affirmative action program. Subsequent to this, a group of white firefighters filed a reverse-discrimination action. The district court dismissed, holding that because the white firefighters had notice of the prior action but had elected not to intervene, the matter was res judicata as to them. The U.S. Court of Appeals for the Eleventh Circuit reversed, and the United States Supreme Court granted review.

ISSUE: May a party be bound by a judgment rendered in an action in which he was not a party, if he had knowledge of the action?

HOLDING AND DECISION: (Rehnquist, C.J.) No. A party may not be bound by a judgment rendered in an action in which he was not a party, even if he had knowledge of the action. It is a principle of general application that one is not bound by an in personam judgment in a litigation in which one is not designated as a party or has not been made a party by service of process. The argument asserted by those defending the consent decree is that by knowing about the underlying action and failing to intervene, the plaintiffs herein waived that objection to being bound. This is incorrect. A party seeking a judgment binding on another cannot obligate that person to intervene; he must be joined. This was the position taken by the Eleventh Circuit, and it was correct in so doing. Affirmed.

DISSENT: (Stevens, J.) In no sense were the white firefighters herein "bound" by the consent decree; rather it was the City that was so bound. The district court properly dismissed the action because the City was fulfilling its legal obligations, not because the white firefighters were somehow bound by the consent decree.

▶ ANALYSIS

Joinder is governed by Fed. R. Civ. P. 19. The rule distinguishes between parties that should be joined and parties that must be joined. Parties may be joined either as defendants or as involuntary plaintiffs.

■═■

Quicknotes

COMPULSORY JOINDER The joining of parties to a lawsuit that is mandatory if complete relief cannot be afforded to the parties in his absence or his absence will result in injustice.

FED. R. CIV. P. 19 Sets forth the rules governing joinder.

INTERVENTION The method by which a party, not an initial party to the action, is admitted to the action in order to assert an interest in the subject matter of a lawsuit.

PERMISSIVE JOINDER The joining of parties or claims in a single suit if the claims against the parties arise from the same transaction or occurrence or involve common issues of law or fact; such joinder is not mandatory.

RES JUDICATA The rule of law a final judgment by a court precludes subsequent litigation between the parties regarding the same cause of action.

■═■

Southern Farm Bureau Life Ins. Co. v. Davis

Life insurer (P) v. Life insurance beneficiary (D)

2010 WL 1245024 (W.D. La. 2010)

NATURE OF CASE: Motion to dismiss interpleader action to determine the proper distribution of life insurance proceeds.

FACT SUMMARY: Southern Farm Bureau Life Ins. Co. (P), which had issued a life insurance policy on the life of Mr. Davis, interpleaded Ms. Davis (D), who had killed Mr. Davis, in an action to determine the proper distribution of the life insurance proceeds under state law, which provided that a named beneficiary who criminally murdered the insured could not recover the proceeds of a life insurance policy.

🏛 RULE OF LAW

A court has jurisdiction to hear an interpleader action where the requirements of either statutory interpleader jurisdiction or rule interpleader jurisdiction are satisfied.

FACTS: Southern Farm Bureau Life Ins. Co. (Farm Bureau) (P) had issued a $95,000 life insurance policy on the life of Mr. Davis. Ms. Davis (D) had been arrested and charged with killing Mr. Davis. Under state law, a named beneficiary of a life insurance policy who had criminally murdered, or intentionally and unjustifiably killed, the insured, was unable to recover the policy proceeds. If a primary beneficiary was disqualified to receive the benefits of the policy and there was no contingent beneficiary, the life insurance proceeds were to be paid to the estate of the insured. Accordingly, Farm Bureau (P) brought an action to determine the proper distribution of the proceeds of the policy on Mr. Davis's life, and interpleaded Ms. Davis (D). Through the interpleader action, Farm Bureau (P) was surrendering the value of the policy to the court in order to be relieved of all its obligations under the policy. While there was complete diversity between Farm Bureau (P) and the defendants, there was not complete diversity between the defendants. Ms. Davis (D) moved to dismiss.

ISSUE: Does a court have jurisdiction to hear an interpleader action where the requirements of either statutory interpleader jurisdiction or rule interpleader jurisdiction are satisfied?

HOLDING AND DECISION: (Minaldi, J.) Yes. A court has jurisdiction to hear an interpleader action where the requirements of either statutory interpleader jurisdiction or rule interpleader jurisdiction are satisfied. The court must have subject matter jurisdiction to hear the case. The requirements for statutory interpleader jurisdiction are set forth in 28 U.S.C. § 1335. That statute provides that a district court has jurisdiction in an interpleader case

where the amount in controversy is $500 or more, and where there is minimal diversity between the claimants. Here, although the amount in controversy exceeds $500, there is no diversity between the defendant claimants. Therefore, there is no jurisdiction under statutory interpleader. The requirements for rule interpleader jurisdiction are set forth in Fed. R. Civ. P. 22, which provides that the action must fall within the general grants of jurisdiction, such as diversity jurisdiction, provided that the complete diversity and amount in controversy requirements are met. Here, the amount in controversy is over $75,000, and there is diversity between the plaintiff and the defendants. Because the requirements for general diversity jurisdiction are satisfied, the court has jurisdiction over Farm Bureau's (P) interpleader action under Fed. R. Civ. P. 22. Accordingly, Ms. Davis's (D) motion to dismiss is denied.

▌ANALYSIS

Statutory interpleader jurisdiction, contrary to rule interpleader jurisdiction, requires only minimal diversity between claimants. Such a minimal diversity requirement has been held to be constitutional. See *State Farm Fire & Casualty Co. v. Tashire*, 386 U.S. 523 (1967).

Quicknotes

DIVERSITY JURISDICTION The authority of a federal court to hear and determine cases involving a statutory sum and in which the parties are citizens of different states, or in which one party is an alien.

INTERPLEADER An equitable proceeding whereby a person holding property that is subject to the claims of multiple parties may require such parties to resolve the matter through litigation.

STATUTORY INTERPLEADER A right pursuant to federal law whereby a person holding property that is subject to the claims of multiple parties may require those parties to resolve the matter through litigation.

Hansberry v. Lee

Black land purchaser (D) v. Party to covenant (P)

311 U.S. 32 (1940)

NATURE OF CASE: A class action to enforce a racially restrictive covenant.

FACT SUMMARY: Lee (P) sought to enjoin a sale of land to the Hansberrys (D) on the grounds that the sale violated a racially restrictive covenant.

RULE OF LAW

There must be adequate representation of the members of a class action or the judgment is not binding on the parties not adequately represented.

FACTS: The Hansberrys (D), a black family, purchased land from a party who had signed a restrictive covenant forbidding the sale of the land to black people. Lee (P), one of the parties who signed the covenant, sought to have the sale enjoined because it breached the covenant. Lee (P) contended that the validity of the covenant was established in a prior case in which one of the parties was a class of landowners involved with the covenant. To be valid, 95 percent of the landowners had to sign the covenant, and the trial court in the prior case held that 95 percent of the landowners had signed the covenant. That case was appealed, and the Illinois Supreme Court upheld the decision, even though it found that 95 percent of the landowners had not signed the covenant, but the court held that since it was a class action, all members of the class would be bound by the decision of the court. Hansberry (D) claimed that he and the party selling him the house were not bound by the res judicata effect of the prior decision, as they were not parties to the litigation. The lower court held that the decision of the Illinois Supreme Court would have to be challenged directly in order for it be set aside or reversed. Otherwise, the decision was still binding. The case was appealed to the United States Supreme Court.

ISSUE: For a judgment in a class action to be binding, must all of the members of the class be adequately represented by parties with similar interests?

HOLDING AND DECISION: (Stone, J.) Yes. It is not necessary that all members of a class be present as parties to the litigation to be bound by the judgment if they are adequately represented by parties who are present. In regular cases, to be bound by the judgment the party must receive notice and an opportunity to be heard. If due process is not afforded the individual, then the judgment is not binding. The class action is an exception to the general rule. Because of the numbers involved in class actions, it is enough if the party is adequately represented by a member of the class with a similar interest. The Hansberrys (D)

were not adequately represented by the class of landowners. Their interests were not similar enough to even be considered members of the same class. Lee (P) and the landowners were trying to restrict black people from buying any of the land, and the Hansberrys (D) were black people attempting to purchase land. When there is such a conflicting interest between members of a class, there is most likely not adequate representation of one of the members of the class. There must be a similarity of interest before there can even be a class. Since there was no similarity of interests between Lee (P) and the Hansberrys (D), the Hansberrys (D) could not be considered a member of the class and so the prior judgment was not binding on the Hansberrys (D). The Hansberrys (D) were not afforded due process because of the lack of adequate representation. The judgment is reversed.

ANALYSIS

Fed. R. Civ. P. 23(c)(3) requires that the court describe those whom the court finds to be members of the class. The court is to note those to whom notice was provided and also those who had not requested exclusion. These members are considered members of the class and are bound by the decision of the court whether it is in their favor or not. The Federal Rules of Civil Procedure allow a member of the class to request exclusion from the class, and that party will not be bound by the decision of the court. Since a party must receive notice of the class action before he can request exclusion from the class, the court must determine if a party received sufficient notice of the action or if sufficient effort was made to notify him of the action. The rules state if the court finds that the party did have sufficient notice and was considered a member of the class, he is bound by the decision.

Quicknotes

CLASS ACTION A suit commenced by a representative on behalf of an ascertainable group that is too large to appear in court, who shares a commonality of interests, and who will benefit from a successful result.

COVENANT A written promise to do, or to refrain from doing, a particular activity.

FED. R. CIV. P. 23 Sets forth the requirements in order to maintain a class-action suit.

Phillips Petroleum v. Shutts

Gas and oil company (D) v. Class of lessees (P)

472 U.S. 797 (1985)

NATURE OF CASE: Appeal of a judgment in a class-action suit.

FACT SUMMARY: Shutts (P) filed a class-action suit against Phillips Petroleum (D) for allegedly underpaying royalties on gas leases.

🏛 RULE OF LAW
A state may exercise jurisdiction over absent plaintiffs in a classification suit even if the plaintiffs have no contacts with that state.

FACTS: Phillips Petroleum (Phillips) (D) had gas and mineral leases with numerous individuals. Royalties were based on the selling price of the final product. When prices were raised, Phillips (D) would often pay royalties at a lower price. Shutts (P) filed a class-action suit on behalf of over 33,000 individuals, seeking damages. A Kansas court certified the class. Letters were sent to all members of the plaintiff class. A plaintiff had the right to opt out of the class or be bound by the judgment. About 3,000 opted out. A judgment for the plaintiffs was entered. The Kansas Supreme Court rejected an appeal by Phillips (D) claiming that Kansas could not exercise jurisdiction over plaintiffs not residents of Kansas. Phillips (D) appealed to the United States Supreme Court.

ISSUE: May a state exercise jurisdiction over absent plaintiffs in a class-action suit, if the plaintiffs have no contacts with that state?

HOLDING AND DECISION: (Rehnquist, J.) Yes. A state may exercise jurisdiction over absent plaintiffs in a class-action suit even if the plaintiffs have no contacts with that state. The "minimum contacts" rule is a matter of personal liberty, not state sovereignty. It exists to protect defendants from being hauled into a distant forum unfairly. A plaintiff in a class-action suit is in a much different position. He is in no danger of a loss of freedom or assets and, in fact, can sit back and let others do the work for him. His ability to opt out of the class further protects him; he is not forced to enter a class unwillingly. Affirmed in part, reversed in part, and remanded.

▶ ANALYSIS

The Court stated in this opinion that minimum contacts is an issue of liberty, not sovereignty. This issue has been touched upon since *Pennoyer v. Neff*, 95 U.S. 714 (1877). The Court here held that the opt-out procedure was a sufficient protection of personal liberty.

Quicknotes

CLASS ACTION A suit commenced by a representative on behalf of an ascertainable group that is too large to appear in court, who shares a commonality of interests, and who will benefit from a successful result.

MINIMUM CONTACTS The minimum degree of contact necessary in order to sustain a cause of action within a particular forum, consistent with the requirements of due process.

Standard Fire Ins. Co. v. Knowles

Insurer (D) v. Insured class action representative (P)

568 U.S. 588 (2013)

NATURE OF CASE: Appeal from remand of a proposed class action from federal court to state court.

FACT SUMMARY: Knowles (P), an insured of Standard Fire Ins. Co. (Standard) (D), filed a proposed class action in state court against Standard (D), stipulating that the class would seek less than $5 million in damages. After removal to federal district court, the court remanded, finding that the amount in controversy fell below the $5 million jurisdictional threshold of the Class Action Fairness Act. Standard (D) contended that the jurisdictional amount had been met based on an aggregation of all potential claims.

🏛 RULE OF LAW

A class action representative plaintiff's stipulation as to the amount of damages the class will seek is not binding for purposes of determining a jurisdictional amount-in-controversy.

FACTS: Knowles (P), an insured of Standard Fire Ins. Co. (Standard) (D), filed a proposed class action in state court against Standard (D), stipulating that the class would seek less than $5 million in damages. However, Knowles (P) sought to certify a class of "hundreds, and possibly thousands" of similarly harmed state policyholders, and if all these potential claims were aggregated, the total amount of damages would exceed $5 million. After removal to federal district court, the court remanded, finding that the amount in controversy fell below the $5 million jurisdictional threshold of the Class Action Fairness Act (CAFA). CAFA provides that in determining the threshold amount, the "claims of the individual class members shall be aggregated." Standard (D) contended that the jurisdictional amount had been met based on an aggregation of all potential claims, and that the district court should not have held that Knowles's (P) stipulation was binding. Standard (D) appealed, but the court of appeals in its discretion denied review. The United States Supreme Court, however, granted certiorari.

ISSUE: Is a class action representative plaintiff's stipulation as to the amount of damages the class will seek binding for purposes of determining a jurisdictional amount-in-controversy?

HOLDING AND DECISION: (Breyer, J.) No. A class action representative plaintiff's stipulation as to the amount of damages the class will seek is not binding for purposes of determining a jurisdictional amount-in-controversy. Here, the precertification stipulation can tie Knowles's (P) hands because stipulations are binding on

the party who makes them. However, the stipulation does not speak for those Knowles (P) purports to represent, because a plaintiff who files a proposed class action cannot legally bind members of the proposed class before the class is certified. Because Knowles (P) lacked authority to concede the amount in controversy for absent class members, the district court wrongly concluded that his stipulation could overcome its finding that the CAFA jurisdictional threshold had been met. Although Knowles (P) concedes that federal jurisdiction cannot be based on contingent future events, he asserts that the amount he stipulated is not contingent. Nevertheless, because a stipulation must be binding and a named plaintiff cannot bind precertification class members, the amount he stipulated is in effect contingent. CAFA does not forbid a federal court to consider the possibility that a nonbinding, amount-limiting, stipulation may not survive the class certification process. To hold otherwise would, for CAFA jurisdictional purposes, treat a nonbinding stipulation as if it were binding, exalt form over substance, and run counter to CAFA's objective of ensuring that federal courts consider interstate cases of national importance. Finally, Knowles (P) points out individual plaintiffs may avoid removal to federal court by stipulating to amounts that fall below the federal jurisdictional threshold. Although that is true in cases where the stipulations are binding, that is not the case here, since the stipulation cannot be legally binding on any class members other than Knowles (P). For these reasons, the district court erred in remanding the case to state court. Vacated and remanded.

▶ ANALYSIS

The key to this decision is that the class had as yet not been certified. Neither a proposed class action nor a rejected class action may bind nonparties, and a non-named class member is not a party to the class-action litigation before the class is certified. Thus, for example, a damages limitation cannot have a binding effect on the merits of absent class members' claims unless and until the class is certified.

Quicknotes

AMOUNT IN CONTROVERSY The value of a claim sought by a party to a lawsuit.

JURISDICTION The authority of a court to hear and declare judgment in respect to a particular matter.

Wal-Mart Stores, Inc. v. Dukes

Retail giant (D) v. Female employees (P)

564 U.S. 338 (2011)

NATURE OF CASE: Class action based on gender discrimination.

FACT SUMMARY: A small group of women filed a gender discrimination claim against Wal-Mart Stores, Inc. (D). A class was certified, and the original small group of women who filed the claims wanted to represent the class. The class was the largest in history.

🏛 RULE OF LAW

(1) A class consisting of more than one million women employed by a single employer nationwide cannot be certified as a class if they do not meet the "commonality" threshold for class certification under Fed. R. Civ. P. 23(a)(2) because they cannot demonstrate all class members were subject to the same discriminatory employment policy.

(2) Claims for monetary relief may not be certified under Fed. R. Civ. P. 23(b)(2) where the monetary relief is not incidental to the injunctive or declaratory relief.

FACTS: Betty Dukes (P), a Wal-Mart "greeter" at a Pittsburg, Calif., store, and five other women filed a class-action lawsuit in which they alleged that the company's nationwide policies resulted in lower pay for women than men in comparable positions and longer wait for management promotions than men. The U.S. District Court for the Northern District of California certified the class, finding plaintiffs satisfied the requirements of Rules 23(a)(2) and 23(b)(2). The certified class was estimated to include than 1.5 million women, all women employed by Wal-Mart nationwide at any time after December 26, 1998, making this the largest class action lawsuit in U.S. history. Wal-Mart (D) argued that the court should require employees to file on an individual basis, contending that class actions of this size—formed under Rule 23 (b) of the Federal Rules of Civil Procedure—are inherently unmanageable and unduly costly. The U.S. Court of Appeals for the Ninth Circuit upheld the class certification three times.

ISSUE:

(1) Can a class consisting of more than one million women employed by a single employer nationwide be certified as a class if they do not meet the "commonality" threshold for class certification under Fed. R. Civ. P. 23(a)(2) because they cannot demonstrate all class members were subject to the same discriminatory employment policy?

(2) May claims for monetary relief be certified under Fed. R. Civ. P. 23(b)(2) where the monetary relief is not incidental to the injunctive or declaratory relief?

HOLDING AND DECISION: (Scalia, J.)

(1) No. A class consisting of more than one million women employed by a single employer nationwide cannot be certified as a class if they do not meet the "commonality" threshold for class certification under Fed. R. Civ. P. 23(a)(2) because they cannot demonstrate all class members were subject to the same discriminatory employment policy. The class action is "an exception to the usual rule that litigation is conducted by and on behalf of the individual named parties only." In order to justify a departure from that rule, "a class representative must be part of the class and 'possess the same interest and suffer the same injury' as the class members." Rule 23(a) ensures that the named plaintiffs are appropriate representatives of the class whose claims they wish to litigate. The Rule's four requirements—numerosity, commonality, typicality, and adequate representation—effectively "limit the class claims to those fairly encompassed by the named plaintiff's claims." Proof of commonality—the second of the Rule's four requirements—necessarily overlaps with the group's argument that Wal-Mart (D) engages in a pattern or practice of discrimination. Under Title VII, the central inquiry involves the reason for a particular employment decision, and the plaintiffs wish to sue for millions of employment decisions at once. Without something holding together the alleged reasons for those employment decisions, it would be impossible to say that examination of all the class members' claims will produce a common answer to the crucial discrimination question. The testimony of the plaintiffs' social science expert who claimed that Wal-Mart's (D) culture was susceptible to gender bias is unpersuasive. The testimony is useless to the question of whether the plaintiffs could prove a general policy of discrimination. Also rejected is the use of aggregate statistical analyses and the mere existence of gender disparities in pay, promotion, or representation to meet the commonality burden. Instead, to show commonality, a plaintiff would at least need to demonstrate store-by-store disparities. Third, affidavits from 120 individuals, or one out of every 12,500 class members, did not constitute "significant proof" that Wal-Mart (D) operates under a general policy of discrimination. The members of the plaintiffs' group held many different jobs, at different levels of Wal-Mart's (D) hierarchy, for variable lengths of time, in 3,400 stores, across 50 states, with many different supervisors (male and female), subject to a variety

Continued on next page.

of regional policies that all differed. Some thrived while others did not. They have little in common but their sex and this lawsuit.

(2) No. Claims for monetary relief may not be certified under Fed. R. Civ. P. 23(b)(2) where the monetary relief is not incidental to the injunctive or declaratory relief. After satisfying the elements of Rule 23(a), the proposed class must satisfy at least one of the three requirements listed in Rule 23(b). The plaintiffs sought certification under Rule 23(b)(2), which applies when "the party opposing the class has acted or refused to act on grounds that apply generally to the class, so that final injunctive relief or corresponding declaratory relief is appropriate respecting the class as a whole." But Rule 23(b)(2) applies only when a single injunction or declaratory judgment would provide relief to each member of the class. It does not authorize class certification when each individual class member would be entitled to a different injunction or declaratory judgment against the defendant. Similarly, it does not authorize class certification when each class member would be entitled to an individualized award of monetary damages. The "predominance test" established by the Ninth Circuit, which permitted the certification of claims for monetary damages as long as claims for injunctive relief "predominated" over the claims for monetary damages, is rejected. Rather, the "incidental damages" test, which permits certification of claims for monetary relief as long as that relief "flow[s] directly from liability to the class as a whole," which "should not require additional hearings," is more appropriate. The adoption of a bright-line rule prohibiting all money damages from ever being certified under Rule 23(b)(2) is not considered here. The judgment of the Court of Appeals is reversed.

CONCURRENCE AND DISSENT: (Ginsburg, J.) The class should not have been certified under Fed. R. Civ. P. 23(b)(2) because the plaintiffs, alleging discrimination in violation of Title VII, seek monetary relief that is not merely incidental to any injunctive or declaratory relief that might be available. But a class of this type may be certifiable under Rule 23(b)(3), if the plaintiffs show that common class questions "predominate" over issues affecting individuals, such as qualification for, and the amount of, backpay or compensatory damages, and that a class action is "superior" to other modes of adjudication. Whether the class the plaintiffs describe meets the specific requirements of Rule 23(b)(3) is not before the Court, and that matter should be reserved for consideration and decision on remand. But the majority disqualifies the class under 23(a)(2), holding that the plaintiffs cannot cross the "commonality" line, and by doing so imports into the Rule 23(a) determination concerns properly addressed in a Rule 23(b)(3) assessment. The majority errs in importing a "dissimilarities" notion suited to Rule 23(b)(3) into the Rule 23(a) commonality inquiry.

▶ ANALYSIS

This is a landmark case that was thoroughly analyzed in the media when it was released. Many criticized the decision as inappropriately and unfairly raising the bar for certification to the detriment of those with valid Title VII claims. District courts will now be required to scrutinize closely all alleged common questions of law and fact to determine if the proposed common questions generate common answers that are apt to drive resolution in each case. It will not be sufficient for plaintiffs to allege a "general policy" without proving the existence of the policy and its impact on each class member.

■=■

Quicknotes

CLASS ACTION A suit commenced by a representative on behalf of an ascertainable group that is too large to appear in court, who shares a commonality of interests, and who will benefit from a successful result.

CLASS CERTIFICATION Certification by a court's granting of a motion to allow individual litigants to join as one plaintiff in a class action against the defendant.

■=■

Amchem Products, Inc. v. Windsor

Asbestos producer (D) v. Class-action plaintiffs (P)

521 U.S. 591 (1997)

NATURE OF CASE: Appeal from reversal of class certification in mass tort action.

FACT SUMMARY: The district court certified a class (P) of persons exposed to asbestos products in order to affect a settlement of the case.

🏛 RULE OF LAW
Fed. R. Civ. P. 23 requirements for class certification must be met even if the certification is for settlement only.

FACTS: All the asbestos exposure cases pending in federal courts were transferred and consolidated for pretrial proceedings to a single district court. Following this consolidation, the parties began settlement negotiations. The defendants' steering committee (D) made an offer to settle all pending and future asbestos cases by providing a fund from which to pay claims. Eventually, a settlement was reached for pending cases. A second settlement for potential plaintiffs was then reached. The parties then sought certification of this class of potential plaintiffs for purposes of settlement only. Nine lead plaintiffs were named who were designed to be representative of a class of all persons and family members who had been exposed to asbestos products but had not yet filed suit. The district court approved the settlement, certified the class (P), and enjoined class members from filing additional suits. Objectors raised numerous challenges to the settlement, claiming that it unfairly disadvantaged those without current problems. The court of appeals reversed the certification on the grounds that Fed. R. Civ. P. 23 requirements were not met. The defendants appealed.

ISSUE: Must Fed. R. Civ. P. 23 requirements for class certification be met even if the certification is for settlement only?

HOLDING AND DECISION: (Ginsburg, J.) Yes. Fed. R. Civ. P. 23 requirements for class certification must be met even if the certification is for settlement only. Rule 23, authorizing class actions, has several requirements that must be satisfied. These standards are designed to protect absent class members. They may not be disregarded simply because a court believes that a settlement is fair. First, common questions of law or fact must predominate over questions affecting individual members. The district court's reliance on the claimants' interest in a compensation scheme does not meet this requirement. A compensation scheme is a matter for legislative consideration. Secondly, the named parties in a class action must fairly and adequately protect the interests of the class. The district court

failed to break the class into subclasses. Thus, the named parties had diverse medical conditions and diverse interests that could cause conflicts of interest. Furthermore, there are impediments to the provision of adequate notice because there are persons in the class who may not even know of their exposure to asbestos yet. The only proper accommodation that should be made to settlement-only class certification is that the problems of trial administration should be ignored. Accordingly, in the present case, the class was improperly certified because the requirements of Rule 23 were not satisfied. Affirmed.

CONCURRENCE AND DISSENT: (Breyer, J.) The need for settlement in mass tort cases is greater than the majority suggests. Also, settlement-related issues should be given more weight for purposes of determining whether common issues predominate. Settlement is something that should help the class meet the Rule 23 requirements.

▌ *ANALYSIS*

Settlement classes have become more and more common since the advent of Rule 23, which does not make provision for such classes. Many commentators have called for revision to Rule 23 to address the reality of settlement classes. However, others have objected on the basis that settlement classes invite collusion among class counsel and the defense.

■=■

Quicknotes

FED. R. CIV. P. 23 Sets forth the requirements in order to maintain a class-action suit.

SETTLEMENT An agreement entered into by the parties to a civil lawsuit agreeing upon the determination of rights and issues between them, thus disposing of the need for judicial determination.

■=■

Glossary

Common Latin Words and Phrases Encountered in the Law

A FORTIORI: Because one fact exists or has been proven, therefore a second fact that is related to the first fact must also exist.

A PRIORI: From the cause to the effect. A term of logic used to denote that when one generally accepted truth is shown to be a cause, another particular effect must necessarily follow.

AB INITIO: From the beginning; a condition that has existed throughout, as in a marriage that was void ab initio.

ACTUS REUS: The wrongful act; in criminal law, such action sufficient to trigger criminal liability.

AD VALOREM: According to value; an ad valorem tax is imposed upon an item located within the taxing jurisdiction calculated by the value of such item.

AMICUS CURIAE: Friend of the court. Its most common usage takes the form of an amicus curiae brief, filed by a person who is not a party to an action but is nonetheless allowed to offer an argument supporting his legal interests.

ARGUENDO: In arguing. A statement, possibly hypothetical, made for the purpose of argument, is one made arguendo.

BILL QUIA TIMET: A bill to quiet title (establish ownership) to real property.

BONA FIDE: True, honest, or genuine. May refer to a person's legal position based on good faith or lacking notice of fraud (such as a bona fide purchaser for value) or to the authenticity of a particular document (such as a bona fide last will and testament).

CAUSA MORTIS: With approaching death in mind. A gift causa mortis is a gift given by a party who feels certain that death is imminent.

CAVEAT EMPTOR: Let the buyer beware. This maxim is reflected in the rule of law that a buyer purchases at his own risk because it is his responsibility to examine, judge, test, and otherwise inspect what he is buying.

CERTIORARI: A writ of review. Petitions for review of a case by the United States Supreme Court are most often done by means of a writ of certiorari.

CONTRA: On the other hand. Opposite. Contrary to.

CORAM NOBIS: Before us; writs of error directed to the court that originally rendered the judgment.

CORAM VOBIS: Before you; writs of error directed by an appellate court to a lower court to correct a factual error.

CORPUS DELICTI: The body of the crime; the requisite elements of a crime amounting to objective proof that a crime has been committed.

CUM TESTAMENTO ANNEXO, ADMINISTRATOR (ADMINISTRATOR C.T.A.): With will annexed; an administrator c.t.a. settles an estate pursuant to a will in which he is not appointed.

DE BONIS NON, ADMINISTRATOR (ADMINISTRATOR D.B.N.): Of goods not administered; an administrator d.b.n. settles a partially settled estate.

DE FACTO: In fact; in reality; actually. Existing in fact but not officially approved or engendered.

DE JURE: By right; lawful. Describes a condition that is legitimate "as a matter of law," in contrast to the term "de facto," which connotes something existing in fact but not legally sanctioned or authorized. For example, de facto segregation refers to segregation brought about by housing patterns, etc., whereas de jure segregation refers to segregation created by law.

DE MINIMUS: Of minimal importance; insignificant; a trifle; not worth bothering about.

DE NOVO: Anew; a second time; afresh. A trial de novo is a new trial held at the appellate level as if the case originated there and the trial at a lower level had not taken place.

DICTA: Generally used as an abbreviated form of obiter dicta, a term describing those portions of a judicial opinion incidental or not necessary to resolution of the specific question before the court. Such nonessential statements and remarks are not considered to be binding precedent.

DUCES TECUM: Refers to a particular type of writ or subpoena requesting a party or organization to produce certain documents in their possession.

EN BANC: Full bench. Where a court sits with all justices present rather than the usual quorum.

EX PARTE: For one side or one party only. An ex parte proceeding is one undertaken for the benefit of only one party, without notice to, or an appearance by, an adverse party.

EX POST FACTO: After the fact. An ex post facto law is a law that retroactively changes the consequences of a prior act.

EX REL.: Abbreviated form of the term "ex relatione," meaning, upon relation or information. When the state brings an action in which it has no interest against an individual at the instigation of one who has a private interest in the matter.

FORUM NON CONVENIENS: Inconvenient forum. Although a court may have jurisdiction over the case, the action should be tried in a more conveniently located court, one to which parties and witnesses may more easily travel, for example.

GUARDIAN AD LITEM: A guardian appointed by the court to represent a minor or incompetent person in a legal action.

HABEAS CORPUS: You have the body. The modern writ of habeas corpus is a writ directing that a person (body) being detained (such as a prisoner) be brought before the court so that the legality of his detention can be judicially ascertained.

IN CAMERA: In private, in chambers. When a hearing is held before a judge in his chambers or when all spectators are excluded from the courtroom.

IN FORMA PAUPERIS: In the manner of a pauper. A party who proceeds in forma pauperis because of his poverty is one who is allowed to bring suit without liability for costs.

INFRA: Below, under. A word referring the reader to a later part of a book. (The opposite of supra.)

IN LOCO PARENTIS: In the place of a parent.

IN PARI DELICTO: Equally wrong; a court of equity will not grant requested relief to an applicant who is in pari delicto, or as much at fault in the transactions giving rise to the controversy as is the opponent of the applicant.

IN PARI MATERIA: On like subject matter or upon the same matter. Statutes relating to the same person or things are said to be in pari materia. It is a general rule of statutory construction that such statutes should be construed together, i.e., looked at as if they together constituted one law.

IN PERSONAM: Against the person. Jurisdiction over the person of an individual.

IN RE: In the matter of. Used to designate a proceeding involving an estate or other property.

IN REM: A term that signifies an action against the res, or thing. An action in rem is basically one that is taken directly against property, as distinguished from an action in personam, i.e., against the person.

INTER ALIA: Among other things. Used to show that the whole of a statement, pleading, list, statute, etc., has not been set forth in its entirety.

INTER PARTES: Between the parties. May refer to contracts, conveyances, or other transactions having legal significance.

INTER VIVOS: Between the living. An inter vivos gift is a gift made by a living grantor, as distinguished from bequests contained in a will, which pass upon the death of the testator.

IPSO FACTO: By the mere fact itself.

JUS: Law or the entire body of law.

LEX LOCI: The law of the place; the notion that the rights of parties to a legal proceeding are governed by the law of the place where those rights arose.

MALUM IN SE: Evil or wrong in and of itself; inherently wrong. This term describes an act that is wrong by its very nature, as opposed to one which would not be wrong but for the fact that there is a specific legal prohibition against it (malum prohibitum).

MALUM PROHIBITUM: Wrong because prohibited, but not inherently evil. Used to describe something that is wrong because it is expressly forbidden by law but that is not in and of itself evil, e.g., speeding.

MANDAMUS: We command. A writ directing an official to take a certain action.

MENS REA: A guilty mind; a criminal intent. A term used to signify the mental state that accompanies a crime or other prohibited act. Some crimes require only a general mens rea (general intent to do the prohibited act), but others, like assault with intent to murder, require the existence of a specific mens rea.

MODUS OPERANDI: Method of operating; generally refers to the manner or style of a criminal in committing crimes, admissible in appropriate cases as evidence of the identity of a defendant.

NEXUS: A connection to.

NISI PRIUS: A court of first impression. A nisi prius court is one where issues of fact are tried before a judge or jury.

N.O.V. (NON OBSTANTE VEREDICTO): Notwithstanding the verdict. A judgment n.o.v. is a judgment given in favor of one party despite the fact that a verdict was returned in favor of the other party, the justification being that the verdict either had no reasonable support in fact or was contrary to law.

NUNC PRO TUNC: Now for then. This phrase refers to actions that may be taken and will then have full retroactive effect.

PENDENTE LITE: Pending the suit; pending litigation underway.

PER CAPITA: By head; beneficiaries of an estate, if they take in equal shares, take per capita.

PER CURIAM: By the court; signifies an opinion ostensibly written "by the whole court" and with no identified author.

PER SE: By itself, in itself; inherently.

PER STIRPES: By representation. Used primarily in the law of wills to describe the method of distribution where a person, generally because of death, is unable to take that which is left to him by the will of another, and therefore his heirs divide such property between them rather than take under the will individually.

PRIMA FACIE: On its face, at first sight. A prima facie case is one that is sufficient on its face, meaning that the evidence supporting it is adequate to establish the case until contradicted or overcome by other evidence.

PRO TANTO: For so much; as far as it goes. Often used in eminent domain cases when a property owner receives partial payment for his land without prejudice to his right to bring suit for the full amount he claims his land to be worth.

QUANTUM MERUIT: As much as he deserves. Refers to recovery based on the doctrine of unjust enrichment in those cases in which a party has rendered valuable services or furnished materials that were accepted and enjoyed by another under circumstances that would reasonably notify the recipient that the rendering party expected to be paid. In essence, the law implies a contract to pay the reasonable value of the services or materials furnished.

QUASI: Almost like; as if; nearly. This term is essentially used to signify that one subject or thing is almost analogous to another but that material differences between them do exist. For example, a quasi-criminal proceeding is one that is not strictly criminal but shares enough of the same characteristics to require some of the same safeguards (e.g., procedural due process must be followed in a parole hearing).

QUID PRO QUO: Something for something. In contract law, the consideration, something of value, passed between the parties to render the contract binding.

RES GESTAE: Things done. In evidence law, this principle justifies the admission of a statement that would otherwise be hearsay when it is made so closely to the event in question as to be said to be a part of it, or with such spontaneity as not to have the possibility of falsehood.

RES IPSA LOQUITUR: The thing speaks for itself. This doctrine gives rise to a rebuttable presumption of negligence when the instrumentality causing the injury was within the exclusive control of the defendant, and the injury was one that does not normally occur unless a person has been negligent.

RES JUDICATA: A matter adjudged. Doctrine which provides that once a court of competent jurisdiction has rendered a final judgment or decree on the merits, that judgment or decree is conclusive upon the parties to the case and prevents them from engaging in any other litigation on the points and issues determined therein.

RESPONDEAT SUPERIOR: Let the master reply. This doctrine holds the master liable for the wrongful acts of his servant (or the principal for his agent) in those cases in which the servant (or agent) was acting within the scope of his authority at the time of the injury.

STARE DECISIS: To stand by or adhere to that which has been decided. The common law doctrine of stare decisis attempts to give security and certainty to the law by following the policy that once a principle of law as applicable to a certain set of facts has been set forth in a decision, it forms a precedent that will subsequently be followed, even though a different decision might be made were it the first time the question had arisen. Of course, stare decisis is not an inviolable principle and is departed from in instances where there is good cause (e.g., considerations of public policy led the Supreme Court to disregard prior decisions sanctioning segregation).

SUPRA: Above. A word referring a reader to an earlier part of a book.

ULTRA VIRES: Beyond the power. This phrase is most commonly used to refer to actions taken by a corporation that are beyond the power or legal authority of the corporation.

Addendum of French Derivatives

CHATTEL: Tangible personal property.

CY PRES: Doctrine permitting courts to apply trust funds to purposes not expressed in the trust but necessary to carry out the settlor's intent.

IN PAIS: Not pursuant to legal proceedings.

PER AUTRE VIE: For another's life; during another's life. In property law, an estate may be granted that will terminate upon the death of someone other than the grantee.

PROFIT A PRENDRE: A license to remove minerals or other produce from land.

VOIR DIRE: Process of questioning jurors as to their predispositions about the case or parties to a proceeding in order to identify those jurors displaying bias or prejudice.